Bold Bearers of His Name

Forty World Mission Stories

Bold Bearers of His Name

William N. McElrath

BROADMAN PRESS
Nashville, Tennessee

Dewey Decimal Classification: J266.09
Subject headings: MISSIONS—MISSIONARIES
Library of Congress Catalog Card Number: 87-8061
Printed in the United States of America

Library of Congress Cataloging-in-Publication Data

McElrath, William N.
  Bold bearers of His name.

  Includes index.
  Summary: Describes the work and experiences of individual Christian
missionaries and those who have supported them all over the world, from the
United States to Sweden to Indonesia.
  1. Missionary stories—Juvenile literature.
  [1. Missionaries] I. Title.
BV2087.M36 1987   266 [920]   87-8061
ISBN 0-8054-4339-8

"Then I heard the voice of the Lord saying,
  'Whom shall I send, and who will go for us?'
Then I said,
  'Here am I. Send me!'"
                      —Isaiah the Prophet, eighth century BC

"Send them on their way in a manner worthy of God.
For they went out for the sake of the Name."
                      —John the Apostle, first century AD

          "O that in me my Lord may see
            A bearer of the Name;
          That men may see his love so free
            From age to age the same.
          ....
          If others stop to count the cost,
          For fear of earthly treasures lost,
            I'll count it gain to die for Thee;
            Send me, O Lord, send me."
                      —Ross Coggins, 1956

Acknowledgments

All Scripture quotations marked RSV are taken from the Revised Standard Version of the Bible, copyright 1946, 1952, by the Division of Christian Education of the National Council of the Churches of Christ in the United States of America.

All Scripture quotations marked NASB are taken from the New American Standard Bible, copyright 1960, 1962, 1963, 1968, 1971, 1972, 1973, 1975, by the Lockman Foundation.

The two Scripture quotations on the dedication page are Isaiah 6:8, NASB, and 3 John, verses 6b-7a, NASB.

The third quotation on the dedication page is taken from the hymn "Send Me, O Lord, Send Me," words by Ross Coggins, stanzas 3a and 2b. © Copyright 1956 Broadman Press. All rights reserved. Used by permission.

Several chapters in this book originally appeared in print in an earlier form. The author expresses his thanks to several publishers for permission to adapt and reuse the following:

Chapter 4, adapted from *Crusader*, June 1976. Copyright © 1976, Brotherhood Commission, Southern Baptist Convention, Memphis, Tennessee. Used by permission.

Chapter 7, adapted from *Adventure*, November-December 1964. © Copyright 1964 The Sunday School Board of the Southern Baptist Convention. All rights reserved. Used by permission.

Chapter 21, adapted from *Junior Musician*, October-November-December 1964. © Copyright 1964 The Sunday

Contents

The Reason for This Book.. 13

I.   Namebearers Among the Nations
   1. Namebearer with Many Names: Kiayi Paulus Tosari of Indonesia..................................... 17
   2. Mother of Orphans: Pandita Ramabai of India 24
   3. Murderer Turned Missionary: Ko Tha Byu of Burma... 32
   4. Always on the Go: Erik Nelson of Sweden, the USA, and Brazil 39
   5. Stubborn Saxon Seed Sower: Gottlob Bruckner of Germany and Indonesia 44
   6. Grandmother with Good News: Ji-wang of Taiwan 52
   7. Liberty Under God: Lott Cary of the USA and Liberia 60
   8. Angel on the Waterfront: Marie Buhlmaier of Germany and the USA...................................... 67
   9. Steadfast South Sea Islanders: Ruatoka and Tungane of Rarotonga and Papua New Guinea 75
  10. Last Chief of the Leni-Lenape: Charles Journeycake of the USA 84
  11. Son of the Samurai: Kanzo Uchimura of Japan 89
  12. Strong-willed Schoolmistress: Ida B. Hayes of the USA, Mexico, and Puerto Rico 95
  13. Pastor of His People: V. Samuel Azariah of India 101
  14. Mill Girl, Missionary, Magistrate: Mary Mitchell Slessor of Scotland and Nigeria 108
  15. Seafarer of the Spice Islands: Joseph Kam of the Netherlands and Indonesia............................ 116
  16. Home Missionary on a Foreign Field: Lula F. Whilden of the USA and China........................ 123

17. Apostle to the Arawaks: William Henry Brett of England and Guyana 130

18. Bold Barefoot Prophet: William Wadé Harris of Liberia, Ghana, and the Ivory Coast 137

19. God's Trusting Traveler: Amanda Berry Smith of America and the World 144

20. God's Soldier of Peace: Deu I. Mahandi of the Philippines 149

II. **They Held the Ropes**

21. The Man Who Wrote "America" 155

22. The Cowboys' Favorite Preacher 160

23. From Kentucky to Chile with Love 166

24. Breakfast Biscuits, Drums, and a Money Jug 169

25. When Lightning Strikes a Church 172

III. **Might-Have-Been Mission Stories**

26. A Church in Lunga-og 177

27. Missionary Kid at the Book Factory 183

28. A Spirit Who Cannot Be Fooled 189

29. Flying Doctor 195

30. *Begitu Saja!* (Just Like That!) 200

31. Voyage of the *Messenger* 206

32. Rosalina Finds Friends 211

33. Mr. Garden, the Popcorn Preacher 218

34. Elijah and the Jungle Pilot 223

35. A Round-the-World Story at Miguel's Church 228

IV. **Modern-Day Martyrs**

36. Faithful unto Death: The Sohn Family of Korea .. 235

37. Gospel Grass Fires: The Wallamo Christians of Ethiopia 244

38. Tortured for the Truth: Kartar Singh of India and Tibet 250

39. On Guard for the Gospel: Watchman Nee of China 255

40. Two Arrows and a Wedding Ring: The Lesnussa Family of Indonesia 263

Topical Indexes 271

The Reason for This Book

Bold mission deeds sometimes start with bold mission stories.

That has been the experience of many boys and girls. They hear and read about brave deeds of William Carey in India, of Adoniram Judson in Burma, of Luther Rice and Annie Armstrong in America, of David Livingstone in Africa, of Lottie Moon in China. And in God's long purpose, those boys and girls grow up to be missionaries.

That has been my own experience and my wife's experience.

But bold mission deeds must be supported by bold praying and bold giving. Many boys and girls have heard and read those same stories and have felt that same thrill of response. Yet in God's long purpose they have stayed at home so others could go.

That has been the experience of our fathers and mothers, our sisters and brothers.

Bold Bearers of His Name brings together daring deeds from many lands. It tells many ways of spreading the good news all over the world.

A psalmist had the right idea when he wrote:

> Things that we have heard and known,
>   That our fathers have told us,
> We will not hide them from their children,
>   But tell to the coming generation
> The glorious deeds of the Lord, and his might,
>   And the wonders which he has wrought.*

That's the reason for this book.

---

* Psalm 78:3-4, RSV (with modified capitalization and punctuation).

I.
Namebearers
Among the Nations

All the men and women told about in the first half of this book were alike in one way: All of them bore the name of Christ among the nations of the world.

Only one of these "Namebearers Among the Nations" did I ever meet in person: Deu I. Mahandi, in his native Philippines (chapter 20). The others lived before my day or beyond my travels. Yet it is still possible to walk where they walked.

I was baptized into the membership of the church in Kentucky that bought the *Buffalo* for Erik Nelson to sail up and down the Amazon (chapter 4).

In a Bible society museum I have held in my hands the Burmese Scriptures translated by Adoniram Judson, the missionary who won Ko Tha Byu to Christ (chapter 3).

I have mounted that high pulpit of carved wood in the old stone church at Semarang, Central Java, Indonesia, where Gottlob Bruckner used to preach (chapter 5).

I have walked steep city streets in Macao and muddy country lanes in Guangdong Province, where Lula Whilden used to walk (chapter 16).

Not all the men and women told about in this book went out from America or Europe to other countries. Many of them were Asians or Africans who bravely bore the name of Christ.

Not all of the stories are new, for some are always worth

retelling. But many of them have rarely, if ever before, been shared with boys and girls of today.

Not all of the Christians told about in this book were members of the same church. Some of them were from denominations most of us have never heard of. But all of them loved the Lord Jesus Christ and boldly obeyed His Great Commission.

Not every country or even every continent is represented in this book, but there is a measure of balance. When you remember that China, India, and Indonesia are three of the world's five largest countries by population, it doesn't seem out of proportion to have more than one story from each.

Not many of the stories tell about mission work in the United States of America. But that doesn't mean home missions is less important than foreign missions. In this book you will find many stories about people who tried in many ways to win their own countries for Christ. The need for that is greater than ever before—in your homeland and mine, and among all nations.

1
Namebearer with Many Names
Kiayi Paulus Tosari of Indonesia

The war year of 1812 was a year of great names.

Charles Dickens was born in 1812, and Robert Browning, and Flotow the opera composer, and Krupp the maker of guns.

In that same year of 1812, a boy was born to an Indonesian family on the island of Java. His parents named him Kasan. But he had many other names in his lifetime. And he became a bearer of the greatest Name of all.

Kasan's father was a hard-working farmer who didn't pay much attention to religion. But Kasan's mother saw to it that the boy prayed five times a day and went to the village mosque on Fridays, as a good Muslim should.

Every day Kasan helped herd his father's goats. Every night he looked around for something fun to do. The most fun would be when a puppeteer would use flat leather figures to tell the great old legends of Java. Kasan would sit for hours in flickering lamplight, watching shadows on the screen that acted out the story. He would listen to poems chanted during intermissions in the drama.

Sometimes Kasan and his friends even hiked to another village where they had heard there would be a shadow play. When there were no puppet shows, they passed the evening hours learning how to play gambling games.

Kasan's Muslim mother frowned to see her son getting into mischief. She ordered him off to school—an Islamic school. At first Kasan managed to play hooky most of the time. But little by little he got interested in what his teacher had to say.

Soon Kasan was the star pupil. The schoolmaster predicted, "Kasan himself will be a teacher of religion someday." The schoolmaster's words would come true . . . but he could never have dreamed how it would happen.

When Kasan could quote by memory five chapters from the Holy Koran, his mother gave a party in his honor. When he turned fifteen, she held his coming-of-age ceremony. Following ancient custom, he dropped his childhood name of Kasan. People started calling him Jaryo instead.

Now Jaryo seemed well on his way toward becoming a Muslim teacher. Sometimes the village priest even let his eager young helper shout the call to prayer from the minaret: "God is great! God is great! There is no god but Allah, and Muhammad is the prophet of Allah!"

Trouble started when the priest sent Jaryo to lead Islamic prayers that must open every party held in the village. Before long Jaryo was enjoying the parties more than the prayers.

Jaryo's mother tried to enter him in another Muslim school. But the new schoolmaster said Jaryo would have to start all over again learning what the Holy Koran meant. Jaryo balked at that.

Then his mother found a young wife for her nearly grown son. She hoped starting a family would help Jaryo settle down. But two months later he deserted his wife and ran away from home.

Now Jaryo became a cotton merchant. He learned every trick of the trade to make more money. He married again, picking out a bride for himself this time. Soon he and his wife had a baby boy named Satipah. People began calling Jaryo "Father of Satipah," or Pak Satipah.

Some of the other cotton merchants in East Java liked to gamble. Pak Satipah remembered his childhood games and began gambling with them. Some of the merchants liked to drug themselves with opium. Pak Satipah started doing that, too.

Little by little his cotton business went to pieces. He had to sell his horse to pay gambling debts. Then he sold his golden-handled dagger, a special gift from his mother. Finally Pak Satipah was down to the clothes on his body. In hot steamy Java, that could mean as little as a headband and a loincloth.

Pak Satipah borrowed another dagger from his brother-in-law. He made one last bet on it . . . and lost. The man he was gambling with shouted, "You'll have to work at my house to pay this off!"

From proud cotton merchant to lowly houseboy—that was too much. Pak Satipah began to wander from village to village, homeless and hungry. When he made a little money, he spent it on drugs.

One day in a daze he stumbled into a town that somehow looked familiar. His aimless wanderings had brought him back home. He found his wife and child sick and his old mother at her wits' end. She hugged him tight, sobbing, "No more of this! Turn from your evil ways!"

Pak Satipah felt as if he were waking up from a bad dream. He began to buy and sell cotton again, but he tried to stay away from merchants who gambled and used opium. Instead, he watched shadow-puppet plays, as he had done in his boyhood.

People in the village whispered that his wife had been untrue to him while he was gone. So he sent her back to her parents along with his son Satipah.

A year later Pak Satipah got married for the third time: to the Widow Gadung. His mother said nothing good would come of this marriage because the Widow Gadung made such a long list of demands: Pak Satipah must give her a tray full of coins. He must pile seven large trays high with rice and other foods. And he must break off completely from drugs and gambling.

Pak Satipah did everything the widow wanted. And to his mother's surprise, he lived in peace and happiness with his third wife. His business prospered. People in the village began to look up to him with new respect.

One day a villager named Kariman brought Pak Satipah startling news: "Allah has two sons!" he cried. "When the older one died, then the younger one came down from heaven to raise him back to life again."

Pak Satipah stared in amazement. He found it hard to believe that Allah had even one son, let alone two. "Where did you hear about this?" he asked his friend Kariman.

"From a landlord in a distant village, who is also a great teacher of religion," Kariman explained. "My father and I plan to go and see him again. Would you like to come along?"

And so it was that Pak Satipah first heard about the Son of God. The landlord was a tall man with a long beard, the son of a Dutch father and a Javanese mother. Carefully he explained again what Kariman had misunderstood before.

A cooking fire burned near the place where the four men sat talking. "How many fires do you see, Pak Satipah?" asked the teacher.

"Only one," replied Pak Satipah.

"Yet there is heat, and light, and the burning wood itself—three in one. So it is with the one God Allah—Father, Son, and Holy Spirit."

Pak Satipah sat in silence. Such breathtakingly new ideas took awhile to sort out in his mind.

All that week Pak Satipah stayed in the landlord's village. He saw farmers gather on Sunday to worship in ways he had never known before. He heard them recite the Ten Commandments and a prayer beginning "Our Father." How strange to think of the great and far-distant Allah as a Father!

The peasants told Pak Satipah, "Our teacher is a man of power. No one dared to clear this jungle till he came. Everyone thought it was full of evil spirits. But even when melted rock and ash shot out from the great volcano yonder, our village was kept safe from harm. The teacher says his power comes from Allah, who sent His Son to be our Lord and Savior."

The landlord's sermon text that Sunday was, "Blessed are the poor in spirit, for theirs is the kingdom of heaven."* Pak Satipah thought back over his life. He remembered being good and being bad, being rich and being poor. Never before had he heard that his past sins could be forgiven. And he longed to enter the kingdom of heaven.

Back home again, Pak Satipah told his wife Gadung all he had seen and heard and felt. He taught her and their children to repeat after him the prayer that began, "Our Father."

From that day a great change began. Not everything ran smoothly for Pak Satipah and his family: He had to learn a whole new way of doing business, and sometimes the temptation to cut corners was still too strong. Yet he and all his household felt a growing hunger for the heavenly kingdom.

His friend Kariman sold out and moved to the great teacher's village. Finally Pak Satipah and Gadung decided to do the same. They bought a team of oxen, to help clear new jungle lands for farming. They said good-bye to Pak Satipah's weeping old mother, who used every argument she could think of to stop them from going.

On the way to their new home, Pak Satipah decided he must also have a new name. He chose "Tosari," which means "Morning Dew" in the Javanese language. He felt that this name expressed the fresh new day now beginning for his whole family.

The tall landlord welcomed Tosari and Gadung and their children. He showed them a piece of land they could clear and farm. Day by day he taught them more about the kingdom of heaven.

---

* Matthew 5:3, NASB.

Tosari proved to be a fast learner. As a special reward, the teacher gave him a Holy Book . . . but it was not the Holy Koran. Eagerly Tosari began to read it. How sad he was to learn that wicked men had nailed the Son of God to a tree and left Him there to die! How glad he was to read of Jesus' resurrection!

But the more Tosari read, the more puzzled he became. It seemed that Jesus had been killed, not just once, but four times. And four times He had risen to life again.

The tall landlord explained: "There were four men named Matthew, Mark, Luke, and John. Each wrote the story of Jesus in his own way. But the story is one, just as God is one."

Soon Tosari himself was leading Thursday evening prayer meetings in the village. Then he was sent to another town to visit a Christian who had been thrown in jail by an official of the colonial government. (Tosari knew that the tall half-Dutch landlord was different from other Dutch colonials. "The very idea of Javanese wanting to become Christians!" That was what many of the Dutch thought about it. "Just as if Javanese were as good as we are!")

Tosari not only encouraged the brother who was being held in prison. He also marched boldly into the colonial official's presence and answered every one of his questions about Christianity. A few days later, the man in jail was set free.

When Tosari and Gadung were baptized, they both chose new names from their Holy Book. Tosari became Paul (or Paulus in the Indonesian language). Gadung became Lydia.

Now Paulus Tosari began to experience what his friend in prison had faced. He traveled all over East Java spreading the gospel. Often he felt like his namesake Paul. He especially met persecution when he crossed a narrow sea to the isle of Madura, where his ancestors had come from. No one there would listen to his message.

But many people on Java did listen. When the Dutch governors changed their minds and missionaries began to be allowed to land on Java, they were amazed to find how many Javanese Christians there were already. Paulus Tosari was delighted to welcome more helpers in telling people about the Son of God.

He found one very special way of telling the good news. He remembered how as a boy and as a man he had sat spellbound the whole night through watching Javanese shadow-puppet plays. Now he began to write poems, using the same style of verses as those chanted during intermissions in the ancient folk dramas. But Paulus Tosari's Javanese poems told about Jesus Christ the Son of God and about the difference He makes in human lives.

Because his Christian poems were so popular, Dutch missionaries collected them and printed them in a book. Because Paulus Tosari was so widely respected for his goodness and wisdom, other Indonesians began calling him *Kiayi*. This is a title reserved for religious teachers of highest rank.

Toward the end of his life, Kiayi Paulus Tosari longed to see a stone church house built in his own village. Foundations were laid, and walls began to rise.

By the time the dedication service was held, the old man could not leave his bed. But before he died in the year 1881, he knew his village church would stand strong through wind and weather. So would the congregations of believers he had planted throughout East Java. Even a hundred years later, Indonesian Christians would speak the name of Kiayi Paulus Tosari with respect and loving memory.

Kiayi: kee-AH-yee	minaret: MIN-ah-ret
Paulus: pah-OO-loose	Satipah: sah-TEE-pah
Tosari: toe-SAH-ree	Pak: POCK
Kasan: KAH-sahn	Gadung: GAH-doong
Koran: KOE-rahn	Kariman: kah-REE-mahn
Jaryo: JAR-ee-yo	Madura: mah-DOO-rah

2
Mother of Orphans
Pandita Ramabai of India

Imagine a little girl five years old being married to a grown man. Five weeks or five months or five years later, the man dies . . . and the young widow gets blamed for it. "He died because of his wife's sins!" people say.

So the little girl becomes a slave to her late husband's family. They hack off her hair and steal her ornaments. They leave her only one sleazy dress to wear and give her only one meal a day. Sometimes they may treat her even worse.

That's what used to happen to young widows in India—during the 1800s and before. All women were looked down upon. No girl went to school. A woman could hope for nothing, in this world or the next, unless she gave herself completely to her husband, even to letting herself be burned alive with his dead body.

God raised up a man to stop such cruelty: William Carey, pioneer Baptist missionary to India. He fought the burning of widows until at last it was made against the law.

Then God raised up a woman to continue the struggle. She was a woman of India, of the highest caste. She was a great scholar in the religious and literary traditions of her own people.

In God's plan she changed forever the place of women and girls in the great subcontinent of India. And more than that: to all who would listen, she pointed the way to new life in Jesus Christ.

In western India stands a mountain eight thousand feet

high. A Hindu priest and teacher lived there with his family. There he could bring up his children as he thought best. Other Hindus called him a heretic and a radical, for he insisted that girls should be taught as well as boys.

The old priest taught his children all he knew. The brightest of them, his younger daughter, was born in 1858. As a child she could quote thousands of Hindu teachings in poetry. They named her *Ramabai,* meaning "Delight."

When Ramabai was still tiny, she and her family moved away from the mountaintop. Too many poor pilgrims had come to that holy place, and the old priest had been too generous in giving them food, clothing, and shelter. Now he and his own household in their turn must become pilgrims. They must live off the charity of those who honored their holiness.

It was a hard way to grow up. By the time she was a teenager, Ramabai figured she had hiked at least seven thousand miles.

Then disaster struck. When Ramabai was sixteen, famine and disease swept across India. Both her father and her mother died of starvation, only six weeks apart. Not long after, her older sister died of cholera.

Ramabai and her brother wandered on in misery. Once they both tried to commit suicide. Little by little they lost their faith. If there were a god, any god, then why did he let them suffer so?

Ramabai was twenty years old when they arrived in Calcutta. To their surprise, her fame had already reached that great city before them. Times were changing in India, and ideas were changing as well. "We want to meet this high-caste Hindu girl," religious leaders said to one another. "Is it true she can quote verses by the thousand? Is it true she can make up new verses herself on any topic you give her?"

Ramabai did not disappoint those who were eager to see and hear her. Newspapers printed her speeches. Modern-minded people cried, "You see, girls can be educated after all!" They began to call her *Pandita* Ramabai or "Great Woman Scholar." (The same word has become the term *pundit* in English, meaning a wise or learned person.)

Many invitations came to Pandita Ramabai and her brother. One was different from the rest: it came from a group of Christians. Ramabai remembered once hearing the name *Yesyu Krista* when she was a child. But she did not understand the Christians' way of praying. Nor did she understand the Holy Book they gave her.

Many young Hindus proposed marriage to Ramabai. But she refused them all because her brother now fell sick and she nursed him faithfully. Only after he had died did she agree to marry. And she married one of her brother's friends.

Her husband had once studied at a mission school, but he was not a believer. Neither was she, for all her great religious learning. So they were married in a civil ceremony, not at a church or a temple. The next year Ramabai had a little girl. They named her *Manoramabai:* "Heart's Delight."

From a friend of her husband's, Pandita Ramabai learned more about *Yesyu Krista.* She was impressed with what she heard and read. She began to pray again, even though she wasn't sure to whom she should pray.

Then . . . an epidemic struck again. Her husband died of cholera, after only nineteen months of married life.

"Look what comes of schooling for women!" many people now taunted. "Pandita Ramabai married beneath her caste, and then her husband died before his time."

Other people encouraged the young widow. They were glad to know she still believed in a woman's right to education and a decent chance in life. When she wrote a book called *Morals for Women,* people flocked to buy it.

One day friends brought to Ramabai a ragged, trembling child. "She's a widow, too," they told her. "She was five when she got married, and still five when her husband died.

Her mother-in-law screamed, 'She's a demon! She killed my son!' "

Ramabai drew the little girl into her arms. "You poor dear," she sighed. And she took care of the child along with her own small Manoramabai.

Pandita Ramabai yearned to help friendless orphans of India. But she needed to know how. With money from sales of her book, she bought steamship tickets. She and little Manoramabai sailed away to England.

Friends welcomed her there—Christian friends. Few people in India knew that Ramabai had been studying the Bible more and more. In 1883, at a little English church, she was baptized as a follower of Christ.

Six years Ramabai and her daughter lived abroad—three years studying in England, three more in Canada and the United States. She wrote another book, telling about child widows of India. Friends helped her start a special mission society. They collected money to send Ramabai back to India as their representative.

When Ramabai came home in 1889, she started out with only two little girls. Three months later, she had twenty-two. What tales they told her! She heard about beatings, and starvings, and brandings with a hot iron. One child had even been hung up by her hands where smoke from burning peppers would torture her nose and throat and lungs.

Often Ramabai made speaking tours, telling about her home for child widows. Never did she ask for money. But special gifts kept coming in.

Pandita Ramabai described her life work like this: "Christ gives different gifts to different people: prophets, preachers, teachers. Since I have become a Christian, Christ has given me the gift of being a sweeper. I want to sweep India clean of all that has hindered the spread of the gospel among women."

Many of Ramabai's supporters in India were not Christians. They insisted that she not try to convert her orphans, and at first Ramabai agreed. "Let each worship in her own way," said Ramabai.

But her own eight-year-old Manoramabai came to Mama's room early every morning to read the Bible. Other little girls followed, so that many of them were hearing God's Word.

"Close your door when you read Christian books and pray, Pandita!" some people insisted.

"Oh, I can't do that," said Ramabai. "My door is always open to anyone who needs me. How could I close it only at that one time?"

Many of Ramabai's girls had never known any other mother. Nor had they ever known a mother's discipline. Some of them stole; some scratched in garbage piles, even though given enough to eat; some rebelled against any rule Ramabai made.

Her way with them was firm and down-to-earth. Near her door stood a great stone hand mill, too heavy to be turned by one girl alone. Pandita Ramabai set naughty girls to grinding grain, two by two. "This is exercise for your body, rest for your mind, and a chance to learn cooperation," said Ramabai.

It was only a matter of time before the light of the gospel began to shine in the shadows. In 1894 one of Ramabai's girls asked to be baptized.

What a fuss she kicked up! "It's all just a front," people cried. "Pandita Ramabai doesn't really care about those children. All she wants to do is force them to become Christians!"

Of sixty-two children in the orphans' home, twenty were promptly yanked out. Newspaper articles warned people not to support Ramabai's work any longer. Unsigned letters even threatened that she would be killed.

But Pandita Ramabai would not back down. Public criticism turned out to be unpaid advertisements for what she was trying to do. Soon the forty-two girls still left were joined by many more. And no less than fifteen of them had asked to be baptized.

Ramabai rejoiced. She herself had recently come to a deeper spiritual life. "At first I became a Christian because the Christian religion was the highest and best I had ever known," she admitted. "But now I know it isn't just a religion. It is a personal surrender to Jesus Christ as Lord and Savior."

With her faith newly strengthened, Ramabai felt led to make a strange prayer request: "Lord, give me not just fifteen souls, but fifteen times fifteen!"

At that time there were 49 girls in Ramabai's home at Poona. She has room for only 65. Yet she was praying for 225! And God answered her prayer.

Once again times of famine came to India. Pandita Ramabai, a lady of the highest caste, went out to find dirty, starving street urchins whose families had died. With loving hands she gathered them in and led them toward a new life. Once she even dared to go into the jungle at midnight to rescue two little girls being stalked by a hungry wolf!

Within a year and a half, Ramabai had her "15 times 15" or 225 children. Then there were 300, 500, 1,000, nearly 2,000. Many among them became followers of *Yesyu Krista.*

How could Pandita Ramabai take care of so many?

First of all, she leaned on the Lord. One of her favorite verses was this: "I am poor and needy;/but the Lord takes thought for me."* She never asked people for money, even though sometimes she gathered the children around her at nighttime to pray for the next day's food. And somehow the money always came in.

Pandita Ramabai also came more and more to depend upon her own daughter Manoramabai. Like her mother, she was beautiful, talented, and well educated. Many young men came to see her. But she stayed single, dedicating her

---

* Psalm 40:17, RSV.

life to Ramabai's work. And Manoramabai proved to be an even better manager than her mother was.

Other workers came to join them. Some of the helpers were paid, but many were volunteers for the cause of Christ.

Ramabai's first children's home in Poona had long since been outgrown. Now the second one was running over. So Ramabai went out south of the city and bought land.

"Oh, Pandita, this land is no good!" people warned her. "See how stony the soil is. Nothing will grow here."

"Dig a well," said Ramabai. And with water from that well, she and her workers made the wilderness turn green.

When Ramabai and her orphans moved in 1899, they had to live in thatched huts at first. One by one she added buildings: a church, a dormitory, a school, a storehouse. And she called her new village *Mukti:* "Liberation."

Not all who lived at Mukti were child widows. Other orphans came, too—at first only girls, but later boys as well. Some were blind, and Ramabai taught them with the most modern methods of her time. Some were girls whose families had thrown them out when they had had babies without being married.

Everyone had to work at Mukti. Great fields grew crops to feed many mouths. Cows and goats gave milk for many children.

Pandita Ramabai herself never stopped working. She wrote more books. Once she even translated the whole Bible from its original languages into a dialect of India. All profits from sales of her writings were plowed back into the soil of Mukti.

She even started her own print shop at Mukti. "Oh, Pandita, you know girls can't run a printing press!" people told her. Ramabai smiled. She knew girls could do many things people thought they couldn't.

But the products of Mukti that brought most joy to Pandita Ramabai were not books neatly printed and bound. Nor were they barns filled with fruits of field and orchard. They were Christians. Not just individual Christians but Christian families, fostered by girls and boys who had grown up at Mukti. And not just at Mukti, either. From Mukti the good news of Jesus Christ spread across the subcontinent of India.

Pandita Ramabai, mother of orphans, died in 1922. Manoramabai is dead, too. But the great Christian center at Mukti lives on. And India will never be the same again.

Pandita: pahn-DEE-tah

Ramabai: RAH-mah-bye

Yesyu Krista: YAY-shoo
   KREES-tah

Manoramabai:
   mah-no-RAH-may-bye

Poona: POO-nah

Mukti: MOOK-tee

3
Murderer Turned Missionary
Ko Tha Byu of Burma

When you think of an American, what kind of person comes to your mind?

Probably a person much like yourself. Yet when you stop to think about it, you know there are many different kinds of Americans. Americans come in different colors, speak in different languages, live in different ways.

The same is true of other countries in the world. For instance, about one tenth of the people of Burma are not ethnic Burmese. They are members of tribes known as the Karens.

Two centuries ago, Karen people were backward and despised. None of them could read; their language had never been put into writing. They had long been pushed down by the proud Burmese. As a result most of them were timid, lazy, and slow to learn. Many Karens stayed drunk day after day.

Burmese had no use for Karens. "Wild men of the jungle," they were called or "Karen pigs." A Burmese proverb said, "You can teach a water buffalo; but a Karen? Never!"

All of that is different now. Karens are among the most advanced tribal peoples of Asia. Schools and churches dot the countryside. Some two hundred Karens—an average of one for every thousand church members—have gone out as missionaries. Karens have become bold bearers of the name of Christ among other "wild tribes" of Burma, and across the border into China, and as far away as the Andaman Islands.

Whom did God use to bring to the Karens the gospel of His Son, which has made such great changes in their lives? He used a most unlikely man: a murderer.

Tha Byu was born about 1778 in a village near the great Irrawaddy River. He grew up wild, always getting into fights; his parents could do nothing with him. When he was fifteen years old, he ran away from home.

Soon Tha Byu fell in with other boys and men more wicked than himself. They taught him how to steal and what to do if someone tried to fight back. They taught him all they knew, and he learned it all too well. By his own confession, Tha Byu murdered or helped to murder at least thirty people.

Wartime came to Burma in the mid-1820s. Tha Byu was nearly fifty years old by that time, so people called him *Ko,* the common Burmese title for a middle-aged man. Maybe Ko Tha Byu thought he was getting too old to run away from the scenes of his crimes anymore. For whatever reason, he tried honest work for a change: at a port city, in a print shop run by an American missionary.

Ko Tha Byu could not read the books he helped to print. Yet he pricked up his ears when he heard that they were books about religion. Like all Karens, he knew ancient legends about people from across the sea. Someday they would come to bring his tribe a long-lost book written by the great Creator-God.

The missionary printer tried to teach Ko Tha Byu what the books said. He listened. But he wasn't ready yet to change his way of living. He left the print shop and plunged again into a life of wickedness.

After a time he turned up in another city—on the slave block! According to ancient Burmese law, a man who couldn't pay his debts could be sold as a slave. Ko Tha Byu owed twelve *rupee.* (Probably he had lost the money gambling.)

A Burmese Christian recognized the slave being sold. He

paid twelve *rupee* and took Ko Tha Byu home with him. But the old Karen proved to be a sorry servant. The Burmese Christian was about ready to give up when he thought of Dr. Judson.

Adoniram Judson had been a Baptist missionary in Burma for many years, even longer than the printer Ko Tha Byu had worked for before. Dr. Judson's wife and children were dead. But he faithfully kept on translating the Scriptures and sharing the good news with all who would listen.

When the Burmese Christian begged for help, Judson paid off the twelve *rupee* and took over the services of Ko Tha Byu . . . for whatever that was worth. He found the old murderer had a fierce temper. But Adoniram Judson had survived prison and torture and sentence of death, and he feared no one but God. Gradually his steadfast witness made a dent on his hardhearted servant.

Slowly Ko Tha Byu learned to read the Burmese New Testament. At first he couldn't believe that God's love in Jesus Christ included him. A thief? A murderer? Yet it was so, and he joyfully accepted it.

Burmese Christians were not so eager. They refused at first to baptize this strange new convert. All their prejudices against Karens came to the front.

For a wonder, Ko Tha Byu kept his temper—most of the time. It took twelve long months to prove that Jesus Christ had made a change in his life. Only then did doubting church members agree to accept him into their number.

But then his baptism was delayed again. A homeless group of Karens had turned up in the city. Among them were an orphaned teenage girl and her two little brothers. The Baptists took them all in. When a missionary planned to move to Karen country in the far south, he decided to take along the three young orphans.

The girl was thirty years younger than Ko Tha Byu. Yet it seemed God had planned them for each other. That was why the baptism had been delayed again: Ko Tha Byu was too busy preparing to move south with his bride and her brothers.

In May of 1828, after they had all moved, Ko Tha Byu was finally baptized. He was the first Karen man ever to become a baptized believer in Christ. Only ten months later, his wife became the first Karen Christian woman.

But Ko Tha Byu did not settle down with his missionary friend on Burma's southern coast. "I want to take the good news to my fellow Karens," he said.

Now it was the missionary's turn to feel doubtful. Ko Tha Byu had been a believer barely a year. His background could hardly have been any worse. He was still ignorant about many teachings of Christianity.

Yet who could say no in the face of such enthusiasm? With the missionary's blessing, Ko Tha Byu set out as a traveling lay evangelist. What if converts or inquirers asked questions too hard for him? He could always bring them into town where there were other Christians who knew more than he did.

Thus began one of the most remarkable missionary careers in all the records of Christianity. In twelve short years God used Ko Tha Byu to change the whole course of Karen history.

He began with Karen villages nearby. Two men followed him home to learn more about the gospel. Soon they were baptized, becoming the first fruits of Ko Tha Byu's missionary ministry.

One of the two was the brother of a village chief. When Ko Tha Byu visited the village a second time, ten men followed him home; among them was the chief himself.

Not long after, the chief's mother died. The chief was afraid his relatives might insist on a funeral in the olden way. So he quickly built an open-sided assembly hall near his mother's grave, and invited Ko Tha Byu to come preach the gospel there.

This "funeral evangelism" brought twelve more converts,

two of them chiefs. Now whole villages began to turn to Christ.

Sometimes Ko Tha Byu's American missionary friend went out with him on his tours. The missionary would preach first in Burmese; then Ko Tha Byu would repeat all he could remember in Karen. But the missionary got sick and died, only a day after his last jungle trip. Ko Tha Byu had to carry on alone.

Again and again he pressed on to new villages. Once he brought back forty new believers with him. Once he even reached the border between Burma and Thailand, where Thai officials turned him back.

Once he accepted the invitation of an elderly high chief and started a long journey southward. Ko Tha Byu fell sick on the way. He urged his companions to go on with the old chief, so more Karens could hear the good news. He himself won many people in the village where he had to stay till he grew strong again.

Finally another Baptist missionary from America came to replace Ko Tha Byu's friend who had died. Now the old Karen became more eager than ever to travel around spreading the gospel. Once his boat was nearly swamped in a storm. He cried out, not "God, help me!" but rather, "O, if I drown, I can never more preach the Word of God to the Karens!"

From city to city, from village to village, Tha Byu looked for Karens everywhere. Sometimes he had to wade through flood waters up to his chest. Sometimes he had to face opposition from Burmese Buddhists. But he would not turn back. Beside the road, in the marketplace, from house to house he boldly carried the good news.

Less than nine months after Ko Tha Byu had been set free from other duties to spend full time as a wandering evangelist, a missionary in a port city wrote a letter to Adoniram Judson:

"For the last several days, my house has been thronged.

There are so many Karens in Ko Tha Byu's house that he complains it is breaking down. Men, women, and children are all anxiously inquiring about the religion of Jesus. They are eager for schools and offer to build churches if someone will come to teach them.

"There are very many who already keep our Sunday, read our tracts, and try to teach one another as best they can. They have left off drinking, and as far as they understand, they try to practice the teachings of our Scriptures.

"What shall we do? Ko Tha Byu is only one among a thousand. We need at least four men to preach the gospel, and we certainly need as many more for schoolmasters. Can you send us any assistance?"

Dr. Judson got the letter and sent several Karen laymen to help. As for Ko Tha Byu, he pushed on into the interior. When persecution broke out in one place, he moved to another. There he found two thousand Karens who were open to his message.

By late 1837, the old man's health began to fail. His bones and joints ached; his eyes were half blind. So he stayed at home awhile, teaching new believers. Yet when another new area was opened in early 1840, Ko Tha Byu begged to go along, with his whole family. In just the first few months, four more Karen converts had been baptized.

But Ko Tha Byu's ministry was nearly over. His rheumatism got worse. His lungs ached. Sometimes his old temper flared up again; at other times, he bore his pain with patience. Death ended his suffering on September 9, 1840.

In twelve years the number of baptized Karen believers had grown to more than twelve hundred. What was more, these tribal Christians were scattered all across central and southern Burma where their witness could touch the lives of many others.

Today there are more than two hundred thousand Karen Christians in Burma, gathered in more than two thousand self-supporting churches. In a city near the banks of the

Irrawaddy stands Ko Tha Byu Memorial Hall, seating fifteen hundred people. A Karen plays its great pipe organ. Other Karens preach, and teach, and lead their own people in "the religion of Jesus."

A fellow mission worker once said, "Ko Tha Byu was an ignorant man, and yet he did more good than all of us, for God was with him."

Ko Tha Byu:
    KOE THAH BYOO   Irrawaddy: ear-ah-WAH-dee
Karen: kah-REN   rupee: ROO-pee
Andaman: ANN-dah-mahn

4
Always on the Go
Erik Nelson
of Sweden, the USA, and Brazil

"Mama, Erik is gone again," announced Papa Nelson, a tall Swedish farmer.

"Oh, that boy!" scolded Mama Nelson. "He's always on the go!"

Where could a six-year-old boy go in a strange city? He spoke only Swedish, and the city was Liverpool in England.

Was he lost? Was he kidnapped?

After several hours of worry, Papa and Mama Nelson found little Erik. "I just went walking to see the sights," he chirped.

Erik wasn't afraid of strange sights and sounds in the busy port of Liverpool. In fact, Erik Nelson wasn't much afraid of anything. Even before he left Sweden, the thin blond boy had learned to drive big farm horses.

Now it was April of 1869, and three hundred Swedish Baptists were sailing for a land where they could worship God as they chose. Erik had fretted during the first part of the cruise. That was why he had disappeared during the stopover in Liverpool: He wanted to stretch his legs before the long voyage across the Atlantic.

Soon the ship steamed out of Liverpool harbor. Like the Pilgrims in 1620, the Nelsons were looking for freedom of religion. After they landed in America, they still had a long way to travel: first on crowded trains, then on a covered wagon pulled by oxen. Finally they reached their new farm in Kansas.

Papa Nelson put Erik to work as a herd boy. Every morning Erik drove his cattle out onto the open prairie. Till sunset he watched them there. When he got hungry, he would catch a tame cow and milk her. When he got thirsty, he would peel off his clothes and dive to the bottom of the river. There he would gulp cool water that no hoofs had muddied.

Two big changes came in Erik's life the year he turned fourteen. New laws made Papa Nelson fence in his pastures, so Erik had to learn new jobs on the farm. And in a revival meeting near the Nelsons' home, Erik gave his life to Jesus Christ as Lord and Savior.

By the time a thin blond boy had grown into a tall blond man, the Nelson farm seemed too small for him. Off he rode to Texas on a cattle drive. Later he hauled timber to make railroad crossties. For awhile he even became a bronco buster.

One big black horse had thrown every man who tried to mount him. But Erik knew a trick the other cowboys didn't. He led the black stallion to a dry riverbed. Suddenly he leaped astride that broad back. In knee-deep sand, the bronco couldn't buck or twist. Before long Erik was riding him.

During his wild West days, Erik Nelson had almost forgotten about Jesus Christ. But after three years, he came back home to Kansas. Now he realized that Christ wanted him to preach the gospel. And preach he did—in Kansas, Missouri, Illinois, Indiana—always on the go.

One day Erik read a letter printed in a Swedish Baptist paper. The letter was from W. B. Bagby, pioneer Baptist missionary in Brazil.

"That's the place!" God seemed to say. Once Erik had thought of seeking his fortune as a cowboy in Brazil. Now he knew he must go there to tell people about Jesus Christ.

He sailed from New York on a Brazilian ship. One dark Friday night in 1891, he landed at Belem with just sixteen dollars left in his pocket. Erik wondered: "How long can I live on that?"

The next morning Erik took another walk around another harbor, as he had done long before when he was a little boy in Liverpool. He met several ship captains who invited him to preach on board the next day.

After Erik had held Sunday services, a captain told him, "Lots of sailors here are dying from yellow fever. There's no one to look after 'em. And even the healthy sailors need a missionary, that's for sure!"

So Erik went to work as a waterfront missionary. Some of the captains paid him enough to live on.

Erik knew he needed help. So he wrote to Ida Lundburg, the girl he'd left behind him. Not a penny could he send her to buy a ticket from Kansas to Brazil. Even after Ida had paid her own way and landed in Belem, Erik had to borrow money for their wedding supper. But Ida knew God wanted her to be a missionary in Brazil, too. She was glad to become Erik's wife and helper.

Besides witnessing to seamen, Erik also sold Bibles to Brazilians. This was a risky business in those days. More than once people tried to kill him. But Erik wouldn't quit. By 1897 there were several Brazilians in Belem who had trusted in Jesus Christ.

Other missionaries came to help organize a Baptist church. They ordained Erik as its first pastor. And they worked things out so that Erik and Ida Nelson could become regular missionaries, supported by tithes and offerings from Baptist churches in the USA.

By that time Erik was getting restless again. For six long years he had stayed in Belem. Now he jumped at the chance to visit Manaus, more than a thousand miles up the Amazon River. He began to realize how few people along that great valley really knew about Jesus Christ.

Soon he started riding river steamers, selling Bibles, and telling the good news. He had to travel the cheapest way. This meant swinging his hammock just above live animals that slipped and slid in the stinking hold of the vessel. It meant being bothered at all hours of the night, whenever the boat stopped to load or unload. It meant being waked up early by the cook as he jerked a cow or pig or sheep over to the rail and slaughtered it right there for food.

Erik Nelson put up with all of this in order to share the story of Jesus. But he knew that many river coves were not being reached by any steamboat.

In 1910 Erik began to roam the river in his own little canoe. He had it loaded with Bibles and food. For weeks at a time, neither Ida nor anyone else would know exactly where he was.

Once a doctor warned him, "You're about to die of malaria." Erik crawled into his canoe and drifted five hundred miles downstream. By that time he felt so much better that he paddled five hundred miles back again. Another time he rowed seven hundred miles against the current, to preach to Brazilians in a distant spot.

One of those he won to Christ was Mark, who suffered from Hansen's disease. (Some people call it leprosy.) In spite of his illness, Mark was a good carpenter. He carved and fitted a beautiful little boat for the missionary. Erik built a palm-leaf roof to keep out sun and rain. He added an outboard motor, and he named the boat *Noah's Ark.*

Now Erik could reach many more places. People would hear the noisy putt-putt of *Noah's Ark.* They would blow hunting horns to call their neighbors together. Then they would hang a white cloth in a tree to guide Erik toward a riverbank preaching point.

Still Erik was restless. *Noah's Ark* couldn't get to everywhere he wanted to go. Then in 1920 a Baptist church in Murray, Kentucky, bought him a fine launch. It had a cabin with two bunks, a kitchen, electric lights, and mosquito screens. It was sturdy enough to ride out river storms, or fast enough to outrun them.

Hearing the roar of that powerful oil-burning motor, Erik

remembered his wild West days. He named his new launch the *Buffalo*.

At last Erik Nelson could go wherever he wanted to. He piloted the *Buffalo* up and down sixteen thousand miles of navigable waters in the Amazon Valley. He nosed his craft into side streams and swampy lakes where few other boats ever went. Sometimes he had to shove his launch between overhanging trees or cut a path through dense floating grass. Everywhere he went, he told Brazilians about the Savior of the world.

In May of 1939 Erik Nelson was seventy-six years old. Yet he was still on the go. With a younger missionary, he started a complete survey of the Amazon Valley. He wanted to plan more mission work for the future.

But after only a few weeks out on the river, Erik Nelson got sick. The other missionary had to steer the *Buffalo* back home to Manaus. The brave old man kept on planning other trips as he lay in his bunk, till he died on June 15, 1939.

Other mission launches churn up and down the Amazon today. Other missionaries—Brazilians and foreigners—bear the name of Christ to distant river coves. But no other person has ever preached throughout that great valley as much as Erik Nelson did. He was always on the go.

Belem: bay-LANE   Manaus: mah-NAH-oos

5
Stubborn Saxon Seed Sower
Gottlob Bruckner
of Germany and Indonesia

The greatest of all missionaries, Paul of Tarsus, once wrote: "I planted, Apollos watered, but God gave the growth."*

This is the story of a missionary who planted seed. He was a stubborn Saxon from Germany who never knew when to quit.

Gottlob Bruckner was born in 1783. He was one of six sons of a farmer in the Saxon village of Linda. His very name tells of his parents' faith, for "Gottlob" means "Praise God" in German. Often young Gottlob's father sang hymns with his boys. In the evenings he read to them from Christian books.

When he was twenty, Gottlob Bruckner left home to seek his fortune. His father wept to see him go. "Remember Jesus Christ, who is risen from the dead!" Gottlob's father reminded him.

Gottlob Bruckner had no money for easy travel. He walked the road northward for eight days till he came to Berlin.

As he met other young workingmen in the city, Gottlob began to doubt what he had been taught from the Bible. But he also met a preacher whose sermons made him think and pray. For the first time he became a follower of Jesus Christ on his own, not because of what his parents believed.

The Berlin pastor often read aloud reports from William

---

* 1 Corinthians 3:6, RSV.

Carey. Carey had once been an ordinary craftsman like young Gottlob Bruckner. Gottlob was still a boy plowing his father's fields in Saxony when Carey the cobbler had left England to go as a missionary to India. For seven long years he had told the good news there before even one person would believe. Now reports reaching Berlin told of many Christians in India.

A voice deep inside Gottlob Bruckner seemed to say, "You must be a missionary, too." His friend and pastor directed a missionary training school. That was a good thing because Gottlob probably could not have enrolled anywhere else for lack of schooling when he was younger. A year and a half he studied with the Berlin pastor. Then he was sent to Holland for more training.

It wasn't easy for a Saxon farmboy to learn Dutch, even though that language is a lot like German. But Gottlob Bruckner was stubborn. He stuck to the task and studied for three more years.

By 1811 a mission society in the Netherlands was ready to send out Gottlob Bruckner with two of his fellow students. But how could they? The Emperor Napoleon with his wars had torn up the map of Europe. Holland was under the heel of France. No ship could get permission to sail, lest it help Britain, Napoleon's great enemy.

At first the mission society sent Bruckner and his friends back to Germany again for another year of study. Then at last they thought of a plan: The three would be disguised as workingmen. (In fact they were workingmen, as well as being missionaries.) They would be smuggled from Germany to Denmark, from Denmark to Sweden, and from Sweden to England.

Bruckner never knew when he might need to run. So he couldn't take a trunk or even a suitcase—just one small bundle. He never knew when his pockets might be searched. So the Dutch mission society didn't dare give him a letter of introduction to Christian friends in England: He might get shot as a British spy!

German police in Hamburg made trouble for the three travelers. Finally they escaped across the border into Denmark. They sailed to Sweden, and then sailed again to England. Their roundabout journey took two months.

English Christians were happy to greet the three new recruits. But before appointing them as missionaries, there must be some testing done. Of course the tests were given in English . . . and of course nobody passed. "You must study some more," the English mission society decided.

A less-stubborn man might have gone home to Saxony. Not Gottlob Bruckner. He studied English as hard as he had studied Dutch. After a year in an English seminary, he was ordained and appointed a missionary.

Where should he be sent? Some said Guyana, in South America. Some said the great island of Madagascar, near Africa. Some said Java, another large island, with even more people than Madagascar. England had taken over Indonesia from the Dutch during the Napoleonic wars. Now the way lay open to send missionaries there.

By this time Napoleon had nearly been beaten. Peacetime travel was beginning again. So Gottlob Bruckner's trunks could at last be shipped across the Channel to England. But the warehouse where they were stored caught fire; everything in it burned up.

Gottlob Bruckner forgot about his disappointment and loss. On New Year's Day 1814, he sailed away toward the mission field. His ship nearly went down in a storm near the equator. Then it limped into port in South Africa. There Bruckner and his friends preached to white people and black, till another ship took them on toward Indonesia.

The three missionaries landed at Jakarta, the capital. A British governor welcomed them. Then Bruckner sailed on alone toward Semarang, a large seaport on the north coast of Java. Twice his ship was attacked by pirates. After going ashore again, he had to hike through forests where tigers roamed.

In Semarang he became pastor at a great stone church, built by the Dutch long before he was born. His church members were mostly Dutch, too, or people from mixed Dutch and Indonesian families.

Only four months after he arrived in Semarang, Gottlob Bruckner married the daughter of an old Dutch pastor. Children came into their home one by one, till there were eight of them in all. But tropical fevers often strike little ones, and there were no miracle medicines in those days. Four of the Bruckner babies died.

While Bruckner was visiting other cities of Java, a new missionary family arrived in Semarang. They were Mr. and Mrs. Thomas Trowt, Baptists from England. Gottlob Bruckner and Tom Trowt were the same age. Soon they became best friends. Bruckner admired Tom's keen mind and the way Tom set to work learning the Javanese language.

Bruckner himself had learned the Malay or Indonesian language by now; he found that many of his church members didn't really understand sermons in Dutch. What was worse, many of them didn't really understand what it meant to be a Christian at all. Bruckner became more and more sad to see people who lived like the devil all week and yet came to church on Sunday. And he had to welcome them at the great stone church as if they were the truest believers on earth.

Bruckner talked with Tom Trowt. He thought more and more about what baptism really means. He studied what the Bible says about it.

Finally he made up his mind. On the last Sunday in March of 1816, he climbed the winding steps to the high wood-carved pulpit. From the great Dutch Bible there he read his text: "You search the Scriptures, because you think that in them you have eternal life; and it is these that bear witness of Me."*

Then he gave his congregation a shock. "I plan to be baptized," he announced. "I now believe the Scriptures teach baptism by dipping, *after* a person believes in Christ and not *before.*"

The next Sunday, Tom Trowt baptized Gottlob Bruckner in the river that runs through Semarang into the sea. Many Dutch church members came to watch. But the Sunday after that, the great stone church was half empty. It wasn't long before Bruckner was turned out of his pulpit.

He still had a house, and he invited the Trowts to share it with his own family. But only six months later, Tom Trowt was dead of a tropical fever. No new missionary could come from England to take his place. The wars were over now, and Indonesia had been handed back over to the Dutch.

Bruckner wrote letters to William Carey in India and to other Baptists in England. In due time he himself was appointed to take Thomas Trowt's place.

The new Dutch governor of Java ruled, "All English missionaries must leave." But Bruckner could prove he was a German who also spoke Dutch. So they let him stay.

Tom Trowt had started working on a dictionary and a translation of the New Testament into Javanese. He hadn't gotten very far, and a lot of what he had done was lost. Now Bruckner, the stubborn Saxon, took up the task.

Javanese was far, far harder than any other language he had ever tackled. Morning after morning he struggled with books and teachers. Evening after evening he tramped through the villages, trying to make sounds that people could understand.

No Javanese people would listen when he told them the good news. Java seemed to be an even harder mission field than India had been when William Carey first went there.

---

* John 5:39, NASB.

Bruckner realized more and more that he needed to have the good news in writing. So he kept plodding away on his translation. By 1819, the four Gospels were done; by 1820, the whole New Testament; by 1823, he had revised it all and felt it was ready for the printer.

But how to get it printed? The Dutch governor would not allow anything that might stir up the natives or cut profits from the great plantations on Java. Christians in England sent Bruckner a printing press, but no one on Java knew how to make it work. Besides, the Javanese language used letters different from any other language on earth.

Even the stubborn Saxon was about ready to give up. Then one day he received a letter from India. William Carey was still serving there, after thirty-five years. Carey invited Bruckner to come see him . . . and to bring along that precious manuscript of the New Testament in Javanese.

In 1828 Bruckner said good-bye to his wife and his two little daughters. With his two sons, he sailed away toward India. He never dreamed he would be gone for three long years.

First, he had to teach William Carey's printers how to make type faces that looked like Javanese letters. Then he had to check every page they printed: No one else in all India knew what those strange-looking squiggles meant. His oldest son, a boy of thirteen, caught a tropical fever and died—far from mother and home. Bruckner himself got so sick he had to take a cruise to Malacca and rest awhile.

Finally the great job was finished. With his one remaining son, Bruckner set sail for Indonesia. The hold of the ship held precious cargo: two thousand Javanese Testaments, twenty thousand tracts, bundles of paper for printing, and a set of type faces with Javanese letters.

Near the island of Kalimantan (or Borneo), a typhoon struck the ship. Bruckner and his boy had to hug the mast to keep from being washed overboard. Even the hardened sea captain screamed, "There's no hope!" But God heard the

prayers of a Saxon seed sower that day. A battered vessel
crawled into harbor on Java.

Gottlob Bruckner hardly had time to greet his wife and
daughters. The next five days were full of excitement. Seven
thousand Javanese tracts were passed out into brown hands
of people who seemed eager to read them.

But the Dutch army had been fighting in Java for five
years. The colonial government had just put down a rebel-
lion led by a Javanese prince. What if these new leaflets
roused the people up again? Soldiers seized the rest of the
tracts and all but a few of the Testaments. They locked
Bruckner's lifework inside a safe in Jakarta.

Yet the stubborn Saxon never knew when to quit. He still
had his paper and his Javanese type faces. Quietly, a little at
a time, he still printed tracts. And thus the good news in
writing still spread through the land.

Bruckner also took two of his remaining Testaments and
mailed them far away. One he addressed to the king of the
Netherlands and one to the king of Prussia. The king of
Prussia sent Bruckner a gold medal for his great achievement. The king of Holland did something even better: He
used his influence to change the Dutch colonial government
in Indonesia.

Little by little the contents of that safe in Jakarta were
sent back to Semarang. And Gottlob Bruckner saw to it that
those Testaments and tracts reached the people of Java.

Still, so few of them would believe! The Baptist mission
society in England kept telling Bruckner he should give up
and move to India. Yet the stubborn Saxon stayed on, sowing
gospel seed in stony soil.

Finally he began to see the harvest. Strange . . . the first
fruits came not in Semarang or nearby but far away in East
Java. When Gottlob Bruckner was nearly sixty years old, he
sailed along the coast to Surabaya. In that great port city he
found a few true believers. When he traveled inland, he
found even more.

"How did you come to know about the Lord Jesus?" Bruckner asked an old man who led a village congregation.

"For twenty-four years I was the Muslim priest here," said the old man. "Then one day someone gave me this." And he handed Gottlob Bruckner one of his own Javanese tracts.

What joyful days Bruckner spent with those village Christians! How thankful he was for the seed that had sprouted and grown!

To the end of his life Gottlob Bruckner never saw many direct results from his own faithful preaching and teaching. And for nearly a century after he died in 1857, no other Baptist from anywhere helped spread the good news in Indonesia.

But other helpers came. Near the end of Bruckner's long life, the Dutch government began to change its attitude toward missions. Before he died, he welcomed many new missionaries sent out from Holland by other churches.

When they arrived, they found a field prepared for them. They found the New Testament already in the Javanese tongue. They found gospel tracts, and hymns, and word lists and dictionaries, so that they could quickly start talking with Javanese people.

Today there are hundreds of thousands of Christians on Java—more than in any other place on earth where Islam is the strong majority religion. And this has come to be because in the beginning there was a stubborn Saxon seed sower named Gottlob Bruckner.

Gottlob: GAWT-lawb	Trowt: TROUT
Bruckner: BROO-k'nur	Malay: MAY-lay
Linda: LEEN-dah	Malacca: mah-LAH-kah
Hamburg: HAHM-boorg	Kalimantan: kah-lee-MAHN-tahn
Jakarta: jah-KAR-tah	Surabaya: soo-rah-BAH-yah
Semarang: suh-MAH-rahng	

6
Grandmother with Good News
Ji-Wang of Taiwan

High mountains form the backbone of the island of Taiwan. Many fierce tribes live there. They are not Chinese like the lowlanders: They are closer kin to the peoples of Malaysia, Indonesia, and the Philippines.

Through long centuries the mountaineers of Taiwan have kept their own languages, their own customs. When lowland farmers crowded them out of ancient homelands, they struck back with fire and sword. Young tribesmen who piled up the highest heaps of heads were most likely to win pretty wives. In the marriage ceremony, bride and groom would kneel on a bloodred cloth and drink cups of human blood.

Christians in Taiwan began to pray for these fierce hill tribes. For many years they asked God to open a way to spread the gospel into the mountains. Yet the door always seemed to stay shut . . . till one day someone thought of sending a grandmother with the good news.

Ji-wang had not always been a grandmother, of course. She was born in 1872 as the daughter of a hill-tribe chieftain. By age-old custom her face was tattooed green and purple; hill people thought that made her more beautiful.

Ji-wang was a bright, pretty maiden with many friends. One young warrior picked her out for his own.

But one day a stranger came to Ji-wang's village: a Chinese merchant with strange goods for sale. Out of his bundle he took what looked like a heavy stick. He lifted it to his shoulder. Then—fire shot out the end of it!

Ji-wang's father, the chief, had never seen a rifle before. He and his braves realized how useful it would be in their wars with lowland farmers. But the Chinese merchant drove a hard bargain. He had noticed Ji-wang's pretty face, too. And in return for his rifles he would take no lesser price than a bride.

Ji-wang wept when she left her highland home. But she quickly learned the life of a lowland merchant's wife. Because she was clever, she could soon speak Chinese as well as her own tribal language. She picked up Japanese, too; in those days the Japanese were beginning to conquer the island of Taiwan.

From her mother-in-law Ji-wang first heard about someone named Jesus Christ. But she forgot about that when new troubles came. Her highland sweetheart had never forgiven or forgotten. One day he ambushed and killed her Chinese husband.

Yet Ji-wang did not go back to the mountains as the wife of a murderer. She already knew a different way of life. Not long after, she married another merchant. They moved to a city and made money there.

By this time Japanese colonial rulers were about to lose patience with the hill tribes. They planned to burn off a whole section of mountains. This would drive fierce warriors out of their caves.

Before taking such a drastic step, the Japanese tried one more time to settle things peacefully. They asked Ji-wang to help. She was one of the few people in all Taiwan who knew life as a lowlander and life as a highlander. And she could speak Japanese, Chinese, and one of the tribal languages.

Ji-wang made a success of her mission as a diplomat. She even earned a new nickname: "Ji-wang the Peacemaker." Her tribal relatives were left alone in their mountains without being bothered. But they had to agree to obey the laws and to let their children go to Japanese schools.

The colonial government paid Ji-wang well for her services. They gave her gold bracelets, necklaces, and earrings. They let her set up a trading post near the hills.

For several years Ji-wang's life seemed smooth and easy. Then her greedy husband ran away with all her gold and all the profits from her store. Dead broke and downhearted, Ji-wang moved to a port city with her children.

One day in the year 1924, a Chinese pastor heard someone sobbing in a back room of his church. There he found Ji-wang. She was middle-aged now and in despair. Life had left her nothing good.

Gently the Chinese pastor told her about Jesus Christ who offers new life and love to anyone, anywhere, in any circumstances. Joyfully Ji-wang listened and believed. She was baptized at the age of fifty-two.

Immediately Ji-wang began to tell her neighbors about Jesus the Peacemaker. Some of them pointed at her tattooed face and called her a savage. She answered them boldly: "It's you who are savages, if you don't accept the Savior!"

By 1929 Christians in Taiwan had still found no way to get the good news to mountain tribes. That was the time when someone finally thought of sending a grandmother.

"Me?" gasped Ji-wang when they asked her about it.

"Why not?" they said. "You're the only tribal Christian we know who speaks Chinese. And Chinese is the language used at our Bible school."

"But I'm fifty-seven years old!" she protested. "I'm a mountaineer with marks on my face! How could I go to school with girls from the lowlands—girls young enough to be my grandchildren?"

Yet in the end that is exactly what Ji-wang did. For two years she studied at the Bible school. Her body was aging, and she looked small and frail. But her mind was still quick. In 1931 she was officially appointed a missionary. She began to travel upland trails, taking the good news wherever she went.

The Japanese authorities were displeased. They had been

trying to stamp all Taiwan with their own mold. The official language must be Japanese. The official religion, too, must be Japanese. Shinto shrines had been built throughout the hills.

Security police came to see Ji-wang. They spoke politely to the woman who was still honored as "Ji-wang the Peacemaker." But their words were plain: "You may not roam around teaching this foreign religion!"

Ji-wang smiled to herself after they had gone. "Maybe they can stop me from roaming," she said. "But they can't stop me from teaching."

Clever as ever, she settled in a cottage at the foot of the mountains. Through friends she sent word of her new location. Those who had already been attracted to her message were not just women and children. Some of them were village chiefs. They would slip out of the hills under cover of darkness. Some would walk as far as twenty miles. Dodging Japanese guards, they would hide in Ji-wang's hut.

First she would serve them a hot nourishing meal. Then she would teach them more about the good news, till time came for them to fade away again. Morning light must not catch them there.

Without meaning to, the Japanese government helped Ji-wang spread the gospel. The Bible had not yet been translated into tongues of the hill tribes. But mountain children were forced to attend Japanese schools . . . and Ji-wang saw to it that they got Japanese Bibles to read. More and more of her people came to believe in Jesus Christ.

In 1941 World War II reached Taiwan. All foreign missionaries were driven away. All Christians were suspected of being spies. All Bibles—even Japanese Bibles—were thrown into public bonfires.

Ji-wang herself was still unharmed. But some of those who visited her at night got caught. So did other hill-tribe Christians who dared to tell people about Jesus the Peacemaker.

Some were killed. Some were thrown in prison. Some

were beaten on the ears till they went deaf. Some were tortured till they went crazy. Then they were carted around in cages like animals as a warning to others.

Did persecution stop the spread of the good news? No, just the opposite. The stubborn hill people became curious: "Ji-wang's religion gets the Japanese all stirred up," they said to one another. "Maybe we ought to find out more about it."

So they held worship services in hidden hollows. Watchmen would warn them when Japanese soldiers came near. Others would go out together to weed rice fields . . . and "just happen" to talk about their Lord during rest times.

Ji-wang smiled to herself every time she thought about one way her friends were spreading the gospel, under the very noses of her enemies. The Japanese liked sports. They took a champion wrestler from village to village to show off his strength. But they never guessed what he was saying in a tribal language to those who came to watch. For the wrestler was one of Ji-wang's converts, too!

One day Ji-wang got tired of staying cooped up in her cottage. "I'm going to visit the Christians at Mikasa Yama," she announced.

"Don't do it!" her friends warned her. "The Japanese security police have been more nosy than ever lately. They might punish you!"

Ji-wang smiled. "Who's going to bother an old grandmother just going to see her children?" she said. So she got on the train. By this time railroads had made mountain regions easier to reach.

Friends at Mikasa Yama greeted her. But before they could take Ji-wang home with them, a man asked, "Hey, who's this stranger?"

"Oh, just our dear grandmother," Ji-wang's friends answered. For she was truly like a loving grandparent to all the hill-tribe Christians.

"Oh, is that so?" retorted the man. He was not a believer.

Ji-wang found that there were now fifteen Christian families in Mikasa Yama. Besides that, there were several young men visiting from a village higher up the slopes. What fun and fellowship Ji-wang enjoyed with her spiritual grandchildren!

Suddenly she heard a trumpet blast. "That's the danger signal!" cried local Christians. "The police must be looking for you. Quick, let's hide in the hills!"

Ji-wang shook her grey head. "I'm too old to climb quickly any more," she sighed.

One of the young men from up the mountain had a bright idea. "We'll take turns carrying you piggyback!" he decided. And so they did. Two youths strode in front, two behind, to watch for danger. Up rocky trails they hurried till they reached their own village.

How happy the village Christians were to see Ji-wang! "But you're not safe here, either," they warned. So a fresh team carried her farther yet, to still another village.

"Oh, if only someone had cut the telephone wires!" wailed Christians in the third mountain town. "Then the police here wouldn't have heard that our beloved grandmother is somewhere out in these hills."

Japanese police began raiding one end of the village. The young men smuggled Ji-wang out the other end of it.

"If we could only get her to Bat-king!" they said. "Then maybe she could get home safely by train."

At Bat-king the police had posted three hill tribesmen to guard the railroad station. Two were watching; one had fallen asleep.

"Ssh! Don't make a sound!" warned the two men. They were Christians, too . . . but the sleeping watchman wasn't. Silently they bought a ticket and bustled Ji-wang on board the train. "Hide in the washroom till the police give up the search," they hissed.

The train clanked away into the darkness. But soon it slowed down again for another station. Six policemen jumped aboard.

A young Christian stood on the station platform. He guessed who the security guards must be looking for. Boldly he pushed his way onto the train and ran from coach to coach. When he found Ji-wang, he laid a large cloth on the seat beside her. "Be my carry-on luggage, Grandmother!" he whispered.

The little old woman sat on the middle of the cloth and hugged her legs tight. The young man tied up the four ends of his cloth. When the police came along, he sat quietly with what looked like a big bundle of clothes beside him. And Ji-wang got safely home at last.

All through those years of wartime, Ji-wang never stopped spreading the gospel. And she was never content unless new believers studied God's Word and shared it with others.

One young Christian said, "Grandma Ji-wang told me not to try to preach till I had studied the Bible at least three months."

"Did you obey her?" someone asked him.

"No," he admitted. "Before I finished that three-month Bible course, I had already led twenty-five other people to Christ!"

When the war ended in 1945, Ji-wang was seventy-three years old. She was sick and weary and worn. But her reward was great. From her own tribe alone, there were already four thousand Christians, not counting those from other hill tribes.

These new believers began to come down out of the mountains. One by one, family by family, they started turning up at lowland churches. "Baptize us!" they begged.

Many were poor and hungry. Yet their first request was not "Give us food" but "Give us Bibles."

After being baptized, they climbed the hills again. There they built their own churches, mostly of bamboo and thatch. Even in poverty they sacrificed for their faith. One village Christian tore down his own house, so that its strong roof beams could be used in God's house of worship. Another lifted the door from his house and mounted it again at the new church.

Ji-wang died in 1946. Christians of her hill tribe raised a gravestone in loving memory. And in 1961 the Ji-wang Memorial Church was dedicated to the glory of God.

But there is an even better monument than either of these: It is the fact that more than 50 percent of Taiwan's hill peoples now follow Jesus the Peacemaker.

Ji-wang: JEE-wahng	Mikasa Yama: me-kah-sah-YAH-mah
Shinto: SHIN-toe	Bat-king: BAT-king

7
Liberty Under God
Lott Cary of the USA and Liberia

Liberty. What does that word mean to someone born a slave? Someone whose skin color meant he had no hope of being fully accepted by the majority race in his native land? Someone who knew no letters, no liberty of thought that comes from reading the thoughts of others?

Lott Cary lacked all those kinds of liberty. Yet he realized his lack of yet another kind of liberty, which was more important than all. The apostle Paul called it "the glorious liberty of the children of God."* Lott Cary found that liberty and claimed it as his own. In liberty under God, he found the way to other kinds of liberty as well.

Lott Cary was born on a plantation near Richmond, Virginia, sometime in the early 1780s. His slave parents had no way of marking down the day or month or year. Lott was their only child. He was brought up singing spirituals and hearing stories about the Lord Jesus.

When Lott Cary moved to the city in 1804, he left home teachings behind him. His master hired him out to work in the Shockoe tobacco warehouse. Soon he was drinking and cursing and brawling with the worst of the other young blacks there.

There were a few people in Richmond who cared. They opened the doors of their church on Sunday afternoons. Darkskinned worshipers came to hear an elderly Baptist

---

* Romans 8:21, RSV.

pastor who had once been a chaplain in George Washington's army.

One Sunday afternoon in 1807, the old man preached on the text, "You must be born again."* Somehow Lott Cary found himself longing for new birth in the Spirit of God. When the invitation was given, he walked to the front. His friends shouted for joy.

Another person who cared was Lott Cary's boss at the warehouse. He noticed a change in work habits of the strong, broad-shouldered young man. So Lott began to get extra jobs on the side, and extra pay as well.

Soon he had earned enough to buy himself a Bible. Other young men at the warehouse helped him learn to read it. They studied at spare minutes now and then, before work and at lunch times.

A Baptist deacon cared about the black people of Richmond, too. He started a school that met three nights a week. Lott Cary was the brightest of his twenty students.

The deacon taught reading, writing, and arithmetic. He also taught about God's Word and about God's world. Lott Cary's heart beat faster to hear the deacon read letters from missionaries—from William Carey in India, and from Adoniram Judson in Burma.

By this time Lott Cary was a young widower with three little children. In 1813 he proudly paid his master hundreds of dollars which he had saved through the years. Now he and his youngsters could go free.

As shipping clerk and warehouse foreman, Cary drew a large salary. Besides that, he was so quick and helpful that buyers sometimes tipped him as much as five dollars. Money mounted up faster now that Cary no longer needed to send any of it back home to his master on the plantation. Soon he had bought a house and farm of his own near Richmond.

More and more people were hearing about Lott Cary. He

---

* John 3:7, NASB.

started preaching—at first, only to groups of blacks in and around Richmond. Then he began to get other invitations. He traveled as far west as Lynchburg in the mountains and as far east as Norfolk by the sea. In Petersburg he met Nancy, daughter of free blacks, and a faithful Baptist. Soon the three little Carys had a new mother.

World missions kept on tugging at Lott Cary's heart. In 1815 he led in founding the Richmond African Missionary Society. Black Baptists, slave and free, brought their gifts to help tell the good news. They especially hoped and prayed that they could send the gospel to Africa.

Africa was in the minds of many people during those years. Some Americans thought that the most hopeful future for free blacks might be in the continent their forefathers had come from. In 1783 the British had started an African colony at Sierra Leone as a home for freed slaves. Why shouldn't Americans do the same?

Ideas such as these attracted Lott Cary's attention. But he wasn't interested in going to Africa only as a colonist: Christ had called him to be a missionary.

Warehouse owners in Richmond offered him a 20 percent raise in salary if he would stay. Cary said no. He sold his house and farm to help pay for the voyage. The Richmond African Missionary Society gladly gave him what money they had collected.

The deacon who had been Cary's teacher called together his fellow Baptists. Lott and Nancy Cary and five others were organized into a new church—a church soon to travel across the wide Atlantic. Cary was ordained as their pastor.

The Carys and their friends planned to sail in January of 1821. At a farewell meeting Lott Cary preached before a huge congregation of Baptists, black and white.

"I don't know what may become of me," he admitted. "The ship may sink on the way over. Or I may be killed by savage men or more savage beasts on the coast of Africa. But I'm not anxious. I long to preach to Africans the way of life and salvation. And God has promised in His Word that just as He 'did not spare His own Son, but delivered Him up for us all,' so will He also 'with Him freely give us all things.'*

"No, I'm not worried. In fact, I'm more afraid for some of you than for myself. Someday many Americans will blush when the Savior reminds you about His Great Commission. Jesus may ask each of you, 'Where have you been? What have you been doing?' "

After a stormy voyage of forty-four days, the Cary family landed at Sierra Leone. Nothing but trouble met them there. The British colonial government refused to let them spread the gospel among native Africans. They were instead given farms and told to get to work. To make matters worse, Nancy Cary fell sick with an African fever. In August of 1821 she died.

Finally friends in America sent more money to buy land from an African chief. Cary and his children gladly moved away from Sierra Leone. But they had to face new troubles in the new colony. None of them were used to the six-month rainy season of West Africa. Food and shelter ran short. Fever still brought sickness and death, even though Lott Cary studied medicine and became a doctor through practical experience.

Many of the colonists gave up. Some turned back to Sierra Leone. But Lott Cary stood firm. He talked many more into staying with him. They moved uphill into healthier country and cleared the jungle for a new settlement.

A new governor arrived, sent by Americans who supported the little colony of freed slaves. The governor's high-handed ways made him few friends. Yet when jealous African tribes attacked the little town, he bravely led in its defense.

In wartime Dr. Lott Cary coolly went about his work. He bandaged the wounded as bullets whizzed about his head.

---

* Romans 8:32, NASB.

For three weeks the Americans fought on, outnumbered ten to one. At last a pipe-smoking woman used a live coal to set off a cannon. The explosion terrified enemy warriors. They fled shrieking into the jungle.

Now, at last, the settlers had breathing space to make a good start. They named their country *Liberia*—"because the love of liberty brought us here," they said. They named their town *Monrovia*, in honor of President James Monroe.

Cary reorganized the little Baptist church. By death and desertion its numbers had fallen from seven to three. Soon it grew to over sixty members.

The high-handed young governor caused a revolt. Cary was brave enough to be a spokesman for the rebels. Then the governor got sick with an African fever. Dr. Cary nursed him back to health and won his love and respect at the same time. The result? New laws that gave more freedom to the people of Liberia.

Cary started schools and Sunday Schools for children of settlers and for children from nearby tribes. He was delighted one day to meet a young African named John.

"Me been to S'a Leone," John said in his halting English. "Me see all men go to church house. Me go, too. The man speak, and one word catch my heart." Dramatically the young African laid his hand on his chest. "Go to my home. My heart be very heavy, and trouble me, too. Something tell me go pray to God. Me fall down to pray. Me say, 'Lord, have mercy!' Then light come in my heart. Make me glad, make me light, make me love the Son of God, make me love everybody."

In simple faith John had walked eighty miles to Monrovia. He had heard that there he could learn more about the Son of God. Lott Cary joyfully baptized him. He was the first native church member in all of Liberia. Then Cary gave him three Bibles and sent him home to win others.

Again and again friends in America invited Lott Cary to come back for awhile. Several times he planned to go, but always one of his many jobs kept him too busy. He was missionary, doctor, teacher, preacher, and leader of Liberia.

Once he traveled eighty miles from Monrovia to buy more land from tribal chieftains. At the same time he visited "John the Baptist," whom he had baptized over a year before. He found John faithfully witnessing, though bothered by Mandingo Muslim priests.

"Why don't you move somewhere else?" Cary suggested.

"Me not pay for wife yet," John admitted.

Lott Cary had learned about the African custom of buying a bride. He promised to help John find the money. Later Cary was glad John had been delayed in moving away because he won another young man to Christ. Together they began to walk from house to house, telling the good news.

In 1826 Lott Cary was elected by his fellow settlers to the second highest position in Liberia. When the governor's poor health made him go home in early 1828, Cary became acting governor of the colony. "I plan to ask that you replace me permanently," said the sickly young governor as he boarded a ship for America.

Governor Cary worked hard during his term of office. He bought more land. He settled new colonists on their farms. He saw to it that guns and cannons were cleaned and oiled. As the rainy season ended in November, he looked forward to more progress for Liberia.

But a shout from the lookout at Monrovia harbor changed his plans: "Slaver off the coast!"

Cruel men still carried human cargo up and down the coasts of Africa. Brave soldiers and sailors of Liberia had fought them off many times. Now a Spanish slave ship was again trying to break the law.

Governor Cary declared war. He mustered his army. He called every ablebodied Liberian into active duty.

"We're short of cartridges," the captain reported. Cary himself took on the tedious job of filling cartridges with gunpowder. A team of four men helped him. When night fell, they went on working by the only kind of light available: a candle.

At midnight Governor Cary stood up to go. He needed to check on other preparations for battle. But as he left, three boys—too excited to sleep—dashed into the armory. One of them nudged the candle with his elbow, and . . . eight people died in the explosion.

Lott Cary did not live to see his troops march off to defeat both Spaniards and slave-trading tribesmen. He did not see new missionaries come to carry on his work. He did not see tens of thousands of Liberians find life and liberty under God. He did not see Liberia become the first independent republic on the entire continent of Africa—and for more than a century, the only republic.

But Lott Cary did live to see liberty: liberty from slavery, liberty from ignorance, liberty from sin, liberty to serve the Lord Jesus Christ. He saw and found his land of liberty, and he gave his very life for it.

Monrovia: mun-ROE-vee-ah   Mandingo: man-DING-o

8
Angel on the Waterfront
Marie Buhlmaier
of Germany and the USA

On the base of the Statue of Liberty in New York Harbor is inscribed a famous poem by Emma Lazarus. It ends with these words:

> Give me your tired, your poor,
> Your huddled masses yearning to breathe free,
> The wretched refuse of your teeming shore,
> Send these, the homeless, tempest-tossed, to me:
> I lift my lamp beside the golden door.

These lines picture the attitude Americans like to think they have always had toward newcomers from other lands. But as a matter of fact America has often seemed like anything but a "golden door" standing open to welcome weary wayfarers.

Nowadays most immigrants to the USA have sponsors before they come. People know they are coming, and promise to help take care of them when they arrive. International airports are dotted across the countryside; many newcomers can be greeted by friends or kinfolks soon after they step onto American soil.

It wasn't like that in the late 1800s and early 1900s.

Between 1890 and 1924, twenty million immigrants thronged into the USA. In just one year, 1907, more than one and a quarter million of them landed in America.

Suppose you had been one of those one and a quarter million people. Suppose you were an immigrant, say, from

Austria. After a long hard train trip to a North German port, you make a rough crossing of the stormy Atlantic. (It's always rough crossing the ocean when you have to travel in steerage, the cheapest part of the vessel.)

Then the ship lands in, say, Baltimore. You and hundreds of others are herded across a bridge onto a big covered area of the dock. It is freezing in winter, steaming in summer, overrun with tired travelers.

American officials check your passport, your visa, your other papers. Most of them speak little or no German, or else they have such bad accents that you can't be sure what they mean. Government doctors check to make sure you have no infectious diseases. Did a member of your family break out in a rash on the way across? Sorry about that; he or she may have to stay behind, and maybe you, too, to care for the sick one.

Probably you're not planning to stay in Baltimore; you have saved back enough money to buy a train ticket to somewhere else. But first you must change your European money into American dollars, and this can be a hassle. Then you must struggle to the proper ticket window.

Everybody seems to be in a hurry. Everybody seems to be yelling instructions at you, and frowning when you don't understand. Everybody seems to be pushing you on toward the next step in the process.

With a sigh of relief you finally make it to the stairs. Be careful! Many a weary newcomer has taken a bad fall down those rough wooden steps.

When you get to the bottom, you find an even bigger room. It's still on the dock; through cracks between planks you can see the ocean surging underneath.

A few hardbacked benches stand here and there, but those in line ahead of you have already plopped down on all of these. Where can you rest while waiting for your train? You guessed it: others are already sprawled all over that filthy, drafty floor.

What's that mountain at the ocean end of the dock? Luggage! And now the customs inspector expects you instantly to dig out of that mountainous heap every trunk and box and suitcase you brought with you from the old country. You sweat and heave and fumble with your keys. At last everything is cleared. You try to tie it all back together again so it can be loaded onto the train.

Clang! Clang! Trains are pulling up on tracks in the street just outside the other end of the dock. How can you tell which train is yours? How can you climb aboard with all that baggage? Where can you find a seat? Who will look out for younger members of your family and make sure they don't get run over or left behind?

Then a woman walks toward you—a smiling woman who wears a huge kitchen apron. Her eyes twinkle behind granny glasses. She speaks . . . and you want to fall into her arms. For the motherly little woman in the big apron is speaking your own language!

"Yes, yes, I know it's hard, but I'm here to help you," she clucks in clear German with a country twang. "Let's see, where is it you want to go to? O yes, not to worry, that train won't be here for half an hour yet. The little ones are thirsty? Just you rest here, I'll get 'em cups of water from the faucet yonder. And here's something written in good old German for you to read while you wait."

Out of the pockets of her apron she hands you tracts and booklets. You and your family begin to read in your own language about the loving Lord Jesus, who said, "Come to Me, all who are weary and heavy-laden, and I will give you rest."*

Soon the little woman is back again, with cool refreshing drinks. She helps you know how much to pay for snacks at the food stalls. She answers your questions about the train trip to your new home. Gently, lovingly, she tells you more

---

* Matthew 11:28, NASB.

about the Lord Jesus Christ. When you show that you are interested, she digs deeper into those bottomless apron pockets and presents you with a German New Testament for your very own.

Locomotive bells begin to clang again; like a mother hen she guides you through the maze of gates and tracks onto the right train. She shooes other passengers into closer clumps on the seats, so you and your family can sit together. With a prayer and a smile she waves good-bye. And you wonder whether the angels in heaven will give you any warmer welcome than the lady in the kitchen apron.

That was how Marie Buhlmaier must have seemed to many of those millions dumped onto our shores: like an angel on the waterfront. For a quarter of a century she was a missionary to immigrants.

Marie Buhlmaier knew firsthand what it felt like. She came to America in 1868 when she was nine years old.

It was not an easy move. Marie's prized dollhouse had to be left behind in Germany. Her father the village blacksmith had gone on ahead to prepare the way, and Marie was the oldest of four children. She and her mother felt helpless to load on three sleepy little ones and all the luggage when their train arrived late at night. Two young men stepped forward to help the Buhlmaier family. Marie never forgot about that.

After being seasick all the way across, Marie smiled to see her father's face again in New York City. But hardly had they arrived when he lost his job.

Marie volunteered to go to work. She earned seventy-five cents a week crocheting trimmings for dresses. She worked hard, and later she was promoted to doing baby shoes, at a dollar fifty a week.

The other little Buhlmaiers passed from grade to grade. Marie studied their books at home by lamplight. She never got to go to school in America, the land of opportunity.

When Marie was fourteen, her family moved to a new

neighborhood. There she met a famous doctor and his daughters. Once a rainstorm drove Marie and her girl friends inside. She heard the doctor leading family worship. Marie had known Bible stories all her life, but never before had she heard anyone pray as if he really knew the Lord.

The doctor's daughters invited Marie to Sunday School. The very first time she came, the teacher was absent. Marie's friends insisted that she teach the lesson. It turned out to be one of the Bible stories Marie knew well, so she did teach that day. By October of 1873, Marie Buhlmaier was a baptized member of a German-speaking Baptist church. So were her mother and her father.

Not long after that, the doctor asked Marie to start working part-time as a missionary for the church. She would be paid a little to visit in the neighborhood two afternoons a week, telling people about the Lord Jesus.

Marie was frightened. She was not yet fifteen years old. She was shy, she had little education, and she spoke broken English. Yet she resolved to try.

She walked all the way across New York City to get some gospel tracts in German. Then she and the doctor planned which streets she should start out visiting.

On the first day Marie walked all the way around the block because she was too scared to go into any of the houses. Then she threw back her shoulders like a soldier, marched straight to the first apartment she saw, and knocked on the door.

Through the years that followed, Marie Buhlmaier worked sometimes as a home missionary, sometimes as a housemaid, sometimes as a seamstress. Once when she was sewing in the home of a German-speaking woman, she led both the woman and her husband to trust in Jesus Christ as Lord and Savior.

The next summer that family vacationed in Maryland. They told a Baltimore Baptist pastor about the little seamstress in Brooklyn.

And so it happened on the same day in August of 1893 that

Marie Buhlmaier received letters from three people she had never met. One was from the German-speaking Baptist pastor in Baltimore. One was from Miss Annie Armstrong, great leader of Baptist women. One was from an official of the Southern Baptist Home Mission Board. All three letters asked the same thing: "Would you come and be our missionary to the immigrants pouring into Baltimore?"

At first Marie thought they must have gotten her name mixed up with someone else's. Gradually she came to realize that the Lord had been preparing her through all the years for just such a job as this.

She stopped by Miss Armstrong's office on the way: "Miss Strong Arm," as Marie later called her, only half in fun. "Be sure to come to me anytime you need help," said Annie Armstrong with a smile. "I want you to know I'm your friend."

Marie worked on the waterfront every time a passenger ship docked. She also helped at a mission church nearby. She put her sewing skills to good use by starting classes in many a foreign neighborhood. Women and girls learned to use their needles, and they learned about the Lord Jesus at the same time.

But always, always there were more people stumbling onto the immigration dock. They never forgot that friendly, bespectacled face beaming above the apron full of tracts and Testaments.

Marie spoke the Swabian dialect of German. Many Poles, Hungarians, and Russians could understand her, as well as Germans and Austrians. "Miss Strong Arm" helped Marie build up her kitchen cabinet supply of giveaways. Little by little she got together gospel literature in many languages of Europe.

Occasionally Marie Buhlmaier took a few days off from work to go traveling with Annie Armstrong. Together they visited Baptist women's meetings. To her amazement Marie found herself standing before hundreds and thousands of people. Eagerly they listened to the stories she could tell:

• There was the boy who thought he had lost a precious slip of paper. It told the name and address of the only person he knew in all of America.

• There was the girl who danced for joy on the dock when she got a Bible all her own. In the old country she had only been able to borrow one from her pastor.

• There was the mother who had been persuaded against her will to leave the old country. Then her husband had died on the way across, and here she was with four children, begging to be sent back home.

• There was the grieving young father with a baby ten days old; he had buried the mother at sea. When he exchanged all his money, it came to just seventy-two cents.

• There were three hungry little ones in the bitter cold of winter. Their mother had had to use her last penny to buy tickets. She had nothing left to feed her children during their twenty-four-hour trip by train.

• There was the man on an outgoing ship whom Marie did not spot till the vessel was starting to steam away. She trotted along the dock and managed to poke a few tracts into his outstretched hand. Two months later he was back. He said the tracts had been welcomed so eagerly in the old country that people had read them to pieces. "Please, kind lady, give me all you can spare," said he, "so I may send them more as soon as possible."

• There was the shipload of families in which nearly all the children had caught measles. That day the whole dock floor was covered with moaning little bodies. Mothers desperately tried to ease the pain . . . and Marie Buhlmaier hurried from group to group, bringing hope.

• There was the girl who insisted that Marie take a dollar as thanks for her help. Marie used the dollar to start a scholarship fund, so younger missionaries could get a better education than she herself did.

Not till World War I did the tide of immigration from Europe begin to ebb. By that time Marie Buhlmaier's health had begun to break under the burdens she bore for others. She lived on until 1938 and followed the Lord faithfully all her days. But she is best remembered for that crucial quarter century from 1893 till 1918 when she walked the waterfront at Baltimore, welcoming men and women and boys and girls into the kingdom of God.

Buhlmaier: BULE-my-er   Swabian: SWAH-bee-ahn

9
Steadfast South Sea Islanders
Ruatoka and Tungane of Rarotonga
and Papua New Guinea

Many years ago, in the middle of the nineteenth century, two tan-skinned children were growing up on the South Sea Island of Rarotonga. On that coral atoll under the tropical sun, they played on warm white sand and swam in cool green water. When they got bored with the beach, they could always walk inland toward coconut, banana, breadfruit, and orange trees that shaded lush green hillsides.

Who would ever want to leave such a lovely place? The tall boy Ruatoka and the little girl Tungane thought they would spend their whole lives on Rarotonga. The nicest thing of all about growing up there was that Ruatoka and Tungane knew about the Lord Jesus, and loved Him, too. A generation before they were born, Christ's namebearers had reached the South Sea Islands.

Ruatoka's father was old before he became a Christian. Often he told his son about the olden days. "There sat the high chief," said Ruatoka's father, pointing toward a great throne of volcanic rock. "And there, the high chief's enemies were killed by having their heads bashed in."

Ruatoka shuddered. He could still see dark red stains on the huge altar stone. How glad he was that Christ had changed Rarotonga!

As Ruatoka grew older and taller, he kept on studying at the mission school. One day a new teacher arrived from Scotland. His name was James Chalmers, but in the island dialect he was called *Tamate*. Ruatoka loved his lessons with the lively young Scotsman. He came to feel that Tamate was his spiritual father.

By this time the childhood friendship between Ruatoka and Tungane had blossomed. One fine day they went to church and became man and wife. Together they began to build a Christian home.

Often Tamate and other missionaries spoke about Papua, an island much larger than Rarotonga. It lay a thousand miles and more to the west. "The people of Papua are still savages," Tamate explained. "Some are even cannibals. How they need to know the good news of Jesus Christ!"

Among the first young Rarotongan Christians to volunteer as missionaries were Ruatoka and Tungane. But some of the church leaders objected: "Look how tall and thin Ruatoka is," they said. "Like a palm-tree sapling! He'll never last. What's the use of sending him to Papua?"

Only Tamate spoke up for Ruatoka. "Don't think he's weak just because he's skinny," insisted Tamate. He managed to convince the others. So Ruatoka and Tungane were appointed in a special ceremony. Then they and other Rarotongan missionaries were sent away to the far west.

For many days Ruatoka and Tungane voyaged. At last they landed on Papua. But the village where they settled turned out to be unhealthy. Many of the young South Sea Islanders fell sick, and some of them died. The rest sailed away again, to find a better place.

A sea captain had recently explored far down the southern coast of Papua and had named a bay after himself: Port Moresby. It didn't look like much when Ruatoka and Tungane arrived there in 1871. Instead of white sandy beaches like those on Rarotonga, there were muddy swamps. Instead of neat villages, huts perched on bamboo platforms that jutted out over the water. Instead of green hills, bare stony mountains. And who knew where cannibals might be hiding in the tall jungle grass?

They tried to make the best of it. Ruatoka put up a small

wooden house near the bamboo huts. There he and Tungane cared for their little children.

Some of the other South Sea Island missionaries were better teachers than Ruatoka. But they soon moved on to other mission stations. Only Ruatoka was left to open a school at Port Moresby.

At first the schoolchildren of Papua didn't like Ruatoka. They whined and dawdled, and asked to be paid for each letter of the alphabet they learned.

Grown-up Papuans weren't much friendlier, either. A witch doctor got angry when Ruatoka taught that black magic was meaningless and wrong. Many a night Ruatoka and Tungane had to sit up watching long after the children were asleep. They were afraid the witch doctor and his sons would do them some harm.

In 1874 new missionaries arrived from Rarotonga. Ruatoka and Tungane helped them during those first hard weeks of learning a new language and a new way of life. But many of them got sick and had to hurry off to a healthier climate. And many of them died. Ruatoka buried them on a low hill near his house.

In 1877 he joyfully welcomed Tamate, his special friend among the missionaries. Tamate and Ruatoka hiked off into the jungle with several helpers. They looked for tribes that might be open to the gospel.

For one whole day they tramped without meeting another living soul. Then they made camp beside a wide river swarming with crocodiles.

Early the next morning they were on the trail again. Suddenly they came face-to-face with a large band of Papuans!

Their dark faces had been made darker still with soot and grease, then decorated with white powder. Their mouths were strawberry red from chewing betel nut mixed with tobacco. Their noses were pierced with animal bones . . . or were they human bones? Their eyes flashed with hate and suspicion. And their hands held sharp spears.

Ruatoka smiled as he stepped forward to greet them. With one hand he held his nose; with the other he pointed to his stomach. "Quick, do what I do!" he hissed to Tamate. Ruatoka had already learned what those strange gestures meant in Papuan sign language: "We come in peace."

That wasn't the only strange thing about Papuans' lifestyle. Some of them not only lived on mountaintops; they also built their huts in the tops of the tallest trees there. Some of them thought they could drive away rain by spitting at it.

Tamate began to pioneer for Christ in Papua. Boldly he traveled everywhere, meeting wild and wary tribes. He found places where other missionaries could follow and settle down to spread the gospel.

During those years, somebody had to stay in Port Moresby. Somebody had to keep the mission school running. Somebody had to welcome new missionaries. Somebody had to help them guard their health, learn the language, and get a good start living in Papua.

For many years Ruatoka and Tungane held the fort in Port Moresby. Other missionaries, from East and West, might have been more talented than they were. But none outdid them in steadfastness. Ten years, twenty years, thirty years and more they faithfully served their Lord.

The first Papuan who believed was Tungane's convert, not Ruatoka's. Ruatoka was gone on one of his hikes with Tamate when somebody knocked on the door at midnight.

"Who's there?" asked Tungane.

"Me," answered a man's voice.

Tungane wasn't surprised at his answer; she knew Papuans didn't like to speak their own names to others. But she had her children to protect, as well as several girls from the mission school who were sleeping at her house.

"What do you want?" she asked again.

"Open the door, and I'll tell you," said the voice.

Tungane tried to persuade him to wait till morning. But

the man's urgent need seemed genuine. Finally she got up, lit a lamp, and unlocked the door. "Now, what is it?" she asked again of the Papuan standing before her.

"I'm not sure, ma'am," he said with a troubled look. "But I think the Holy Spirit you told us about must be working in my heart. I'm afraid to go to sleep lest I die, for I'm a very wicked man."

Gently Tungane told him how the Lord Jesus drives away wickedness and fear. He listened eagerly, prayed with her, and then left. Before dawn he was back again, begging to hear more.

That man became the first Papuan baptized upon profession of faith in Jesus Christ as Lord and Savior. Later, he became a deacon in the little church Ruatoka and Tungane were building in Port Moresby.

More and more foreigners appeared in town these days: gold had been discovered in the mountains. Ruatoka greeted the newcomers politely, even though some of them looked down on him as "just another one of the natives."

Papuan tribal peoples got nervous about the inrush of white-skinned gold miners. Rumors flew that they were planning a massacre in the mountains.

"I must stop this," said Ruatoka to Tungane when he heard it.

"Don't go!" Tungane begged him. "They'll kill you!"

But Ruatoka struck out into the jungle toward the white men's camp. In his limited English he told them about the danger. "I go speak black man he no kill you," Ruatoka offered.

"Good for you!" cried the miners. "We'll go along, and take our guns."

"No!" Ruatoka forbade them. "Black man see gun, he throw spear, then you shoot. Better I go speak peace."

"They'll kill you, Ruatoka!" the miners warned him.

But Ruatoka slipped away again into the jungle. He hurried toward the place where he had heard tribal warriors were gathering. Boldly he stepped out into a clearing amid hundreds of armed savages.

"What's all this?" he demanded in their language. "Are you thinking of fighting the white man? Hear me: This is foolishness!"

Instantly twenty spears were aimed at Ruatoka's chest. "You're on their side!" they accused him. "They take our land. They make the spirits of our ancestors angry. We'll kill them all—yes, and kill you, too!"

"Why?" Ruatoka asked calmly. "If you kill these white men, others like them will come and burn down all your villages. Let them dig the yellow stuff out of the hills; to you it means nothing, but they like it. And they will give you good axes and other useful things if you make peace with them."

Some grumbled, but Ruatoka's words won the day. Then he invited all those war-painted braves to kneel, and he asked God's blessings upon them. And he sent them home in peace.

Yet problems kept on coming up between Papuans and new settlers. There was no real government to settle disputes. The missionaries began to feel it would be wiser if the whole eastern end of Papua or New Guinea were taken under the protection of the queen in faraway Britain.

One day in 1884, five tall British men-of-war sailed into the harbor at Port Moresby. "How can we persuade Papuans that we mean well?" the commodore asked.

"There's only one way," answered Ruatoka and the other missionaries. "We must go in person and tell their chiefs."

So Ruatoka boarded one of the big ships and sailed west. Tamate boarded another and sailed east. Papuan chiefs, brightly dressed in paint and feathers, gathered to watch the British flag being pulled up the pole at Port Moresby.

"What does all this mean, Ruatoka?" asked the puzzled chiefs.

"It means that no one can take away your land," explained

Ruatoka. "If anyone tries, the great queen will punish him. It means you may not make raids and murders. It means you must bring your disputes to the queen's officer and let him settle them."

As he sat by countless campfires, Ruatoka explained in simple words how the new government could help the peoples of the jungle. But some things even the colonial government could not control.

One Sunday Ruatoka was leading morning worship when a deafening racket drowned everything out. Ruatoka dismissed the congregation and strode out of church, an English Bible in his hand. Nearby a Scottish settler was hammering on an iron roof. "Say, come down!" Ruatoka ordered him.

The Scotsman glanced at him, then went on working.

"Say, you no savvy?" demanded Ruatoka. "I speak come down!"

The Scot began to shout insults and curses at the tall darkskinned man standing near the ladder below.

Ruatoka waited till the roofer ran out of breath. Then he thundered out: "You talk foolishness! Before, my people eat your people. Then your people send missionary, and my people get good. Then I come here and speak black man that Sunday taboo: no fish, no hunt, no build house on Sunday. Then black man see you, and he say, 'Ruatoka, you make lie!' What for you do that? Come down!"

The Scotsman's boss by this time joined Ruatoka in ordering him down. Ruatoka thrust the Bible at him. It was already opened to the Book of Exodus. "Read that!" he demanded.

The roofer mumbled through the Fourth Commandment: "Remember the sabbath day, to keep it holy."*

"God, He speak," said Ruatoka as he closed the Bible.

---

* Exodus 20:8, RSV.

"You no work now. Put down hammer!" And the rest of that Lord's Day was peaceful in Port Moresby.

Years passed. Ruatoka's black hair turned grey. He became like a father to all the younger missionaries, from Great Britain and from the South Sea Islands alike.

A new chapel was built on the campus of the mission college. Who should dedicate it? Tamate? "Oh, no," replied Tamate and the other veteran missionaries. "Ruatoka was here before any of us. Let him do it."

On that historic day, the queen's lieutenant governor stood out among the crowd. But it was Ruatoka who led the way and unlocked the door of the new chapel. Yet he did not immediately step inside. Only those nearest heard him whisper in the Rarotongan language: "Go in first, my Lord. We will follow."

Sunlight streamed through a special window in the new chapel. On it were inscribed the names of eighty-two South Sea Island missionaries who had given their lives in Papua. Only Ruatoka was left—the one they had thought too frail to last as a missionary!

Now there were young men and women volunteering to replace those who had fallen by the way. Better yet, now there were Papuan boys and girls hearing the call of God to go out as bearers of the name of Christ.

At Easter time in 1901, Ruatoka heard sad news: Tamate, James Chalmers, his spiritual father, had been murdered by Papuan cannibals!

With a heavy heart Ruatoka sat down and wrote a letter:

"My father Tamate's body I shall not see again, but his spirit I shall see in heaven. Hear my wish: The remainder of my strength I would spend in the place where Tamate died. In that village of murderers I would live, to teach the Word of Jesus Christ."

Bold words . . . but Ruatoka was getting old now, and his body was not as strong as his undaunted spirit. After Tamate's death, his health began to fail. By 1903 he, too, was dead.

Three quarters of a century later, Papua New Guinea became an independent nation. At that time it was announced in the capital, Port Moresby, that more than 90 percent of all the new country's citizens were followers of the Lord Jesus Christ.

Ruatoka: ROO-ah-toe-kah   Rarotonga: rah-ro-TAWNG-ah
Tungane: toong-AH-nay   Tamate: TAH-mah-tay

10
Last Chief of the Leni-Lenape
Charles Journeycake of the USA

White men called them Delawares. Indians called them Leni-Lenape: "Real People" or "Original People." They were ancestors of all the Algonkian tribes that roamed the eastern half of North America. The proud Delawares once ruled from the Potomac River to the Hudson River and far into the interior.

It was Delaware Indians who made a treaty with William Penn so that persecuted Quakers could live at peace in Pennsylvania. It was Delawares who first turned to the Lord Jesus Christ when Moravian missionaries came to live among them. It was Delawares who tried to keep other tribes from fighting and killing during the French and Indian War and during the American Revolution.

But by the 1820s, hard times had come upon the once-proud Leni-Lenape. White men had broken treaty after treaty. Settlers kept crowding into Delaware lands. Even when Indians tried to keep the peace, whites attacked their villages, burning and murdering and driving away.

Once, people who pretended to be friendly neighbors borrowed the Delawares' tools and weapons. Then they struck while the Indians were praying and slaughtered ninety-nine of them.

When Charles Journeycake was growing up near the shores of Lake Erie, only one Delaware in all Ohio would claim to be a Christian. That one was Charles's mother.

Sally Journeycake had learned English from her white

mother. She had learned several Indian languages from her Delaware father. When missionaries tried to move into Ohio, the Delawares said no; they had had enough of paleface tricks and paleface teachers. But the Wyandotte tribe nearby let the missionaries stay. Sally Journeycake became their interpreter.

When Charles Journeycake was ten years old, the Delawares had to move again. The trip was long and hard, all the way to where the Kansas and Missouri Rivers meet. It took nearly a year, with a camp for the winter along the way.

The Kansas River was swollen with floods when young Charles first saw it in the spring of 1829. Boldly the boy jumped onto the lead horse to help swim his tribe's livestock across to safety.

As he came up cold and dripping from the water, he saw on the other side a white man wearing a white hat. "Good work, youngster!" the white man called out in the Delaware language.

Charles was impressed to find a paleface speaking his language. Soon he learned the man couldn't talk much. He was a new missionary who had just come to Kansas. But Charles Journeycake himself had learned to speak English, Delaware, Wyandotte, Shawnee, Seneca, and Ottawa. Soon he was helping his mother translate for the missionaries.

When Charles was fifteen years old, he took Jesus Christ as his High Chief. Probably he was the first person of any race ever baptized in what later became the state of Kansas. Two years later his father became a believer. He and Charles's mother were baptized together. When young Charles married pretty Jane Sosha, she became a Christian, too.

The 1830s and 1840s were good years for Charles Journeycake. He and Jane had eight little girls. They owned cornfields and cattle. They rode in a carriage; their horses had silver-tipped harness.

Often Charles and other Delaware braves made hunting

trips as far west as the Rocky Mountains and the Great Salt
Lake. Once a cornered bear turned to chase Charles out of
a cave. The Indian youth beside him dropped his torch in
panic. But in the dark Charles saw the bear's fiery eyes and
brought him down with one shot.

During those same years, Charles Journeycake became
well known as a Baptist preacher. He said no when people
wanted to ordain him. "Let missionaries pastor the churches," he said. "Let me keep on telling the good news as a
layman."

Once Journeycake stopped where Cherokees were holding a gospel meeting. For several days he joined them in
preaching the Word. Another time he met Moses Keokuk,
high chief of the Sauk and Fox tribes. He led Keokuk to stop
drinking the white man's firewater and to start living for the
Lord Jesus Christ.

But good times didn't last for the Delawares. White settlers crowded into Kansas. Some of them brought along
black slaves.

In 1854 Charles Journeycake made the first of many trips
to Washington. There he met with congressmen and other
officials. Again and again he demanded justice and fair play
for the Delawares. Standing straight and tall, he dared to
say, "The white man has lied!"

In 1855 Charles Journeycake was elected chief of the Wolf
clan. In 1861 he was elected high chief of all the Leni-
Lenape. That same year, war split the nation apart. Many
Delaware men marched away to fight for the Union. The
government did nothing to protect families left at home.
Raids and robberies kept on making life miserable for Journeycake and his people.

Finally, in 1868, they packed up and moved one more
time. South of the Kansas state border lay Indian Territory
(now Oklahoma). The Delaware tribe was told to move in
with the Cherokees. Some of the Cherokees didn't like this.
Arguments about land dragged on and on.

The worst thing about moving from Kansas was that churches and missionaries were being left behind. But down in Indian Territory, Chief Charles Journeycake started preaching more than ever. By 1871, fifty of his neighbors on Lightning Creek had been baptized; by 1872, a hundred more.

That same year the Delaware Christians dedicated a new meeting house. At long last Charles Journeycake agreed to be ordained as their pastor. His old mother Sally rejoiced to see the day. It was only five months before she died.

Throughout the 1870s, Delawares kept on turning to the Lord. A tornado blew away the church house in 1876; Cherokee enemies tried to kill Journeycake in 1877 and did kill his brother. But Journeycake kept on telling the good news in spite of everything. By 1880 his church had 226 members.

Journeycake summed up his life when he said, "We have been broken up and moved six times; we have been despoiled of our property. We try to forget these things. But we would not forget that the white man brought us the blessed gospel of Christ, the Christian's hope. This more than pays for all we have suffered."*

The last chief of the Leni-Lenape was growing old now. He needed help as a pastor. New settlers were mostly whites or Indians of other tribes. Journeycake still didn't feel comfortable preaching to them in English. So missionaries came to continue his work. His own daughters went off to college in Ohio, and one of them married a missionary. One became organist and choir director in her father's church.

When Jane Journeycake died in early 1893, a light went out of the old chief's face. He still cheered up when he could mount his pony and go hunting as before. But less than a year later, he had joined his wife in the burial mound.

---

* As quoted in Victor M. Kaneubbe, *Indian Life on New Trails.* © 1955 The Home Mission Board, SBC. Used by permission.

During the days when he was still chief of the Leni-Lenape, Charles Journeycake often remarked, "My people used to have a religion. They worshiped the Great Spirit, and observed many ceremonies. But they did not know Jesus."*

Then he would draw himself up to his full height, looking every inch a proud chieftain. And he would add: "It used to be said that Jesus was the white man's Savior, that He was not suited to the red man. But I know that He has saved one Indian."*

Leni-Lenape:
   LEH-nee-LEH-nah-pee   Wyandotte: WY-an-dot
Algonkian: al-GAHN-ki-un Sosha: SO-shah
Moravian: mo-RAY-vi-un   Keokuk: KEE-oh-kuck

---

* As quoted in S. H. Mitchell, *The Indian Chief, Journeycake* (Philadelphia: American Baptist Publication Society, 1895).

11
Son of the Samurai
Kanzo Uchimura of Japan

The samurai are noble warriors of Japan. In olden times they defended their emperor from attack. Nowadays the code of the samurai still inspires Japanese people to high achievement.

Kanzo Uchimura was born in Tokyo in 1861. His father and grandfather were sons of the samurai. So were their ancestors for two hundred years before.

Kanzo's father was a government official and a classical scholar. He paid little attention to religion. But young Kanzo was different. Each time he and his brothers passed a Shinto shrine, Kanzo stopped to kneel in worship. Each time they played make-believe, Kanzo took the part of a Shinto priest.

Kanzo was sent to the best schools and learned English as well as Japanese. His father hoped he would become a great statesman. And statesmen must learn the international language.

Then Kanzo with several of his classmates transferred to a new type of school far to the north. There they studied practical subjects needed in building a modern Japan: agriculture, trade, forestry, fisheries.

Upperclassmen told Kanzo about the American educator who had been invited to Japan the year before to start the new school. "He not only taught us skills," they said. "He taught us faith as well." Every one of those older students had become a follower of the Lord Jesus because of their teacher's testimony.

One by one Kanzo's own classmates became believers in Christ, too. But Kanzo himself became more and more angry. He argued with anyone who tried to witness to him. In Shinto temples he prayed that the ancient gods of Japan would rain destruction on this strange foreign religion.

Kanzo's Christian friends would not give up. Their changed lives impressed him more than their words.

At last Kanzo Uchimura, like three fourths of his classmates, gave his life to Jesus Christ. He was baptized soon after his seventeenth birthday.

Now Kanzo joined other eager Christian schoolboys in reading the Bible together each morning. They took turns leading worship services and prayer meetings. Often they met outdoors to sing and pray. Often in the dormitory they talked about their beliefs till late at night.

When Kanzo Uchimura and his friends graduated in 1881, the seven boys with highest grades were all Christians. Kanzo himself came out ahead of them all.

On a visit back home to Tokyo, Kanzo laid on his father's desk a book about the gospel. His father was startled. Even though he cared little about religion, he knew how his family had become samurai: Two hundred years before, one of his ancestors had led in persecuting Japanese Christians.

Kanzo's father promptly threw the book in the wastebasket. Kanzo fished it out and laid it on the desk again. The same thing happened twice. Finally the third time his father was at least willing to open the pages of a Christian book and start reading.

The provincial government in the far north had helped pay for Kanzo's education. Now he took a government job there to repay his debt. So did most of his classmates.

Kanzo and his friends wanted to start a new church. They borrowed money from a mission organization to help put up a small building.

Some of them had been baptized by missionaries from one church, some from another. Instead of splitting up or changing over, they decided to start their own independent church.

This did not please the mission organization that had lent them money. A telegram came, demanding that the loan be paid back as soon as possible.

It was a bitter blow for eager young Christians. Kanzo Uchimura did not drift away from Christ because of it. But for the rest of his life, he had his doubts about churches and missions. He even became known later as the "Leader of the Nonchurch Movement." Yet the Lord used Kanzo Uchimura to strengthen churches and promote missions throughout Japan.

All of that happened later. After the telegram came, Kanzo and his friends scraped together enough money from their small salaries. By the end of 1882, Kanzo delivered the last debt repayment to Tokyo.

Good news greeted him there: His father had become a Christian. So had his whole family!

Kanzo decided to stay in Tokyo this time: first as a teacher and later as a government official. He fell in love with a girl from a Christian school. In early 1884, they got married.

But Kanzo found out that attending a Christian school isn't the same as being a true Christian. The girl soon left him. Then she found she was expecting a baby, so she begged Kanzo to take her back again.

Kanzo said no. Many Christians criticized him for his stubbornness. "Of course, the girl is no good," they said. "But when she repented, Kanzo should have taken her back again."

Kanzo Uchimura felt bitter and confused. In late 1884, he sailed away from Japan. After landing in America, he taught for awhile. Then he studied for awhile and finished an advanced degree. But he found no peace.

The president of the college he was attending knew about Kanzo's troubles. One day he called in the unhappy young foreign student. "Why don't you stop looking inside yourself,

Kanzo?" he urged. "Why don't you look instead to Jesus Christ, who bore your sin on the cross?"

Kanzo Uchimura took the college president's advice. From that day forward, he felt the full power of Christ's forgiving love.

After four years in America, Kanzo Uchimura sailed for home. He had no money, no plan, no job, nothing but a burning desire to win Japan for Christ. But how?

He tried teaching at first and had no trouble finding a position. After a year he married again. The future looked bright.

The late 1800s were troubled times in Kanzo's homeland. For centuries Japan had been a hermit kingdom. In the mid-1800s, Japan had at last begun to look outward toward other nations. But in the late 1800s, a reaction set in. Many people insisted that everything Japanese must be better than anything from abroad.

The emperor sent out a special decree about education. It was decorated with pictures of himself and the empress. In public assembly, every student and every teacher in every school must march to the front and bow before a copy of the imperial decree.

To Kanzo Uchimura, this was almost the same as worship. And he would worship no one but Jesus Christ. When his turn came, he marched forward and stood respectfully at attention. But he would not bow.

What a storm he stirred up! Newspapers and magazines reported the incident, blowing it up out of all proportion. Many Japanese demanded that Uchimura be fired, and he was. Persecution broke out against Christians as "traitors to Japan."

How did Kanzo Uchimura react to all of this? At first he knew nothing about it. He fell sick with pneumonia and lay near death for two long months. His wife wore herself out nursing him. Finally she caught the same disease and died.

Then came the darkest period in Kanzo Uchimura's life.

It seemed everything he had tried to build had come to nothing: a church, a school, a Christian home. His own people hated him—they whom he had hoped to win to Christ.

In desperation he moved from place to place, living any way he could. Late in 1892 he married for the third time. He was thirty-one years old now—no longer a youngster, and it seemed his life had been a failure.

In the depths of disappointment, Kanzo Uchimura somehow began to write. Other samurai had dedicated their swords to the emperor; he would dedicate his pen to the Lord.

First he wrote articles, then books. People liked them. Publishers paid for them. By 1897 he was able to move his family back to Tokyo. There he became a regular columnist in one of Japan's most popular daily newspapers.

Kanzo Uchimura discovered that God had given him rare gifts as a writer. His opinions put down on paper came through loud and clear to every reader. He dared to apply Christian teachings to current problems in Japan. And he did it in ways ordinary people could understand.

In 1900 Uchimura began to publish his own magazine. Its title was simple: *The Study of the Bible.* He dug into God's Word in its original languages. Then he interpreted what it meant for the average Japanese.

More and more people subscribed to *The Study of the Bible.* City folks and villagers, college professors and peasants—all were attracted to what Uchimura had to say about the Scriptures. Soon he became one of the best-known writers in Japan.

Kanzo Uchimura still tried to keep his distance from churches and missions. Yet he gathered hundreds of people on Sundays to hear his "lectures" on books of the Bible. Each person who attended was expected to "pay a fee." Say "sermons" instead of lectures and "give an offering" instead of pay a fee, and it becomes clear that Uchimura was pastoring a large church without calling it that. He taught that all true believers should be baptized. Often he conducted Lord's Supper services.

In summers he would gather together readers of his magazine from all over Japan. For ten days he would lead them in special Bible studies. Christian young people who attended these retreats became leaders in many fields of Japanese society.

Uchimura would accept no missionary offerings for his work. Yet he led his followers to study world missions and to send special offerings to Africa and to China. "It is a contradiction," he once admitted. "But it is a good contradiction!"

Another time he said, "There are two *J*'s that I love. One is *Jesus*; the other is *Japan*. I have given my life in serving these two. The code of the samurai is the best product of Japan, but it has no power to save Japan. Christianity has power to save not only Japan but the whole world."

Kanzo Uchimura did not blindly go along with everything that was done in the name of Japan. When Japan fought China in 1894, he supported the war effort. But when Japan fought Russia ten years later, he opposed it. "War is murder on a large scale," he said. "And murder is the greatest crime."

Like Amos and Hosea in Old Testament times, Kanzo Uchimura was not afraid to speak out against wrongs in society. Till the end of his life in 1929, this son of the samurai dedicated his pen to the Lord Jesus Christ. No one can tell how many Japanese were influenced by his unique ministry.

Kanzo: KAHN-zoe	samurai: SAH-moo-rye
Uchimura:	
oo-chee-MOO-rah	Shinto: SHIN-toe

12
Strong-Willed Schoolmistress
Ida B. Hayes
of the USA, Mexico, and Puerto Rico

Ida B. Hayes never planned to be a missionary. In Minnesota, where she was born in 1856, and in Missouri, where she grew up during the Civil War years and after, she didn't hear much about missions. She became a Christian and a faithful church member. But her whole life was aimed toward becoming a teacher.

Ida got a better education than most girls of the 1800s—better than most boys, too, of the 1800s or now. After graduating from Stephens College, she went on to the University of Missouri. By 1879 she had earned a Master of Arts degree.

In those days many schools had a staff member called the lady principal or the dean of women. Ida Hayes did well as a teacher. Not many years later, she became lady principal of Liberty College in Missouri.

That was still her job in the early 1890s. Then the Foreign Mission Board of the Southern Baptist Convention asked her to go and teach at Madero Institute in Saltillo, Mexico.

Ida said no. She had her work, her position, her friends, her life-style. She especially lost interest when she learned that her salary in Mexico would be only half what it was in Missouri.

But somehow she couldn't feel right about refusing. She knew Christ's Great Commission. She knew Madero Institute was a special kind of school, where Mexican girls could learn how to serve God and country. She heard that a Mexican state governor had said, "Our women must be taught to think." And he had given much of the money to get the new girls' school started.

It was mainly a sense of duty that finally caused Ida B. Hayes to change her mind and go to Mexico. In October of 1893 she arrived at Saltillo, six thousand feet high in the mountains. Saltillo was a small city but an ancient one. It had been founded before the Spanish conquered Mexico in the 1500s.

Most people thought Saltillo wasn't a safe place for a woman to live alone. So Ida moved in with a missionary family, the Moselys. Soon she came to enjoy daily prayers with them. She admired H. R. Mosely's boldness in preaching the good news.

Her own work was with the girls at Madero Institute. Soon she loved them like daughters. In a letter back home she told exactly how many were already baptized believers, how many were Christians but had not been baptized because of fear or family pressure, how many were thinking about trusting Jesus, and how many were strongly opposed.

One Sunday night it was Ida's turn to stay in the dormitory with girls who wouldn't go to church. No one was forced to go, and several always stayed at home.

As Ida worked in her room that evening, she heard a soft knock on the door. "Come in," she said.

Three Mexican girls walked in. Ordinarily they would have greeted their teacher with polite words that were proper for beginning a conversation in Spanish. Not these three; they were too excited about what they had to say.

"We've made up our minds," they began. "We felt you were praying for us. So we've come to tell you: We are resolved at any cost to follow the example and command of our Savior. We want to be baptized."

Ida Hayes smiled as she told them how proud and happy she was. She knew these three girls were some of the strongest characters in the school. No doubt their brave stand would influence many others.

Another night, a strange man turned up at the institute. "I come from a ranch near here where five hundred people live," he explained. "Ten of us have been studying a piece of a Bible which we found somewhere. So the others sent me here to see if we could get a whole Bible." He went home to the ranch happy, with a complete copy of God's Word in Spanish.

Experiences like these were in Ida Hayes's mind when she sat down to write a letter in December 1894: "I can't realize that this will be my second Christmas in Mexico, and yet it is true. I did not want to be a missionary. I did not want to come to Mexico. There was simply no rest until I yielded. And now . . . I am happy here."

Some of Ida's experiences in Mexico were hard ones. Congregations in the mountains were persecuted. People threw rocks and fired shots at church buildings. Missionaries were threatened with death when they baptized new converts. Twice a mob of two hundred men tried to catch Mr. Mosely as he left Saltillo on the train. Finally he was arrested and thrown in prison, then sent home to the USA.

Some people thought Ida Hayes should come home, too. But Ida was a strong-willed schoolteacher. She knew her pupils had to face persecution when they followed Christ. How could she herself show fear in the face of danger?

She taught her girls to give as well as receive. They formed their own mission society and collected money to help send the good news all over the world.

The girl who was secretary of the society said, "I have only one cent. It's all I've had for weeks, and I don't know when I'll have any more. But I want to send it." That girl's one cent became part of a special offering of two Mexican dollars. Ida made an English lesson out of the letter the girls wrote, as they sent their gifts to the Foreign Mission Board in Richmond.

After five years in Mexico, Ida Hayes felt her work there

was done. But when she came back home to the United States, she found that missions was in her blood. Soon she was off again to spread the gospel in Puerto Rico.

No schools in that beautiful island needed Ida to look after them. But her Spanish language and experience in Mexico came in handy. She mounted a little pony and rode uphill and down. For eight years she carried the story of Jesus to homes of Puerto Ricans. Sometimes she told it in spoken words; sometimes she sang it in her rich deep contralto.

Ida was middle-aged now and not in good health. Home she came again, thinking that this time she would stay. But at her sister's house in Texas she quickly grew well and strong again. When the Foreign Mission Board asked her to go back to Saltillo as lady principal of Madero Institute, Ida prayed about it and then said yes.

Missionaries and Mexican Christians welcomed her. Saltillo had changed, and so had the institute. Churches were growing; girls from Madero were making a difference in Mexican society. One graduate left a good position to come back and teach for half her former salary. Ida Hayes knew exactly what that felt like. Best of all was the news that some of the Madero Institute girls were in training to become missionaries among their own people.

In 1912 a revolution broke out in Mexico. A great battle with rebels was fought not far away. Many wounded soldiers were brought back from the front to Saltillo. Their general had been killed.

Some people said the girls' institute should be closed. Everyone was afraid to go out after dark, so all night church services and school activities had to be stopped. Even the consul thought all Americans should hurry across to the other side of the Rio Grande. But Ida B. Hayes was a strong-willed schoolmistress. She kept right on.

Once when she crossed the border into Texas to do some shopping, the rebels cut off all travel back toward Saltillo. It was weeks before trains began to run again. When Ida could finally get through, she found bullet holes in the institute building.

Soon shelling began again. All stores were closed, all businesses stopped. But Ida still kept school.

Later she found out it was a good thing she did. A military officer had seen that fine thick-walled building and had wanted to seize it for army barracks. "But I won't take it if school is still in session," he finally decided.

Conditions in Mexico got worse and worse. Rebels tore up the roadbed of the railway; government forces made emergency repairs. A troop train was blown up with dynamite; many soldiers died. Refugees crowded into Saltillo.

By the end of 1913, Ida Hayes was the only American missionary left in all that part of Mexico. Calmly, she continued her work. She looked after schools and churches and everything else. In a letter she wrote: "In spite of these disturbances we are quietly moving on. Sunday two presented themselves for baptism. The services are well attended, and God is blessing His people in these sad times."

In April of 1914, the U.S. Marines occupied the great port city of Veracruz. Mexicans turned against their neighbors to the north. Ida Hayes had to hide in the British consulate for six long weeks. If she had been seen on the streets of Saltillo, a mob would have killed her, as they would have killed any American.

Even a heartbreaking disappointment like that couldn't stop the strong-willed schoolmistress. She hadn't wanted to be a missionary in the first place. But once she got started, nothing could hold her back.

After Ida finally made it in safety to Texas, she looked around and found many Mexicans living on that side of the border. So she went to work as a home missionary among them, for several years before her death in 1920.

Spanish-speaking people in three countries came to know

Christ because Ida B. Hayes knew it was her duty to obey Christ's Great Commission.

Madero: mah-DAY-roe   Rio Grande: ree-oh-GRAHN-day
Saltillo: sahl-TEE-yoe   Veracruz: veh-rah-KROOS

13
Pastor of His People
V. Samuel Azariah of India

The young man had everything. He was the beloved only son of a village pastor. He had grown up to become a strong Christian. Now he held an important job as leader of a Christian youth movement. He was well known as a speaker in large cities, even in foreign lands.

Then . . . he left it all to go as a missionary to one of the most backward tribes anywhere on earth.

In your mind's eye, are you seeing someone from Europe or America who went out to Asia or "darkest Africa"?

The person whose biography you are reading was born in India. Even when he went as a missionary, he still stayed in his native land.

V. Samuel Azariah was born in 1874 near the southern tip of India. His tribe was one of the lowest in India's caste system but also one of the highest in the number of people who have turned to Christ as Lord and Savior.

Every time young Samuel went to church in a nearby village, he walked across a stone slab at the door. Once it had been the altar where his ancestors made blood sacrifices. Samuel's own tribe had torn down their pagan temple and had used its stones to build a church.

In young manhood Samuel Azariah made two friends for life: a girl and a boy. The girl was one of India's few female college students in those days. Like Samuel, she was a faithful Christian and an outstanding scholar. Soon they became man and wife. The boy was an American who worked for the same student Christian organization that Samuel did. The two young men learned from each other that Christ calls all peoples to Himself, but He does not blot out their differences.

After university days, Samuel Azariah began to work full-time for the organization of Christian students. He traveled all over what is now India, Sri Lanka, Pakistan, and Bangladesh. Everywhere he encouraged young believers to tell others about Christ. As he did so, he himself became more and more dissatisfied.

"Thank God for foreign missionaries!" he said to himself. "Where would India be without them? But . . . why aren't more of my own people going as missionaries?"

He looked at his home area near the southern tip of India. Some 54,000 Christians lived there. Many of them were well educated and well off. Yet they seemed to be doing little to reach the rest of India for Christ.

One night in Sri Lanka, Samuel Azariah came to a point of crisis. He knelt under palm trees on a tropical beach. There he poured out his tears and his prayers. After that, he knew what he must do.

Soon he had organized the youth from churches in his district into their own mission society. Three months later, they sent a fellow Indian as their first missionary to an area far to the north. Backward tribes lived there—people who had no place at all in India's caste system.

Within the first three years, this home missionary reported several dozen converts. Several hundred more had joined inquirers' classes. But that wasn't enough for Samuel Azariah.

He studied census reports from all India. At least one hundred million people were beyond the reach of any church, any mission! He wrote to mission boards in other lands; they told him they could do no more for India than they were already doing.

So Samuel Azariah and his friends called a meeting. Christians gathered from all the places that make up the great subcontinent of India, and from Burma as well. They met at Serampore where William Carey had labored for so many years. In eight different languages they set up the same goal: reaching their own people with the good news of Jesus Christ.

Samuel Azariah became general secretary for the newly formed National Missionary Society. He traveled more than ever. He called on students everywhere to volunteer as missionaries. He urged church members to give sacrificially in support of missions. And still he felt dissatisfied.

Often he thought about that missionary sent from his home district to outcaste tribes farther north. Samuel Azariah's American friend in the Christian student organization visited that area. He described the people there this way:

"They are almost like savages. The men are all thieves and drunkards; the women are all stupid. If a volunteer were to go and spread the gospel among them, he need not hope for much harvest within his lifetime."

Samuel Azariah and his wife talked and prayed about God's will for their lives. They knew what they would face if they volunteered: Although still inside the borders of India, they would be moving to an area as strange to them as if it were at the ends of the earth. Their first home in the north would be a tent with a stockade around it to keep leopards out. After ten years of talking daily with university students, they would have to learn the ways of illiterate peasants. And the language would be entirely different from their own.

Many friends discouraged the Azariahs from volunteering. "You can do so much more for Christ and for the cause of missions in the place where you are now!" they urged. But the Azariahs listened to God's call, not people's advice. In the year 1909, they volunteered to go as missionaries to the outcastes.

Success is not a Christian's major goal in life. The Lord

Himself decides which gospel seeds bear most fruit. But everybody likes to hear a success story. And the missionary ministry of V. Samuel Azariah is one of the greatest success stories in Christian history.

There were already signs of a people movement among the outcastes when the Azariahs moved to that tent inside the stockade. With the Azariahs' help, this turning toward Christ blossomed. Soon believers were counted in hundreds, then thousands. Congregations sprang up in more than twenty villages.

Church leaders noticed this growth. They said, "We need a bishop to oversee the area." Until that time, all bishops in India had been foreign missionaries. But four days after Christmas of 1912, V. Samuel Azariah walked down the aisle of Calcutta's great cathedral. He was glad to see again that day his American friend from past years in student work. For on that day Samuel Azariah became the first son of India ever consecrated as an Anglican bishop.

When you read about Samuel Azariah in books of Christian history, he will usually be spoken of as "the Bishop of Dornakal." But in his heart Samuel never forgot that he was the son of a village pastor. Truly he became a great pastor of his people.

Greatness starts at home. Through the years Mrs. Azariah was his strong companion; her faith never faded. Four sons and two daughters knew their father practiced what he preached. They heard him get up in the dark of early morning to pray and study God's Word. Is it surprising that among those children arose a pastor, a doctor, an editor, and an agricultural expert? All of them faithfully served their Lord in India.

Throughout Bishop Azariah's thirty-five years of service, evangelism always came first. The number of believers in his area grew from a few thousand to a quarter of a million.

Of course, he didn't do it all by himself. His motto was: "Every Christian a witness." Every time Bishop Azariah personally performed the ordinance of baptism, the new convert had to put his hand on his head and repeat the apostle Paul's words, "Woe to me if I do not preach the gospel!"*

Samuel Azariah felt that witnessing need not wait for a pastor, let alone a bishop. What did it matter if a Christian's knowledge was small? Let him share with others what little he knew!

Yet the bishop did not neglect his pastors. When he took over, there were only 6 of them in the area. Eventually their number reached 150. Samuel Azariah prayed for every one of them by name.

For those who were able, he started a seminary. But he never hesitated to ordain a villager with a grade-school education if God's call to the ministry seemed clear.

"You'll give Christianity a bad name!" some people accused Azariah. "People of the upper classes won't want to become believers."

Bishop Azariah quietly went on doing as he thought best. Time proved that he was right: Upper-class people of India saw how much difference the gospel made in the lives of lower-class people. And they became interested in Christianity as never before.

Besides urging everybody to spread the gospel everywhere every day, Bishop Azariah also promoted a great "Week of Witness" once a year. In the hot season, when there was little work to do in the fields, he called on villagers to go out evangelizing. One year no less than 34,000 people took part. They visited 3,000 villages. They recorded the names of 7,250 people who wanted to know more about the good news.

Azariah always encouraged Christians of India to stand alone, without hoping for help from abroad.

---

* 1 Corinthians 9:16, RSV.

"But . . . we have no money, Father," villagers would sometimes say.

"Do you have food, my children?" he would ask.

"Yes, of course."

"Then here's what you can do," he went on. "Every time you cook grain, lay aside a handful for the Lord. On Sundays, bring your grain sack to church. That's the same as city people setting aside part of the money they make."

"But Father," some of the peasants said, still puzzled, "we can't possibly figure out what we make week by week. We have to wait till harvest."

"Then bring first fruits, like God's people in Old Testament times," urged Bishop Azariah. "When a hen first starts to lay, give God the first egg. When a cow begins bearing young, give God the first calf. Then when harvesttime comes, add to all of this a thank offering."

Through such simple methods as these, Samuel Azariah led Christians of the Indian countryside to band together in mission support. He also led them in other ways to give the gospel an Indian flavor—through music, plays, and books that sprang from Indian soil.

All of this he firmly based upon the Word of God. For all Christians who could, Azariah urged private daily Bible reading as he himself did. For those who could not read or who felt weak in faith, he urged daily group gatherings to hear the Word and pray. When Azariah's American friend visited the district, he found twenty thousand Christians meeting together every morning and a hundred thousand every evening.

As the years passed, Bishop Samuel Azariah became known throughout the Christian world. Even as early as 1910, he was chosen to speak for believers of the Third World at a great international conference held in Scotland. But wherever he went, in Europe or America or Asia or Australia, he always came back home again to pastor his own people.

During the Christmas season of 1944, he enjoyed visiting village congregations as usual. But this time he came down with a fever.

It didn't seem serious . . . but Bishop Azariah was seventy years old now. He had spent his strength in the Master's service.

The first day of 1945 was Samuel Azariah's last day on earth. The great missionary bishop of India went to celebrate the new year with the Savior he had followed all his days.

Serampore: SEH-rum-pore   Dornakal: DORR-nah-kahl

14
Mill Girl, Missionary, Magistrate
Mary Mitchell Slessor
of Scotland and Nigeria

Mary Mitchell Slessor wasn't afraid of anything . . . except cows. Somehow it scared her to cross a pasture with a cow in it.

But cannibals—that was different. When her big brother Robert stood on a chair and pretended to be preaching to cannibals in Africa, Mary piped up, "I want to be a missionary, too."

"You can't," said Robert. "Girls can't be missionaries. But you can hide behind me in the pulpit when I preach."

Robert was wrong, of course. Women have been missionaries ever since the days of Priscilla and Aquila, Phoebe and Paul. Many years before Robert and Mary played make-believe missionaries, brave women such as Nancy Judson and Sarah Boardman and Mary Moffat and Henrietta Hall Shuck had gone out to the ends of the earth.

But wrong ideas die hard. And in Scotland of 1848, when Mary Mitchell Slessor was born in Aberdeen, some people thought being a missionary was something a girl could never do.

Mary learned early in life to do things others couldn't. For instance, she stood up to her drunken father one night when he tried to strike her mother. For doing that, she was turned out into the street.

Mary's mother kept her little family together somehow. She took them to church every Sunday. She read them mission stories, too. When Robert Slessor died young, she said,

"John will be our missionary, now that Robert has gone to heaven."

But her husband still came staggering home drunk on Saturday nights, and money was still scarce. First Mrs. Slessor had to go to work in the textile mills of Dundee while Mary kept house. Then eleven-year-old Mary herself got a half-day job. The other half day she was sent to school at the factory. She made good progress in reading and writing.

At last the alcoholic father died. Mary, now fourteen years old, became the main support of the family. She got up at five every morning, for she had to be at her weaving machine by six. With short breaks for eating and resting, she worked till six in the evening. Then she hurried home to help her mother care for the younger children.

Time off on Saturday afternoons and Sundays brought a happy change. But Mary still stayed busy. Besides attending church services, she now taught a girls' Sunday School class.

Trudging to and from the mill, Mary saw other girls and boys in the slums of Dundee whose lives were even harder than hers. When her church opened a mission over a shop, she begged the Sunday School superintendent to let her start a new class there.

A gang of rough-talking boys tried to stop Mary from urging them into Sunday School. The gang leader tied a lead weight to a string. He swung it in a circle, ever nearer and nearer Mary's head.

Mary was a slight fair-skinned girl with strawberry blond hair cut short. She stood straight and still, her blue eyes snapping. The weight grazed her forehead before the young tough lost his nerve.

"She's game, boys," he cried, dropping the string. And he led the whole gang into Mary's class.

That gang leader became Mary's best assistant in winning Scottish slum kids to Christ. Mary visited in their homes. She held their grimy baby brothers and sisters in her lap. She used her precious Saturday afternoon holidays to take them hiking in the country.

Still Mary asked herself how she could better serve the Lord. She needed more education, that was plain. So, like David Livingstone a half century before, she took her books to the mill and studied at every spare moment. Sometimes she even propped her Bible on the loom and read it while threads were spinning smoothly into the weave.

Not that she neglected her work: Mary Mitchell Slessor became known as one of the most skillful mill girls in all Dundee. She earned extra money because of this. Most of it she stored away against the time when her mother and sisters might need it.

One day sad news came from faraway Africa: "David Livingstone is dead! Who will take his place?"

Mrs. Slessor had given up hoping for a missionary in the family. Young John had proved as frail as his brother Robert. He had died in early manhood.

But now Mary Mitchell Slessor spoke up. She asked to be sent to her church's mission in Calabar, Nigeria, West Africa.

Many people wondered why Mary would leave her thriving slum mission work. They wondered why she would go to a place nicknamed "the white man's grave."

"Why not?" asked Mary. "The field of danger is the post of honor."

Mrs. Slessor agreed. So did the mission board. After a few months of training in Edinburgh, Mary Slessor sailed for Africa. She landed where the Cross and Calabar Rivers meet and pour their tumbling waters into the sea.

For four years she taught in a mission school on the coast and studied the language spoken by nearby tribes. Africans said, "She is blessed with an Efik mouth." Older missionaries were amazed at how quickly she could speak and understand the tribal tongue.

But Mary was not content to stay on the coast. Often she would walk a ways into the jungle and climb a tree. Longingly she would look upriver, toward places where witchcraft was common, and trial by torture, and human slavery, and human flesh served at tribal feasts.

Mary took a furlough in Scotland with her mother and younger sisters. Then she came back to Nigeria and moved upstream to a mission station of her own. A human skull on a pole marked the entrance to the village. There she lived in a mud hut with a palm-leaf roof. And there she taught the people about God's love in Jesus Christ.

One day Mary tracked a panting messenger to a hut where twins had just been born. Snatching the two little black bundles from an old woman, she demanded, "What are you going to do with them?"

"Break their backs and throw them into the bush," the old woman answered.

The blue eyes flashed. "Why?"

"Because one of their fathers must have been a devil," the old woman explained. "Why else were two born at once?"

Mary Slessor marched home with the twins. Many people stayed away from her. They thought the twins had a curse on them. Someone even stole the boy baby away and killed him. But Mary saved his sister from certain death.

Other children found their way to her house—sometimes twins, sometimes orphans, sometimes a chief's son sent to learn new ways. Mary loved them all and fed them all from her meager missionary salary. But that first black twin girl held a special place in her heart. "Jeanie," Mary called her, after her own baby sister back home in Scotland.

Once Mary nursed a six-month-old with a high fever. Taking the baby with her, she hiked up a high mountain. There she pitched her tent to spend the night.

In the cooler climate the baby's health improved. But in the night Mary was awakened by a growl. She was horrified to see a panther with the baby in its mouth!

Mary grabbed a burning log from the fire. She rammed it

into the panther's face. The beast howled, dropped its prey, and ran. The baby was unhurt.

A chief invited Mary to his village, still further inland. Thirty-three black oarsmen stroked the royal canoe up the river as Mary sat under an arch of fiber matting. Torches lit the way as darkness fell. The trip took ten long hours.

In the chief's village, Mary bandaged hurts, treated diseases, taught the women how to sew, and twice a day held services of Christian worship. The chief ordered a hundred lashes each for two of his girl wives, and salt rubbed into their wounds afterward. Mary talked him down to whipping them only ten times. As she rubbed healing salve on the two girls' backs, Mary told them about Jesus, the Great Physician.

After two weeks, she came back downriver. A tropical storm and a tropical fever made her return trip a nightmare. But Mary had been infected with something more than fever. She couldn't get the jungle out of her system. She couldn't forget that cannibals needed to know the love of Christ.

Home again she went to regain her strength, and she took young Jeanie with her. Mother Slessor was delighted with the wee black lassie. Soon Jeanie was prattling with a Scottish accent. But Mrs. Slessor was weak and worn, and Sister Jeanie was sick. Mary moved them out of smoky Dundee down to the south of England. Then she and her own Jeanie turned toward Africa again.

It was not long before sad news came to Mary. Her mother and her last surviving sister had died, only three months apart.

"Heaven is now nearer to me than Britain," said Mary. "And no one will worry about me if I go up-country."

So up-country she went! For years Mary had heard of a warlike tribe that ran off missionaries and killed travelers on jungle paths. Not long ago a chief of that tribe had died; eight men and eight women had been buried with him.

Mary's African friends urged her to stay away; but to this very tribe she was certain she should go.

It was pitch-dark and raining when the canoe arrived at last. With her waifs—five of them now—Mary slithered through the black jungle. She was so frightened that she could get no farther praying than the one word: "Father!"

She bedded the children down in a damp, filthy hut. Then she learned that the oarsmen had refused to unload till morning.

"But tomorrow is the Lord's Day!" she snapped. "What a bad example to give!"

Back she sloshed through four miles of mud to the landing place. She threw off the cover of the canoe. She shamed the Africans huddling there till they got up and finished their job. The next morning she led her little flock in worship.

That was the beginning of a new day for the fierce jungle tribes of Calabar. The first boy who offered to help Mary got boiling oil poured over his hands. But she saved many another from death and from torture intended to drive evil spirits away.

Once Mary trudged eight hours through jungle paths in pelting rain to nurse a village chief back to health. Once she talked tribal warriors into leaving their arms behind when they made a visit downriver to a Christian village. When one of the canoes tilted in the river because of an uneven load, Mary spotted swords hidden beneath yams and palm kernels. She yanked them out and threw them onto the bank. The warriors meekly sat down to continue their journey in peace.

When the high chief's son died in an accident, everyone except Mary insisted that there must have been witchcraft. A dozen luckless captives were chained up like dogs. They must drink poison to prove their innocence.

Mary sat blocking the way to the prison compound. Later, she dashed toward a woman about to drink poison. Grabbing the captive's arm, she cried, "Run!" Together the two women raced to safety inside the mission house. Still later, Mary even hid the supply of poison. Finally only a cow was sacrificed for burial with the high chief's son. Long afterward, the high chief himself kneeled and thanked Mary for stopping the shedding of blood.

Once when Mary was tired and ill and ready to leave for furlough, an urgent call sent her on an all-night hike to a distant village. Standing between two angry armies, she ordered them to put down their spears.

One of the leaders proved to be that same chief she had nursed back to health after walking eight hours in the rain. With his help she worked out an agreement for a fine to be paid, instead of a war to be fought.

New troubles threatened when the fine was mostly paid in barrels and bottles of gin. Mary feared what would happen if a drunken party began.

Then she remembered an old African custom: Anything covered by one's clothing was considered to be under personal protection. Quickly she slipped off two of her many petticoats and flung them over the liquor. At last she persuaded the disappointed warriors to go home.

Slowly she saw the fruit of her years in the jungle. Always she was eager to press on to new places. "Let others continue my work here," she would urge. "Send me forward among the cannibals."

For a year she went "gypsying in the jungle," as she called it. Moving from place to place at her own expense, she started new congregations everywhere. Once she fought off an angry hippopotamus with pots and pans—she who had been afraid of cows!

As the Nigerian government improved jungle paths, Mary learned to ride a bicycle. That way she could reach more village churches. When her legs began to fail her, she got a two-wheel cart. Always she found African boys and girls eager to push and pull her on her way.

Through the years Mary kept her flock of little Africans.

Black Jeanie grew up to lovely womanhood and helped her white mother with the smaller ones.

Every evening Mary would sit down on the mud floor and gather her children around her for family worship. By flickering lamplight, she would read them stories of the Good Shepherd. She would teach them songs with Efik words but Scottish melodies, beating time with a tambourine and using it to tap the head of any child whose attention wandered.

So greatly was Mary honored among African tribes that in the early 1900s she was appointed to judge and settle court cases with the rank of vice-consul. And so it was that Mary Mitchell Slessor, mill girl of Dundee, became the first woman magistrate in the British Empire.

Later his majesty the king awarded her a special title. Then a new mission hospital was named after her.

Mary wrote a letter to friends in Scotland: "Don't think there is any change in me because I received this honor. I am Mary Slessor, nothing more and none other than the unworthy, unprofitable, but most willing servant of the King of kings."

And in the year 1915, Mary Mitchell Slessor was called into the presence of her King.

Edinburgh: ED-in-bur-ah   Efik: AY-feek
Calabar: KAH-lah-bar

15
Seafarer of the Spice Islands
Joseph Kam
of the Netherlands and Indonesia

The Spice Islands are what Columbus was really looking for when he stumbled onto America instead. Anyone who's ever been there can tell you those islands are worth searching out.

You won't find the Spice Islands by that name in atlases or maps of today. Look for Indonesia instead. The parts of Indonesia that especially grow spices were already world famous by 1492. These are the islands known today as the Moluccas.

Portuguese seafarers were among the first Europeans in the Moluccas. With them they brought priests who told the story of Christ.

Then the Dutch drove out the Portuguese and the priests along with them. The Dutch brought in their own version of Christianity. But they sent far too few pastors and teachers through the centuries that followed. Little by little Christianity in the Spice Islands became a hollow shell, not a living faith.

In 1769 a little boy was born who in God's plan would change all of that. He was born not in Indonesia but on the other side of the world, in the Netherlands. His name was Joseph Kam.

The Kam family had moved from Switzerland many years before. Joseph's father was a leather worker and a faithful Christian. The little boy grew up hearing Bible stories, and stories about world missions, too. As a youth he committed his life to the Lord Jesus Christ. As a man he announced, "I feel a call to missions."

But how could Joseph Kam become a missionary? His older brother Samuel was already a pastor, and somebody had to carry on their father's leather business. Besides that, there were still two unmarried sisters in the Kam family to be looked after.

Joseph Kam quietly accepted the fact that he would probably spend his whole life in Holland. He got married, and he and his wife had a little girl. When he finally closed down the family leather shop, he took a job as a courtroom clerk. By that time he was already in his late thirties.

Then within two years Joseph Kam lost everything. His wife, his daughter, and his two single sisters died one after another. Even his job disappeared as the Dutch court system was changed.

Joseph Kam grieved for all he had lost. Yet he also began to realize a strange fact: He had now been set free of any responsibility that could hold him back from going to the mission field.

In the year 1808, when he was thirty-nine years old, Joseph Kam went back to school. (One of his teachers was half his age!) Patiently he studied science, history, Bible, theology, and even music, for he learned to become a good organist.

All of this was intended to prepare him for his work as a missionary. But perhaps he learned as much on weekends as during the weeks. On Sundays he tramped to nearby village churches and put into practice what he had been taught.

He ended up studying for five years—in the Netherlands, Germany, and England. Joseph Kam was already past forty-four when at last he sailed for the mission field. But the long years of working and waiting had not been wasted. When he finally reached the Spice Islands, maturity would win him respect.

On the way he stopped awhile at Surabaya, a seaport in

East Java. There he stayed six months, learning the Malay (or Indonesian) language.

He also visited and encouraged congregations of Dutch colonials throughout East Java. In Surabaya he met a few Christians who seemed truly interested in obeying Christ's Great Commission. Joseph Kam organized them into a little mission society. He encouraged them to keep on telling the good news after he was gone. He never knew what a great influence his half year had in evangelizing East Java, for he never got to go back there again.

It was March of 1815 when Joseph Kam reached the place that was to be home for the rest of his life: Amboina, capital of the Moluccas. There he began his great work for Christ as seafarer of the Spice Islands.

Churches in the Moluccas were in a sad state. Some of their buildings had fallen down. Somebody had even planned to use the largest church in Amboina as a warehouse. Members of the churches had forgotten what little they had once known of the gospel since no pastor or teacher had visited them for so long.

At one place, a strange procession greeted Joseph Kam when he came. In front marched several old women, all wearing black dresses that looked a little like robes the Portuguese priests had worn three hundred years before. Each woman was singing as she held a psalmbook in her hands. But neither tune nor text made much sense. Kam noticed that some of the women were holding their books upside down. Then he learned that not a one of them could read!

On another island, all the Christians gathered on Christmas Day to mourn and wail. Somehow they had gotten the idea that Jesus died on December 25. Then at New Year's they all went to church and celebrated Jesus' resurrection day, January 1!

Joseph Kam saw he had his work cut out for him. He wasted no time in getting started. First he majored on Amboina and places nearby. Then he began to move out toward distant isles.

He did not work alone. Only eight weeks after arriving in Amboina, Joseph Kam married for the second time. His wife was half Dutch, half Indonesian; her name was Sara Maria, and she was only nineteen years old.

Sara Maria's husband was two and a half times her own age. Yet she proved to be just the helper Joseph Kam needed. She made their home a place of warm welcome for many people. When Joseph Kam was gone on long journeys, she faithfully carried on his church work in Amboina. And a year after their marriage, she bore him a fine little son.

Each year winds and waves are right for seafaring in the Spice Islands from September till mid-December. So each year Joseph Kam would sail from island to island, visiting scattered congregations. After coming home to celebrate Christmas in Amboina, he would leave again for nearer places he could reach by foot or by sedan chair.

What did Joseph Kam do during those six months or more of every year that he spent in traveling? Here's a sample:

Usually he would arrive in the early morning, often after sailing all night long. Sometimes he rode Dutch colonial government ships, sometimes trading vessels, sometimes even whalers. Sometimes he voyaged in a little sailing craft that he ordered and paid for out of his own pocket. But most often he traveled by swift Malay prau—a long outrigger canoe paddled by dozens of strong darkskinned oarsmen.

As the prau crunched on the sandy beach at dawn, all the Christians would come out to greet their long-awaited pastor. Even the local chief would appear to pay his respects. Schoolchildren would march, playing merry tunes on their bamboo flutes. After Joseph Kam landed, he and his crew would join the happy parade as it reentered the village.

On that first morning, Kam would always inspect the school. All afternoon he would interview those who wanted to become church members, from little children to grandparents. The worship service that evening would include reception of new members, baptisms, Christian weddings, and preparation for the Lord's Supper. Can you imagine how long it must have lasted?

The next morning the Lord's Supper would be celebrated with full reverence. Usually Kam himself had to bring Communion supplies with him in his boat, for few grapes grow in the Spice Islands. At midday Kam had heart-to-heart talks with local church leaders and schoolteachers. In the afternoon there would be another service of worship. In his sermon Kam would always include much helpful advice.

At nightfall he would sail away again, for there was always another island to be visited tomorrow and the next day. Can you imagine how wearying such a journey must have been? And remember, Joseph Kam was already middle-aged before he even began to be a seafarer.

Everywhere he went, Kam saw that Christians had too long been like sheep without a shepherd. Many church members got drunk and had fights. Many used magic charms to bring good luck, and cast spells to curse their enemies. In secret some still sacrificed to idols. Some still decorated their town halls with human skulls.

How sad Kam felt to see such heathenism! How glad he was when Moluccans themselves decided to burn their idols and pull down their jungle altars!

On one island, people heaped all their charms and idols into one long box. Then they turned it over to Joseph Kam. With the help of his oarsmen, he carried the box far out to sea, then cast it overboard. Back on shore again, he joined the village people in a Christian festival of thanksgiving.

Even stranger experiences awaited him in distant islands to the north. The voyage would be many months long, so he took no less than fifty-two men to row his prau. Pirates roamed those seas, so he also carried along two soldiers, four small cannon, and a supply of three-pound shot. There were other dangers: strong winds, high waves, hidden reefs, tropical diseases. Once Joseph Kam lay sick a whole month before he could continue his journey.

Everywhere he found great spiritual need. On one island Bibles were so scarce that he tore several pages out of his own New Testament to leave behind.

For more than six months Joseph Kam was gone to the northern isles. Many Christians in Amboina feared he would never come back alive. When at last he returned, they met him with sad news: His little son had died while he was far away.

But Joseph and Sara Maria Kam would not give in. They kept on building up the Moluccan churches. Others before them had used only Dutch or such high Malay language that few people could understand it. Joseph Kam preached and taught in everyday Malay, the forerunner of modern Indonesian. He also wrote and translated and printed Christian tracts and books.

The Kams' house in Amboina was always open to anyone in need: poor people, youths from distant islands learning how to become home missionaries to their own tribes, new Dutch missionaries just beginning to learn the language.

In the midst of their busy household, the Kams welcomed another baby boy. He grew up strong and straight and served to an old age as an evangelist in the land of his birth.

Still Joseph Kam kept on seafaring. He spied out distant isles to the south where no minister of the gospel had been for twenty, thirty, even forty years. He saw roofless ruins that had once been churches. He met old men who could barely remember when Christian worship had once been held in their villages.

Joseph Kam did not limit his work only to those who already called themselves Christians. He also looked for those who had never even heard the name of Christ. He urged Indonesians everywhere to spread the good news— among their neighbors, among their friends, even among their enemies.

In one year alone, 1825, Joseph Kam baptized no less than 2,560 people. Only the book of life in heaven will tell how many more he turned from the kingdom of darkness to the light of Jesus Christ.

Until four days before his death in July 1833, Joseph Kam was still seafaring in the Spice Islands, still carrying news of salvation. No wonder loving Indonesian Christians carved this on his tombstone in Amboina:

"Joseph Kam, Apostle of the Moluccas."

Moluccas: mah-LUCK-kahs   Amboina: ahm-BOY-nah
Joseph Kam: YO-sef KAHM   prau: PRAH-oo
Surabaya: soo-rah-BAH-yah

16
Home Missionary on a Foreign Field
Lula F. Whilden
of the USA and China

Lula Whilden first went to the mission field when she was two years old. Then she went again when she was twenty-six, and she stayed.

Like many others before and since, Lula was an MK (Missionary Kid) who grew up to become a missionary in her own right.

Some of Christ's namebearers are called foreign missionaries because they go to other countries. Some are called home missionaries because they serve in their native land.

Lula Whilden's mission field was as far away as you can get from where she was born—away over on the other side of the world. Yet she was a home missionary, too. She pioneered language missions in the USA. And her main work, both at home and abroad, was in the homes of Chinese people.

Lula F. Whilden was born in 1846 at Camden, South Carolina. Her father was a Baptist pastor there. Lula's mother believed in world missions with all her heart. When Lula's father announced he was called to go as a missionary, Lula's mother felt her prayers had been answered.

Lula was too little to remember much of the long trip to China in the fall of 1848. But she could remember strange sights and sounds and smells in Guangzhou (Canton), that great port city on the South China Sea.

It was only a little over a year later when Lula's mother died. Her last prayer was that God would raise up more missionaries from among her three children. Lula's heart-broken father sailed for home with his little family before the end of 1850.

Lula was a teenager when she understood for herself what she had been hearing all her life: that Jesus wanted to be her Savior and Lord. From the time of her conversion she became an active church member. While still in college, she started teaching a Sunday School class. She won several of her pupils to Christ. She must have learned something about teaching, too: After graduation she was asked to stay on two more years as a college faculty member.

But Lula Whilden could not forget China, or her mother's prayers. On the first day of May in 1872, she sailed toward Asia for the second time in her life. With Lula traveled her sister and her sister's husband. All three of them had now been appointed missionaries.

Childhood memories came flooding back as the two MK sisters landed again in old Guangzhou. They heard the cries of street sellers whose wares dangled from split-bamboo shoulder poles. They smelled incense being burned before idol shrines. They saw unwanted people being treated like dirt or left to die: poor people, handicapped people, some-times even healthy babies . . . if they happened to be girls.

One of those unwanted people especially attracted Lula Whilden's attention. She was an old beggar woman who lived in a three-by-five-foot hut that leaned against a wall. Lula smiled at her and sometimes gave her something, but longed to do much more. Lula had learned a little Chinese as a toddler. Now she plowed into the language in earnest. She never dreamed it would be so hard. How she wished for words to tell the old beggar about Jesus!

Day by day the old woman grew weaker. After hours of begging on the streets, she barely had strength to crawl into her lean-to at night. Lula began to pray that the beggar would live long enough to learn of Jesus' love.

One day word came that the old woman was dying. Lula

hurried to her side. In broken Chinese, groping for words, she told the good news the best way she could.

The wrinkled face curled into a smile. "Yes, I understand," she croaked. "Yes, I will believe in this Redeemer from sin."

And Lula experienced such joy that day that she almost felt she herself was in heaven as soon as the old beggar woman was.

Those were hallmarks of Lula Whilden's forty years as a missionary: She cared about people. She went to them where they were. And she told them the Old, Old Story.

It kept her busy. Here was her weekly schedule for awhile:

Sundays: Two Sunday Schools in Chinese, two worship services in Chinese, and one worship service in English.

Mondays: Visiting a mission school to hear the girls' weekly review of Bible verses and Christian teachings.

Tuesdays: Visiting a home for blind people and another home for old people.

Wednesdays: Visiting from house to house on the Island of Honan, across the Pearl River from Guangzhou.

Thursdays: Visiting another girls' school in Guangzhou.

Fridays: Visiting still another school on Honan Island.

Saturdays: Studying Chinese with a teacher all morning and writing letters to friends in America all afternoon.

That was an ordinary week. But Lula was no ordinary missionary. Her married sister's health broke down like their mother's years before, and she and her husband had to go back home. But Lula stayed. Yet she didn't stay inside the city and its suburbs. Boldly, she moved out to places where few people had ever seen a foreigner.

There were the boat people, for instance. Some of them— especially women—lived and died on batwinged boats in the Pearl River without ever setting foot on land. Even when riverboat robbers took everything she had, Lula

Whilden kept on searching out boat people who needed to hear the good news.

She ranged out into Guangdong Province, to the south of Guangzhou. For a month at a time she would spread the gospel from house to house in villages eighty miles away.

How did Lula travel on her countryside trips? Sometimes by wheelbarrow. Can you imagine how it must have felt on those rough roads? She was always glad when the wind blew her way because, then, the straining coolie could raise a sail to help them trundle along faster. Often Lula walked— through dust, through mud, through rain, through cold.

Her travels took her as far as Macao, that Portuguese colony perched on the farthest tip of land pointing out to sea. There she entered a home where no other namebearer for Christ had ever been. "Couldn't we pray to Jesus some days and to the goddess of mercy on others?" two women there asked her. Lula left Macao with a sad heart.

Yet there were so many others who were ready to believe!

There was the woman who jumped up and said to her family, "I told you so! I knew there must be a true and living God! But you thought I was crazy." Then she knelt beside Lula like a little child, asking, "Teach me how to pray to Him." After repeating a simple prayer of faith, she rushed out of the room. Everyone could hear her telling others in the back part of the house, "She says God became a man, and they nailed Him to a cross, but He came to life again!"

There was the feeble old man who called out in a weak voice as Lula walked through his village: "Do you have a book that tells about Jesus?" Lula gladly gave him the Book. When she stopped by again a year later, she learned that the old man had read it faithfully. And he had died believing in the Lord Jesus.

There was the farmer's wife who led Lula up to her loft and barred the door. "Yesterday everyone crowded around you," she said. "Today I have you to myself in a quiet place, so I can hear it all and understand it all." And she listened for three hours.

There were half a dozen young girls who had so many questions about prayer: "Must we close our eyes, or look up toward the sky? Must we pray aloud, or whisper? Must we be indoors or outdoors? Must we pray together or by ourselves?" And then the best question of all: "May we begin praying to Jesus right now?"

A grandmother had questions about prayer, too: "I only pray once a day because my grandchildren are so noisy most of the time. And if my daughter-in-law sees me kneeling, she scolds me."

Lula told the old woman she could even pray in bed. Her weathered face brightened.

"I'm glad to hear that," said the grandmother. "In winter I feel the cold so much that some days I can hardly get up, and they bring me my meals in bed. Now I know the Heavenly Father will hear me, even when I cannot kneel. And when I wake in the night, I'll spend those long lonely hours in prayer."

In all her busy ministries as home missionary on a foreign field, Lula Whilden never forgot about people who had no home. Her heart especially went out to blind girls and women. Most Chinese parents felt disappointed anyway if their baby was a girl. And if she couldn't even see, then what was she good for?

Lula took in a little blind girl whose father had sold her for ten dollars. She knew that blind girls in China often ended up as beggars or as women who sold their bodies to be playthings for sex. She was determined that her ten-dollar daughter would not experience that kind of shame. So she wrote to friends in America and got together enough money to start a home for blind girls, probably the first in all China.

A blind woman once crouched close beside Lula. She murmured, "Heaven must be a lovely place. It would be good to be where I was not blind and need not beg."

Little Ah Ng was one of Lula's blind children. She loved to walk with Lula in the girls' home garden. "It's a pity you made poor choices when you got the other little girls," she chirped. "But it's good you got me, 'cause I can walk fast enough to keep up with you."

During the 1880s Lula's health failed. She came home to South Carolina. But she didn't stay at home very long. During the first year of her extended furlough, she spoke at seventy-one missionary meetings!

By 1887 she was feeling stronger. But two doctors agreed she couldn't go back to Guangzhou yet. So Lula Whilden became a home missionary for awhile. She worked with Chinese people in Baltimore, Maryland. Many of them ran laundries. Patiently, Lula peered through clouds of steam as she told them the good news.

One old man had lived in America for twenty-eight years and yet had never heard of Jesus till Lula told him. Another old man acted at first as if he didn't care whether Lula came to see him or not. But one day he told her he had stopped praying to his idols and now prayed only to Jesus.

"Do you love Him?" Lula asked.

"If I didn't love Him," said the old Chinese, "how could I pray to Him?"

Finally in the fall of 1890 Lula returned to her home in Guangzhou. Through the decades that followed, she never stopped her work. During the year when she turned sixty-three, a mission report says that she visited in over six hundred homes.

Robbers struck again in 1914—this time, by night. The shock was too great; Lula Whilden came home to stay, a worn-out old woman.

For months she lay in a nursing home, apparently knowing nothing. Yet when younger missionaries on furlough sang "Jesus, Lover of My Soul" in Chinese at her bedside, she perked up and asked about friends in Christ half a world away.

The end came in September of 1916. Who knows how many Chinese Christians welcomed Lula Whilden home to heaven?

Whilden: HWILL-den	Guangdong: GWAHNG-DONG
Guangzhou:	
GWAHNG-JOE	Macao: mah-KAH-aw
Honan: HOE-NAHN	Ah Ng: AH-UNG

17
Apostle to the Arawaks
William H. Brett
of England and Guyana

Many people know about William Carey. He grew up in England as a humble shoemaker and then went to India to become one of the greatest missionaries of all times. Not as many people know about William Brett. He grew up in England as a humble tailor and then went to Guyana to become one of the greatest missionaries of all times.

In some ways Brett's story is even more remarkable than Carey's. William Carey was a bivocational preacher as well as a shoemaker. He was a family man of thirty-two when he left England for India, and had already had several years of experience as a pastor. William Brett was a youthful layman of twenty-two when he left England for Guyana.

Life was never easy for William Brett. Born in 1818, he started to school with other boys his age. He made good grades, even in Latin and Greek. But his father died while he was still quite young, and his mother married again. William had to leave school to become a tailor's apprentice. He kept on studying languages, and he read every book he could get his hands on.

Apprentices in olden days had to do hard work for little or no pay. But they were guaranteed food and lodging till their years of training were over—that is, unless something happened to their master. William Brett's master the tailor ran out of money before the boy had finished his apprenticeship. So the luckless teenager found himself doing all sorts of odd jobs to make ends meet.

Ever since he was only twelve, William had been teaching other boys in Sunday School. His home was in Dover, near white cliffs that look down on the English Channel. Often he led his Sunday School pupils on long hikes beside the sea.

The pastor lent William a book one day. It was the biography of Henry Martyn. A generation before, Martyn had gone as a missionary to the Middle East. He had burned out for God after only seven years there.

The book lit a flame in William Brett's soul. Like Henry Martyn, he was a boy from the south of England. Like Henry Martyn, he longed to tell the good news of Jesus Christ. But there was a difference: Martyn had gone out as a youth of twenty-four, yet he was highly educated and already experienced as an assistant pastor. Brett had no such training for missionary service.

But the mission society in London decided to send him anyway. The bishop of Barbados had called for missionaries willing to reach Indian tribes on the mainland of South America. Brett and another young man were appointed to meet that need.

The Atlantic was stormy in February of 1840. After a four-week voyage, William Brett and his friend landed safely on the island of Barbados. They spent a month with the missionary-minded bishop there. From him they learned more about the job that lay ahead of them. Then they sailed again to Georgetown, capital of Guyana.

What a babble of voices greeted them there! English, Dutch, Portuguese—all of these were people of Guyana. So were tan-skinned Indians who had come from half a world away to work on sugar cane plantations, and redskinned Indians who paddled their canoes downriver out of the jungle, and black-skinned children of former slaves.

Brett's traveling companion took sick soon after they arrived. He never was able to do the work they had been sent out for. Instead, he was given an assignment in George-

town where the living was easier. So William Brett, twenty-
two years old, turned his face toward the jungle alone.

Forty-three miles upriver, Brett was put ashore at a settlement of ramshackle huts in a clearing. Nearby stood a tum-
bledown church, overgrown with weeds.

An old black woman greeted him with great joy. She and
the children she cared for were almost the only people left
in the deserted village. Bustling back and forth, she set up
a mouldy, thatch-roofed cabin as the young missionary's
new home. There she fed him on plantain broth and fresh
fish from the river.

When money came from London, Brett tried to pay her.
"Oh, dear," she said, "didn't the good Lord send you to ol'
Jeanette same as He send the Prophet Elijah to the widder?
Didn't He make me happy looking after the man of God,
same as the widder was happy looking after Elijah? Ol' Jea-
nette don't want no money."

After his house had been whitewashed and some (not all)
of the bugs, frogs, and lizards had been cleared out of it,
Brett began to do the same for the half-ruined church building. He held regular services there—for old Jeanette, for her
little colony of children, and occasionally for black crewmen
from river schooners. He started a school, too, though for a
long time he only had two pupils, both black.

But William Brett had been sent as a missionary especially
to the redskinned peoples of Guyana. He was delighted to
see a wandering tribe set up camp across the river. They
were cutting leaves to use in thatched roofs.

A black youngster paddled Brett over to the other shore.
He began trying to do the work to which he had been as-
signed. But he got nowhere . . . till he hit on the idea of
pointing to something, listening to what came out of the
Indians' mouths, and then writing down the sounds in his
notebook.

Now at last Brett could invite the Indians to cross the river
and attend church services. But they always refused. When

five of them finally came one Sunday, they got tickled trying
to kneel, since they were used to squatting on their heels
instead. They never came back to church. Two months later,
they all broke camp and left.

A friend told Brett that the wanderers were members of
the Warau tribe. This tribe was not as civilized as other
Indians of Guyana. "Why don't you try the Arawak tribe
instead?" the friend suggested. "They're the ones who live
around here all the time."

Often Brett saw proud-faced Arawaks paddling their
canoes up and down the river. But they paid no attention
when he waved and called them to the bank. Even when he
learned to paddle a canoe himself, they were not interested
in what he had to say about the Word of God.

"My father knew not your Book," one of them explained.
"And my grandfather knew not your Book. They understood more than we. We have no wish to learn what they did
not know."

Even if grown-ups would not listen, Brett hoped they
would want learning for their children. But he was disappointed again. Redskinned people of Guyana would have
nothing to do with black-skinned people, and all of Brett's
other pupils were black. One Arawak did promise to send
his son to school. But he broke his promise, and Brett never
saw him again.

One day a short, friendly faced Arawak father appeared
at William Brett's riverside hut. His hair seemed a little
lighter than the other Indians' and had a bit of curl to it.
Brett was not surprised when the Arawak said his name in
Indian language: "Good-hair."

"Me go down river long time," the Arawak went on in
broken English. "Me travel everywhere: up rivers, forests;
me see many people, many places. Me hear of the Great Our
Father who live in heaven. Me think better to serve Him
than to make magic for devils. Me come to learn."

With the man stood his five-year-old son. Brett eagerly

invited the boy to his school. He encouraged the father to come each weekend to visit, worship, and learn how to serve "the Great Our Father."

Good-hair shook his head. "Another day me leave him here," he said. And he went away.

So Brett was disappointed again. He learned that Good-hair had once been a witch doctor who actually did "make magic for devils." So he expected nothing more to happen.

But Good-hair's interest was genuine. Not many days later, he turned up again. With him he brought both his five-year-old boy and an eight-year-old girl. The next Sunday he came to church with his wife. The Sunday after that, he brought her sisters with their husbands and children.

That was the beginning of a miracle among the Arawak Indians of Guyana. The little church began to overflow. So did Brett's house as redskinned children squatted round him to learn their *ABC's.* And they learned about "the Great Our Father," too.

When Good-hair was baptized, he took the Christian name of Cornelius. Like that Christian soldier of New Testament times, he boldly took the good news to those around him. He helped Brett learn the Arawak tongue. He interpreted when Brett taught and witnessed. When Brett ran out of words, Cornelius himself took up the Story.

One day he explained it all to an old Arawak chief. Brett listened with growing delight. "God sent His Son because He loved us," said Cornelius. "Jesus Christ died because He loved us. His disciples far across the sea sent their messenger to bring us good news because they loved us."

He pointed at William Brett as he continued his testimony to the chief: "This young man crossed the sea at midnight to visit you because he loves you. We came with him gladly because we love him."

Love kept on breaking down barriers among the Arawaks. One afternoon a thunderstorm caused a family of Indians to beach their canoe and take shelter in Brett's schoolhouse.

They were amazed to see Indian children who could read and write. When Brett offered to go visit them, they eagerly invited him.

A year after Cornelius Good-hair first came to meet Brett, half of the Arawaks in nearby villages were attending church. Brett himself fell sick with the dreaded yellow fever. But old Jeanette nursed him back to health. And grateful Indians brought him gifts of fish and fruit and cassava bread.

After Brett was well again, he paddled farther upriver to find Carib Indians. Three weeks later, five canoe loads of Caribs came to church. Another time Brett and his helpers paddled across five miles of open sea from the mouth of the river to accept the invitation of an old Carib chief. More and more Indians of Guyana came to know "the Great Our Father."

Brett and Cornelius worked together to put the Scriptures into Arawak. It was hard work because the language had never even been written down before.

The best translator turned out to be Cornelius's sister-in-law. Brett had gone home to England and brought a wife back with him by now. Cornelius's sister-in-law helped Mrs. Brett around the house. All day long she would quietly listen in the background as Brett and Cornelius and other men wrestled with great biblical ideas that would not fit into Arawak words. After everyone else had gone home, the sister-in-law would shyly come up and suggest the very phrase they had all been searching for.

Again and again Brett's work was interrupted by yellow fever, cholera, smallpox. Other missionaries came out to help him but soon sickened and died. Several times Brett himself was shipped off to England, so sick that none of the weeping Indian Christians ever expected to see him again this side of heaven. But the Lord always healed him and sent him out again as apostle to the Arawaks.

For thirty-nine long hard years, William Brett worked as

a missionary in Guyana. For forty-one long, hard years, William Carey worked as a missionary in India. Both of them crossed cultural barriers to win men and women and boys and girls to Jesus Christ. Both of them put the Scriptures into foreign tongues, so others could more easily take up the task of world evangelism.

William Brett died in 1886. He was old before his time, worn out by years of heavy labor. But his name will be remembered forever in Guyana . . . and in heaven.

Warau: WAH-rah-oo   cassava: kah-SAH-vah
Arawak: AH-rah-wock   Carib: KAH-rib

18
Bold Barefoot Prophet
William Wadé Harris
of Liberia, Ghana, and the Ivory Coast

Most missionaries go out when they are young and serve for years. William Wadé Harris went out when he was old, and served for months. Yet God used "the Prophet Harris" in a way He has used few other missionaries. One historian writes that never has there been another case in modern missions "of such multitudes being brought to God in so short a time by the preaching of a single man."*

Who was "the Prophet Harris"? Where did he come from?

The answer to both of these questions is found in the small West African country of Liberia.

Liberia is unusual in two ways: For many years it was the only free country in West Africa, not a colony of some foreign power. Though all Liberians are Africans, yet they form two entirely different groups.

Liberia was founded by people whose African ancestors had been captured and taken to America. As freed slaves, they later came back again to the continent of their forefathers.

But many tribal peoples had never left Africa. Sometimes they have felt as if Liberians whose parents or grandparents used to be in America were trying to rule everything. Struggles between these two groups of Liberians were still going on late in the twentieth century.

---

* John T. Seamands, *Pioneers of the Younger Churches* (New York and Nashville: Abingdon Press, 1967). Used by permission.

Long before that, in about the year 1853, a Liberian boy was born in a village near Cape Palmas. His tribe was one of those that had never left Africa. More important, his tribe was one of those that had already heard and believed the good news about Jesus Christ.

Young William Wadé Harris grew up knowing Bible stories. He went to mission schools and learned to study the Scriptures for himself, both in English and in his own tribal tongue. When he was twenty-one years old, he gave his life to the Lord Jesus. As he himself told it, "I felt the Holy Spirit come upon me and change me at the moment of my conversion."

For ten years William Wadé Harris taught in one of the mission schools. He also worked as a bricklayer. He made several voyages up and down the west coast of Africa.

Troubles started when Harris was about forty years of age. He and his tribe got tired of being ruled by "Americo-Liberians," as the other group in their country was called.

"We might as well be a colony of some foreign power as be bossed by those stuck-up city folks," grumbled Harris to his friends. He even started flying the British flag above his house.

Three times in the late 1800s and early 1900s, Harris and his tribe rebelled against the rulers of Liberia. Harris ran up the British flag so many times that he got the nickname, "Old Man Union Jack."

Finally in 1910, Harris was locked up for several months. He was still in jail when God called him to be a prophet.

Harris felt he had seen the archangel Gabriel. He had been specially anointed with the Holy Spirit. And he had been told, "Go and obey the Great Commission!"

Was it a dream? Was it a vision?

Whatever kind of experience it was, William Wadé Harris came out of prison a changed man. Immediately he started preaching the gospel.

Liberian police said, "There's Old Man Union Jack again,

trying to get everybody all stirred up." And they threw him back in jail.

For more than two years Harris tried to be a prophet in his own country. But no one would listen to him.

Finally in 1913, when he was about sixty years old, Harris decided to cross over into the Ivory Coast. His home in Cape Palmas lay near the border anyway.

Harris could not speak the tribal languages of the Ivory Coast. Nor could he speak French, the official language of that colony. So he found a man to help him, as Paul the missionary had once found Silas and Luke and Timothy.

With Victor Tano as his helper, William Wadé Harris began to walk the seashores and riverbanks and jungle paths of the Ivory Coast. Barefoot he walked, dressed in a long white robe. Standing tall, with broad shoulders and grey mustache and beard, he quickly drew attention wherever he went.

In his right hand Harris always carried a long bamboo staff in the shape of a cross. In his left hand he carried his Bible. On his belt he strung a gourd filled with dried seeds.

In village after village, the scene was the same: "There is only one God!" Harris thundered. "Throw away your charms and idols! There is only one Savior, Jesus Christ, who died on a cross shaped like this! He died for your sins, so turn to Him and be saved!"

Harris proclaimed the good news in simple English. Victor Tano translated it into whatever dialect the people of that area could understand. And everywhere, everywhere, people listened.

Witch doctors tried to argue. Harris would fix his keen gaze on them, and they would fall at his feet, begging for mercy. Then hundreds more would come, confessing faith in Christ and asking to be baptized.

Harris would make each convert kneel, holding onto his cross-shaped staff. He would lay his Bible on the new Christian's head. "This is God's Book!" he would shout. "You must promise to obey it!"

In every village, Harris taught the believers how to pray. He taught them hymns to sing, keeping time by shaking the dried seeds in his gourd.

"Gather to pray every morning," he told the Christians. "Gather to sing hymns every evening. And on Sundays, hold special services of worship, for that is God's holy day. Appoint a preacher from among your own congregation, along with twelve apostles to help him."

William Wadé Harris knew God had sent him to be a prophet and a missionary. But he also knew practical answers when problems arose.

Sometimes new Christians asked him, "Must we throw away healing herbs the witch doctor finds for us when we're sick?"

Harris smiled. "You may use the herbs. They grow from God's good earth. But you must not let the witch doctor say his spells over you!"

Sometimes tribal peoples thought that Harris's own staff held special powers. "Come and see!" he would say, laughing in his great booming voice. Then he would break the staff across his knee. Cutting two fresh pieces of bamboo, he would tie them together with grass to make a new cross.

"My cross is not important," Harris explained. "But the cross of Christ is. And me, I'm not important, either. I'm just the carpet on which Christ wiped His feet."

Sometimes chieftains and their clans brought rich gifts in gratitude to the one they called "Big Man" or "the Prophet." But Harris would shake his shaggy grey head.

"Give your gifts to the poor," he would tell them. "But now if any of you would be so kind as to cook for me or to do my washing, why, I'd be truly grateful."

Hundreds of Christians became thousands; thousands became tens of thousands. Anyone could tell which way "the Prophet Harris" had passed. He left behind him a string of thatch-roofed church houses and bamboo bell towers. He left behind him villages where stealing was frowned upon, whether stealing of goods or cattle or wives. He left behind him people who no longer got drunk or bowed down to heathen gods.

By mid-1914, William Wadé Harris had worked his way across another border, into Ghana. (In those days people called it the Gold Coast.) Here, too, multitudes listened and believed the good news.

But far away from Africa, great events were happening that would cut short Harris's time as a missionary. Some Africans always claimed Harris himself predicted World War I before it started. He said it was a punishment upon the people of Europe for their sins.

Whether that story is true or not, the situation had changed by the time Harris got back to the Ivory Coast in early 1915. The French were fighting for their lives in Europe. Every available soldier had been called home from the French colonies in Africa.

This made the colonial governor of the Ivory Coast especially nervous about excitement among tribal peoples. So he decided the man they called a prophet had to go.

It was April of 1915 when a French district officer found William Wadé Harris on a beach. He was still proclaiming the gospel to great crowds. The old man did not run away or resist arrest. When the officer's two servants professed faith, he baptized them. Then he quietly gave himself up.

The Frenchman and his party put Harris in a canoe and rowed him back toward Liberia. Part of the three-hundred-mile trip they made by water, part by land. At the border they warned him, "Don't ever try to come back to the Ivory Coast!"

Harris had taught his converts to obey the authorities. Now he practiced what he preached. But he also knew a higher Authority who said, "Go therefore and make disci-

ples of all the nations."* So he kept on walking barefoot from
village to town, telling everyone the good news.

Most people in Liberia either claimed to be Christians
already or else would not listen to his message. Harris found
his heart yearning again toward the Ivory Coast. He remembered those tens of thousands who were so eager to know
the Lord Jesus.

At last he could stand it no longer. Once more he turned
his face eastward. But colonial officials stopped him at the
boundary line.

Eight times during the following years, William Wadé
Harris tried to go back and finish the job God had sent him
to do. Eight times his way was blocked. Once he even saw
the inside of a jail again. There was nothing he could do for
those multitudes of new believers in the Ivory Coast and
Ghana . . . nothing except to pray for them.

By 1926 Harris was an aged widower. He lived in Cape
Palmas with his daughter. In the fall of that year, he wel-
comed two guests. One was his old friend and translator,
Victor Tano. The other? He was a missionary to the Ivory
Coast.

"At last, at last, God has sent you to continue my work!"
the old man rejoiced. "Tell me about my children. I know
my Liberian grandchildren are going to Christian schools
here. But what about my spiritual children? Are they still
worshiping the one true and living God?"

A hundred thousand West Africans had turned to Christ
during less than two years that William Wadé Harris had
preached among them. Not all had stayed true to their Lord.
Some had wavered when colonial authorities burned down
bamboo churches and stopped worship services.

But others had bravely kept on meeting. They had built
new churches, some even of hewn stone. The Ivory Coast
missionary who visited Harris in 1926 could report that after

---

* Matthew 28:19, NASB.

twelve years, there were still tens of thousands of his "spiritual children" growing in the faith.

"The Prophet Harris" had taught great multitudes about a glorious life to come. A long-ago prophet described it in these words: "And those who are wise shall shine like the brightness of the firmament; and those who turn many to righteousness, like the stars for ever and ever."*

William Wadé Harris had turned many to righteousness. Not long after receiving visitors from the Ivory Coast in 1926, he began to experience that glorious afterlife for himself.

Palmas: PAHL-mahs   Tano: TAH-no

---

* Daniel 12:3, RSV.

19
God's Trusting Traveler
Amanda Berry Smith
of America and the World

Amanda Berry Smith never forgot what it was that had set her free from slavery: It was trusting God and working hard. All through her long life she kept on doing both. And she kept on being set free from other kinds of bondage as well.

Amanda's black mother was a slave who trusted God. She prayed that "Miss Celie," her master's daughter, would turn to Christ.

The white girl did, during a Methodist camp meeting. But not long after that she got sick. On her deathbed "Miss Celie" begged her parents, "Promise me you'll let Sam Berry buy his wife and children."

Sam Berry was Amanda's father. He had already bought his own freedom by working overtime. Often little Amanda saw him sit up late at night to make brooms and mats or stagger home long after dark, worn out from extra work on neighbors' farms.

"Miss Celie's" heartbroken parents kept their promise. After Sam Berry had earned enough to buy Amanda's mother and all five children, the Berry family moved from Maryland to the free state of Pennsylvania.

Now Amanda began to see other scenes late at night: She saw black Americans traveling the Underground Railway to freedom. Her father and mother helped many of them make their escape toward Canada.

Not knowing how to read makes a person a slave to ignorance. Young Amanda and her brother walked five miles in summer heat to a six-weeks' school. But they didn't learn much there. The teacher first took care of all the little white children before noticing two small black faces in the back of the classroom.

Sam Berry and his wife could both read. So Amanda cut letters out of newspaper headlines. She asked her mother and father to sort them into words. That was how she learned to read.

Amanda was only thirteen when her mother died. Not long after that she began working for a widow with five children. The whole family liked the way Amanda fried chicken and baked biscuits Maryland style.

One night after work Amanda went to a revival meeting. She was the only black person in church that night. As usual, she sat by the back door.

Suddenly a young woman walked back to where Amanda sat. Weeping, she begged the teenage servant girl to accept Christ. Together they walked down the aisle. Together they knelt at the front. And the white woman put her arms around the black woman and prayed as Amanda resolved to trust in the Lord and live for Him always.

Amanda was only seventeen when she got married in 1854. A few years later, her husband died fighting in the war to set slaves free. Her second husband James Smith was a deacon, but he didn't even go to church as often as Amanda did. He also died while Amanda was still a young woman. She had borne five children in all, but only her daughter Mazie was still alive.

During those troubled years, Amanda Berry Smith kept on working hard—cooking, washing, ironing. And she kept on learning how to trust God.

One day Amanda listened to a great preacher in New York City. She longed to go down front again and renew her life as a Christian. Yet somehow she held back. As Amanda herself told about it later, "They were white and were *there,* and I was black and was *here!*"

As she walked away from the church in New York that day, Amanda remembered a verse of Scripture: "There is neither Jew nor Greek, there is neither slave nor free, there is neither male nor female; for you are all one in Christ Jesus."* From that day forward, Amanda began to know more fully the freedom of trusting the Lord.

Little by little, Amanda Smith realized that God was calling her to preach the good news.

"Why me, Lord?" she asked in prayer. "I'm black, I'm a woman, no money, no schooling. Why me?"

The Lord answered in a dream: Like those letters Amanda had cut out of newspaper headlines long ago, she saw the word *Go*. And a Voice seemed to call, "Go, preach!"

Preach she did—sometimes through speaking, sometimes through singing. People loved to hear Amanda sing. And when she spoke in the pulpit, she trusted God more than ever, and somehow the right words always seemed to come.

"Give me a sign, Lord," Amanda begged, like Gideon in the Bible. The Lord gave her one: He arranged for Amanda's rent to be paid in advance. He even saw to it that she got a new pair of shoes.

The devil taunted her: "Didn't Jesus send His disciples out two by two? If you go out preaching all by yourself, people will think you're just looking for another husband!"

Amanda knew the devil was lying, but she did wonder what people would think. And she did wish for another woman to travel with her. Finally the Lord seemed to say, "You want a traveling companion? Go, and I'll go with you!"

So Amanda Berry Smith began to go out preaching the Word. Dressed like an old-fashioned Quaker dame in plain brown or black, with a poke bonnet and a carpetbag, she became God's trusting traveler.

She traveled to Washington, DC, where she looked for two long days to find a restaurant that would serve her food.

---

* Galatians 3:28, RSV.

She traveled to Knoxville, Tennessee, to the first great all-black church meeting ever held in the South. She traveled to Austin, Texas, and sat alone all night in the train station because she didn't know where she could go that people would take her in.

Then someone invited Amanda to travel all the way to England.

"To England!" she gasped to herself. She didn't even pray about it; such a trip seemed out of the question.

The Lord told Amanda she was wrong: "You're afraid to trust Me. You're afraid to cross the ocean."

"God, forgive me!" Amanda cried. "Give me another chance, and I'll go to England."

In the summer of 1878, when Amanda Berry Smith was forty-one years old, she sailed for England. God even gave her enough money for a first-class ticket. He gave her opportunities to lead worship services on board the ship.

Amanda thought she would be back home in just three months. Instead, it was twelve long years before she ever saw America again. She held evangelistic meetings all over England and Scotland. People listened when she called them to live holy lives before the Lord.

Then God opened the way for His trusting traveler to go on from Europe to Asia, to India and Burma. She preached there for two more years. After that it was Liberia and Sierra Leone in Africa.

During Amanda's eight years in Africa, friends in America suddenly stopped sending their money to support her as a missionary. God told her why: "Amanda, you've stopped trusting in Me. You've started trusting in America instead."

Again she asked for forgiveness. And again generous gifts poured in. Amanda could even arrange to adopt two African children and send them off to school in England.

Amanda felt old and tired when she finally came home to America in 1890. But the Lord still had another job for her to do: After resting awhile, she started a home for black orphan children in a suburb of Chicago.

Till she died in 1915 at the age of seventy-eight, Amanda Berry Smith kept on trusting God, and kept on working hard. When she wrote the story of her life, she ended it with a prayer: that the Spirit of the Lord would come upon younger people who have "better opportunities than I have ever had, and so must do better work for the Master."

20
God's Soldier of Peace
Deu I. Mahandi of the Philippines

Deu Mahandi had always wanted to be a soldier. But not just any ordinary soldier: Deu wanted to be a military officer.

His Filipino ancestors had been fierce fighters. And when Deu was born in 1926 on Tabawan in the Sulu Islands, he longed to follow the example of his forefathers.

Deu's family religion made him want to be a warrior, too. Many Filipinos on other islands claimed to be Christians. But nearly everybody on Tabawan Island was a Muslim. They told young Deu stories of brave soldiers who had followed the great prophet Muhammad in ancient times.

When Deu was eleven years old, a friend talked him into tagging along to a Christian meeting at their school. Deu noticed that many of those attending the service seemed to be true followers of Christ. They were real Christians, not just because their parents were.

Deu listened to the sermon that day. Somehow he felt an inner force urging him to believe in this Jesus Christ. But soon he managed to forget all about that strange feeling inside.

On Deu Mahandi's fifteenth birthday, war came to the Philippines. Japanese invaders struck from the north. Villagers shuddered to hear tales of their cruelty. Filipino troops could not hold them off. Neither could the small American army and air force.

In such times even fifteen-year-olds march away to war—especially boys who want to be soldiers anyway. Before Deu left home, a friend gave him a copy of the New Testament. He took it along to read between battles.

Deu Mahandi was nearly nineteen before the Japanese were at last driven away. The Philippines celebrated its hard-won independence. But the new nation still needed brave men to guard its freedom. Deu knew that a military officer should have a good education. So he moved to Manila, capital of the Philippines, far to the north from his native island. There he studied hard in college.

In 1948 Deu met and married a pretty girl. His Muslim parents might have been shocked to hear the girl was a Christian. She was not just a so-called Christian, either, but a faithful church member and teacher of a Sunday School class. Month by month, year by year, she tried to show and tell her husband who Jesus Christ really is.

After college Deu entered active military service again— this time, in the Philippine navy. Sometimes he went many weeks without seeing his wife and their two little girls.

Deu Mahandi soon made his mark in the navy. He joined a commando team, a crack unit sent to fight Communists and other troublemakers. Danger was part of Deu's job.

The Mahandi family was glad when November of 1954 rolled around. That meant Deu had only one last dangerous mission to perform.

The ship's orders read, "Go to Palawan Island." But winds blew strong against them off Palawan. Finally they turned instead toward the Sulu Islands, Deu's home country.

Mist and rain kept the steersman from seeing far ahead. With a grinding jolt the little ship crunched against a reef. Soon she sank into the South China Sea.

Life rafts were lost in the wreck. Deu and the other commandos and crew clung to bits and pieces of the ship. Hour after hour they struggled to stay afloat. Wind and rain still beat against them.

A day and a night passed somehow. Then another.

After the third night, Deu saw sharks circling. He noticed

how weary his comrades were. One of them half sobbed, "I'm going to die. If anybody makes it, tell my mother how I died."

Deu wondered whether he would be the one to take the message. He was older than that dying boy, and a stronger swimmer.

In such a desperate venture, no one is ashamed to pray. Some called on one god, some on another. Deu tried to pray as his Muslim parents had taught him to . . . but there seemed to be no answer.

Then one of the younger commandos gasped, "Hurrah for Magsaysay!"

Deu knew that Magsaysay was running for president of the Philippines that year.

Suddenly he remembered a Bible verse his wife had taught him: "Every one who calls upon the name of the Lord will be saved."*

A strange thought flashed through Deu's mind: "That poor lad still has the courage to call out the name of Magsaysay, even though Magsaysay can do nothing to save him here. How much more, then, should I have the courage to call upon the name of the Lord!"

Deu Mahandi did just that. He did more than that: He urged the others to trust in Jesus Christ as Lord and Savior. Several of them did so. And Deu himself made a solemn promise: "Give me another chance to live, O Lord, and I will serve You all my life."

Three hours later, the wind at last died down. Afternoon sunshine sparkled on the waves. And before that sun had sunk into the sea again, a ship that had drifted off course from Singapore spotted Deu and his friends. They were safely put ashore on Palawan Island. From there they were airlifted back home to Manila.

Deu Mahandi wasted no time in finding a church. The

---

* Romans 10:13, RSV.

nearest one was Pasay Baptist Chapel. An American missionary there blinked in surprise when Deu told his story.
Who ever heard of a Filipino Muslim becoming a follower
of Christ? The missionary could hardly have guessed that
one day Deu would even become pastor of that same chapel.

Hard times came at the very beginning of Deu Mahandi's
new life in Christ. Two months after he started studying at
the Baptist seminary, word came from Tabawan: "Your father has died, and we need your help. There's trouble brew-
ing in the southern isles."

Indeed there was trouble. After World War II, new settlers had crowded into Palawan, Mindanao, and the Sulu
Islands. Most of the newcomers called themselves Christians. But they knew little of Christ's love, for they began to
push aside Filipinos whose Muslin ancestors had lived on
those lands for centuries. Feuds broke out, then tribal wars.

God showed Deu Mahandi that he must not give up and
go back home. Even when tenant farmers were being shot
down in his family's fields, Deu stuck to his calling.

For fifteen years he faithfully served as a pastor—first at
Pasay, later in Quezon City. Twice his fellow Baptists chose
him as their leader. But often his thoughts turned toward
the southern isles.

By early 1971, fighting between Muslims and so-called
Christians was worse than ever. Gangs of "Black-shirts" ambushed busloads of innocent people. Whole villages had to
pack up and move.

The Mahandis' two little girls were grown women now
with families of their own. Deu felt the time had come for
him to join the battle . . . as God's soldier of peace. He
volunteered to go south as a military chaplain.

"I was brought up among Muslims," he explained. "I
know all their ways. But I also know what a difference Christ
makes—when you really believe in Him." So Deu Mahandi
put on his military officer's uniform and joined a special
"peace and order" team.

From island to island, from village to village he traveled. He begged Filipinos everywhere to settle their differences. "Even if the blood of Christians must be shed," he urged, "let there be peace."

Muslim leaders trusted him because he spoke their language. Christians-in-name-only trusted him because he was a minister of the gospel. Real Christians heard his challenge to stand by the Lord in the face of danger.

One day when Chaplain Deu Mahandi was worn out from his work, he felt as if he were becoming paralyzed. But the feeling passed away, and he didn't worry his wife by mentioning it in a letter.

On he pressed—broadcasting messages of peace by radio, meeting rival chieftains face to face. The Philippine government saw his value as a peacemaker. They gave him a special military medal.

Then in March of 1972 . . . paralysis struck again. Deu Mahandi was rushed to a military hospital. Two days later he was dead.

The government of the Philippines presented his widow with an even higher medal than the first one. They gave it in honor of what Deu Mahandi had done during thirteen months of peacemaking in the southern isles. And God's soldier of peace became the first evangelical chaplain ever to be buried in the Heroes' Cemetery near Manila.

Deu Mahandi:
DAY-oo mah-HAHN-dee   Magsaysay: MAHG-sigh-sigh
Tabawan: tah-BAH-wahn   Pasay: PAH-sigh
Sulu: SOO-loo   Mindanao: min-dah-NAH-aw
Palawan: pah-LAH-wahn   Quezon: KAY-zawn

II.
They Held the Ropes

William Carey was a shoemaker and a bivocational Baptist preacher who earned the nickname: "Father of the Modern Missionary Movement." Late in the 1700s, he led his fellow believers to band together for mission support. Carey himself volunteered to go as a missionary to India where he served for more than forty years.

When William Carey was still in England, other members of the mission society said, "There is a gold mine in India, but it seems about as deep as the center of the earth. Who will venture to explore it?"

William Carey said, "I will venture to go down. But remember that you must hold the ropes."*

The stories in section II of this book are all about people who never became missionaries—at least not in the usual sense of that word. But they all supported world missions—by praying, by giving, by managing mission affairs back home. In other words, they held the ropes.

You may be surprised to find these stories just as interesting as stories about "real live missionaries." Of course, I think this section of the book is especially interesting. For you see, the young dentist told about in "From Kentucky to Chile with Love" (chapter 23) was my father, Dr. Hugh M. McElrath.

---

* As quoted in F. Deaville Walker, *William Carey, Missionary Pioneer and Statesman* (Chicago: Moody Press, 1951).

21
The Man Who Wrote "America"

> My country, 'tis of thee,
> Sweet land of liberty,
> Of thee I sing."

You know the rest. Whether you call it "America" or "My Country, 'Tis of Thee," you have probably been singing it as long as you can remember. But have you ever stopped to think who wrote the words of this beloved patriotic hymn?

"An American, of course," you reply. And you are right. Yet the man who wrote "America" was more than an American. He was an American who had the whole wide world in his heart.

Sam Smith was as American as they come. He was born in 1808, almost in the shadow of a church steeple in historic old Boston. It was the very same belfry to which Paul Revere had looked for that famous lantern, signaling a warning that the British were coming.

Sam Smith was sickly as a little boy. Yet he often climbed Copps Hill and looked across the water to Bunker Hill and Breeds Hill on the point of Charlestown Neck. He knew that many brave Americans had died over there, in the first important battle of the Revolution.

When Sam was a budding poet eight years old (his first poem was "Elegy on a Cat"!), he joined thousands of other Bostonians in cheering for President James Monroe. The tall Virginian wore a revolutionary war uniform: three-cornered hat, blue coat with scarlet borders, and buff-colored breeches. No wonder Boston shouted!

A few years later, a sturdy teenager named Samuel Smith mingled with another patriotic crowd. This time the important visitor was the Marquis de Lafayette. It had been fifty years since Lafayette had helped America win the war. The old French nobleman laid the cornerstone of a monument on Bunker Hill. America's greatest orator, Daniel Webster, made the main speech that day.

The old America was quickly passing away. Only one signer of the Declaration of Independence was still alive, and he was in his nineties. But new ways and new days were coming for Samuel Smith's beloved country. While still in his teens, Sam watched the first steamboat puff its way into Boston Harbor—no sails, no oars.

Yes, the man who wrote "America" was an American. He was loyal, patriotic, always interested in both the new and the old in the life of his native land.

But Samuel Francis Smith knew a higher loyalty. He was true to America, yes . . . but first of all, he was true to the Lord Jesus Christ.

The early 1800s were exciting years for all Americans. They were especially exciting for the people called Baptists. And Sam Smith was a faithful member of a Baptist church.

Since early childhood, Sam had heard about the brave deeds of Adoniram Judson. Judson had sailed away from Massachusetts to become the first American missionary to Burma. War, sorrow, prison, torture—Judson had lived through them all. Still he kept on obeying Jesus' Great Commission by telling the good news to the people of Burma.

For a time Samuel Smith felt the Lord wanted him to be a missionary, too. He knew that for years not a single Burmese had turned to Christ. Then one day while Sam was still a seminary student, he heard that many people of Burma had at last begun to believe what Adoniram Judson was teaching them.

Sam Smith's joy bubbled over in the words of a fine missionary hymn. Many churches still sing it today:

> The morning light is breaking,
>   The darkness disappears;
> The sons of earth are waking
>   To penitential tears.

When he was still a young man of twenty-two, Samuel Smith did something that brought him more fame than anything else in all his long life.

Sam knew the famous musician Lowell Mason. Mason was working hard to improve music in American schools and churches. "Here, young man," cried Lowell Mason to Sam Smith one day. "You can read these books a friend brought me from Europe. But I can't tell what's in 'em."

At a glance Sam saw that the music books in Mason's hands were written in German. He nodded his head, for he could read German (along with fourteen other languages!).

"Look 'em over for me, would you?" continued Lowell Mason. "Find which songs are worth translating for youngsters to sing here in America."

Late one afternoon in February of 1831, as Sam Smith leafed through the borrowed books, he noticed a patriotic German hymn. He hummed the tune and liked the rhythm of it. Snatching a scrap of paper, he began to scribble. In thirty minutes he had written thirty-five lines of poetry. Later he sent his five stanzas with their tune to Lowell Mason and thought no more about what he had done.

On the next July 4, Sam Smith attended an Independence Day service at a big church in Boston. His mouth sagged open in surprise as Lowell Mason directed a choir of boys and girls in singing:

> My country, 'tis of thee,
> Sweet land of liberty,
>   Of thee I sing.

Later on Sam decided to drop the middle stanza of his hymn. He felt it might remind Americans too much of how they had hated the British as their enemies during the war. But the other four stanzas quickly became one of America's top tunes. Boys and girls sang it at school. Civil War soldiers died with its words on their lips.

Even the great American poet Oliver Wendell Holmes quoted it. He was a college friend of Sam Smith's. For their thirtieth class reunion, he wrote these teasing lines:

> And there's a nice youngster of excellent pith—
> Fate tried to conceal him by naming him Smith;
> But he shouted a song for the brave and the free—
> Just read on his medal, "My country," "of thee!"

But to Samuel Francis Smith himself, the most important part of his poem was the prayer in the last stanza:

> Our fathers' God, to thee,
> Author of liberty,
>   To thee we sing:
> Long may our land be bright
> With freedom's holy light;
> Protect us by thy might,
>   Great God, our King!

Samuel Smith knew that the only true freedom and light in the soul of humankind comes from Jesus Christ. That was why he dedicated his life to telling other people the good news.

It turned out that Sam Smith himself never became a missionary. But he did become one of that great host of faithful Christians who stay at home and support the ones who go.

After he finished seminary, Sam became editor of a missionary magazine. He published exciting reports from Adoniram Judson in Burma and from other missionaries all over the world. Then he became a pastor—first in the state of Maine, then back home again in Massachusetts.

For several years Samuel Smith helped direct the work of Baptist missionaries in many lands. He traveled around the world so he could report firsthand on what they were doing. His heart beat faster to hear his own hymn, "The Morning Light Is Breaking," being sung in Burmese, Karen, Telugu, Italian, Spanish, Portuguese, German, and Swedish.

All his life Samuel Francis Smith supported worldwide missions. Somehow he found time to write and edit hymnals, biographies, and mission study books. He lived to see his own son go out to help continue Adoniram Judson's great work in Burma. And when the man who wrote "America" dropped dead at the age of eighty-seven, Sam Smith was climbing onto a train to go out one more time and preach the good news of Jesus Christ.

Karen: kah-REN   Telugu: TELL-oo-goo

22
The Cowboys' Favorite Preacher

Who is the most famous Baptist preacher in the world?

If you asked that question in the last half of the twentieth century, the answer would probably be: "Dr. Billy Graham."

If you asked that question in the first half of the twentieth century, the answer would probably be: "Dr. George W. Truett."

Who was George Truett?

Why is there a Truett Auditorium on the campus of the largest theological seminary in the world? Why is there a Truett Orphanage in Nazareth, Israel? Why are there churches named Truett Memorial in North Carolina, Colorado, and California? Why are there chapels, schools, camps, and hospitals that bear the name of Truett?

George Truett was many things: pastor, friend of missions, world Christian leader. And not least of all, he was the cowboys' favorite preacher.

He got his start far from the western plains where cowboys roamed. George Truett was born in 1867, near the mountain border of North Carolina. Life was hard in those lean years after the Civil War. But the call of Christ comes in bad times as well as good, and George Truett as a teenage boy gave his life to Christ.

George was hungry for learning. By the time he was eighteen, he had already learned all that mountain schools could teach. By the time he was nineteen, he had already started his own school across the state line in Georgia.

That was how it happened that George Truett was in the crowd overflowing a Baptist church in Marietta one day in 1887. The yearly meeting of the Georgia Baptist Convention finally had to move over into the courthouse.

A speaker on the program was urging more support for home missions—especially Christian education for boys and girls in the mountains. "If you don't believe me," he cried, "I'll show you. George! Where are you? George, come up here!"

A pale, slender youth barely out of his teens walked forward. George Truett said afterward that he could actually feel his knees knocking. But before he had finished speaking, strong men wept; rich men opened their wallets to give to missions.

No one present that day ever forgot the mountain boy who came out of nowhere to kindle the fires of mission support. George Truett had that kind of God-given ability to move hearts and minds.

In 1889 George followed his family to Texas. He enrolled in junior college as a prelaw student. But his fellow church members recognized George Truett's true calling, even before George himself did. They almost forced him to accept ordination as a preacher of the gospel.

Then George was drafted to raise funds for Baylor University, a Baptist college about to go under because of unpaid debts. For two years George stumped the state of Texas and brought in offerings totaling ninety-two thousand dollars. That was an unheard-of amount for Southern Baptists in the 1890s.

George Truett himself was still hungry for learning. He enrolled in Baylor University as a twenty-six-year-old freshman. He met and married the pretty daughter of a university trustee. On weekends he pastored a small church nearby.

When he was barely out of college, George was invited to become pastor of First Baptist Church in Dallas. It was one of the largest churches in the state of Texas. George refused because he wanted to go on to seminary. But the church would not take no for an answer.

The pulpit committee explained one of their church's rules: no special offerings for missions.

Young George Truett shook his head. "If I am to be your pastor," said he, "then I must be free to present an appeal for missions whenever the need appears."

The committee members swallowed hard, then agreed.

On his second Sunday at First Church, Dallas, Pastor Truett urged a special offering. He asked the church trustees, "How much do you think we can get?"

"Hmm . . . twenty-five dollars at the most," they answered.

George Truett shot them a sharp glance. "You're not serious," he charged. "I expect to give that much myself. Surely the colonel, here, will give at least a hundred dollars."

The men all roared with laughter. It was a good joke on the colonel. But the special offering came to three hundred dollars, and the colonel plunked in his hundred.

That was the first of many such offerings during the forty-seven years that Dr. George W. Truett pastored the First Baptist Church of Dallas, Texas. He saw his church members increase from seven hundred to seven thousand. And he led them to give millions to missions.

Once Dr. Truett was invited to become president of Baylor University. He turned it down, saying: "I have sought and found the shepherd heart of a pastor."

He didn't come by that "shepherd heart" easily. Early in his years at Dallas, he went quail hunting with a fellow church member, the Dallas chief of police. As the young pastor shifted his shotgun, it blasted off. The wound in the police chief's lower leg didn't seem critical. But then a blood clot lodged in his heart, and he died.

George Truett told his wife, "I'll never preach again." He knew it was an accident. Yet he couldn't stop blaming himself.

Days of misery, nights without rest . . . and then came Saturday evening. George Truett prayed. He read God's Word. Sleep came at last, and with it a dream: Jesus Christ was saying, "Don't be afraid. You're My man from now on."

The tall, broad-shouldered young pastor had hollow eyes when he mounted the pulpit that Sunday morning. But he had a new note of sympathy and urgency in his voice. And he preached the good news of God's forgiving love as he had never preached it before.

During World War I, George Truett crossed the ocean to France. He preached to the troops there, by special appointment of President Woodrow Wilson.

Later, Dr. Truett was elected president of the Southern Baptist Convention for two years. Then he became president of the Baptist World Alliance for five years. He toured Baptist mission fields on four continents. And he always came back home to plead for more mission support.

Yet, some people say George Truett got his greatest joy in life from the times when he himself became a missionary: a missionary to cowboys.

Hundreds, thousands of cowboys gathered at Paisano Pass in the mountains of West Texas. Nearly every summer for forty years, they came from distant ranges. There they spread their tarps and bedrolls, slept and ate under the sky—and listened to George Truett preach.

He never forgot his first sermon for that crowd. It was already late at night. He was worn out from travel, and he had eaten a heavy supper. He was shocked when they asked him to start preaching right then and there.

"Can't you shoot quick, parson?" they challenged him. " 'Cause if you can't shoot quick, I reckon we've done sent for the wrong parson."

"Why, yes," Dr. Truett fired back. "I guess I can shoot quick, if you get me something to shoot at."

"Wal," said they, "we're all plumb anxious to be shot full of holes on this-here gospel proposition. Fire away!"

The big-city pastor looked around at cactus and cotton-wood. "Where can we hold the service?" he asked.

"You kin have the whole range, parson, from here to the mountains!" they cried.

At first George Truett's new congregation wanted to start by singing: "There'll Be a Hot Time in the Old Town To-night." He suggested "Nearer, My God, to Thee" instead.

"All right, parson," they agreed. "We kin make out to sing that-there song fitten to git started with the roping and branding of sinners." And the first of the cowboy camp meetings was underway!

Those weeks once a summer were highlights in George W. Truett's ministry. As he went back to Dallas (and to Washington and to London and to Shanghai and to all the other places where he preached), he told stories of cowboys:

There was Sam, just getting over the shakes from too much liquor. Sam spoke up without waiting for the invitation hymn: "Do you mean, parson, that if I come under to the Master, He'll help me fight these devils that's eating me up?"

Dr. Truett didn't need to answer. The other cowboys did it for him:

"That's exactly right, Sam!"

"That shore is right!"

"You bet your life He will!"

And Sam came under to the Master.

Another time it was old Jim, who gasped out his prayer: "Lord Jesus, the worst man in the world gives up to You—right now!"

What weeping, what shouting in the cowboys' camp that night! They had nearly given up on old Jim, who was known as "the worst sinner west of Fort Worth."

Those West Texas cowboys of years ago have long since gone to the last roundup. So has the cowboys' favorite preacher.

On one of the hottest days in the summer of 1944, twenty

thousand people came to the funeral of Dr. George W. Truett. They mourned the passing of the most famous Baptist preacher in the world. But more than that: They mourned a great friend of missions—missions in the city, missions on the plains, missions in the mountains, and missions around the world.

Paisano: pie-SAH-no   Shanghai: SHAHNG-HI

23

From Kentucky to Chile with Love

How much difference does just one person make in winning the world to Christ?

You can easily see the difference it makes when that "one person" is a great missionary like Lottie Moon or a strong supporter of missions like Annie Armstrong. Special offerings that they helped to start have had an impact all over the world.

You can easily see the difference it makes when that "one person" is a millionaire who gives to missions.

But . . . what if that "one person" is a nobody to most other people in the world? Not rich, not famous, not ever called to serve the Lord in home or foreign missions?

What if that "one person" lives in a small town, off the beaten path? How much difference can that one person's life make in carrying out the Great Commission?

Here's the answer: *You never can tell.* For sometimes in God's great plan just one ordinary person can be used to make a tremendous difference in winning the world to Christ.

That's what happened a long time ago, with the littlest boy in a big family at a small town named Murray, in western Kentucky.

The littlest boy in a big family gets overlooked sometimes. And if he's a slow reader and a poor speller in a family where most of the kids do well in school, then maybe nobody expects much from him.

But this youngest son turned out to be smart enough after all. His grades improved, especially in subjects where he could work with his hands as well as with his brain. When the time came to make a choice, he went away to dental school.

His father died before he got through. He had to borrow money to finish his education and to buy equipment for his office. Not many patients came at first, to a hometown boy just starting out in practice as a dentist. It took him years to pay off his debts.

The young dentist was an active member of the Baptist church in Murray. Ever since he could remember, his mother had taught him from the Bible, and from mission magazines, too.

Every year the church in Murray held what was called in those days a Bible institute. Guest preachers and teachers came for a week, even though to do that they had to leave the beaten path. Murray lies in the westernmost corner of Kentucky, and to get there in those days most people had to ferry big rivers.

In February of 1917, one of the Bible institute speakers in Murray was a Southern Baptist missionary, home on furlough from Argentina. He told how he had recently made a survey trip across the high Andes Mountains into Chile on the western coast of South America. He told how much Baptists needed to tell the good news in Chile, but how little money there was to send more missionaries.

The missionary finished his message and sat down. The pastor stood to dismiss the congregation.

But someone else stood up, too: The young dentist who had led the singing at the beginning of the service. "We're not going home yet," he quietly announced.

The pastor's voice was loud and gruff. "What's that, doctor?" he boomed. "Are we going to spend the night here?"

"No, but . . ." The young dentist turned toward the congregation. "But we *are* going to take a special over-and-above offering to send missionaries to Chile. And I'll start the collection with . . . one hundred dollars."

Somebody gasped. One hundred dollars could buy a lot in 1917.

Then somebody else came forward to pledge a gift. Then another, and another, and another.

Soon two thousand dollars had been raised. A telegram was sent from Murray, Kentucky, to Richmond, Virginia, addressed to the Foreign Mission Board: "Go ahead and appoint missionaries to Chile. We'll provide the funds."

Sixty years and more after that cold winter night in western Kentucky, Baptist churches in Chile numbered in the hundreds with thousands of members. In one year alone, Baptists of Chile baptized twelve hundred new believers and gave two hundred times as much as that first special offering in 1917. Schools, clinics, radio programs, a children's home, a seminary—all are helping Baptists to show and tell Christ's love in Chile.

Of course, to do all of this God has used many people, not just one. But who knows whether any of it would ever have been done . . . if just one person in a little Kentucky town had not stood up, and spoken up, and boldly put a love gift on the line for world missions?

24
Breakfast Biscuits, Drums, and a Money Jug

Here's a riddle for you:

How are breakfast biscuits, drums, and a money jug all alike?

Answer: All three have helped Christian young people make sacrifices, so that missionaries could be sent to tell the good news.

A sixteen-year-old boy in Florida worked after school all year long. He was saving his money to help a young missionary get to California for three months in the summer. But his savings still weren't enough. So he sold his set of drums to help pay travel costs. And that summer missionary boarded a bus, California bound!

A fifteen-year-old girl in South Carolina was too young to go as a summer missionary. But her big brother wasn't; he was already a senior in college. His problem, though, was the same old thing: not enough money.

Oh, he worked hard at his part-time job, all right. But nearly all the cash he could lay aside had to go for payments on his car. He had borrowed money to buy it the year before.

"I really do want to be a student summer missionary," he said. "But if I go out there to Oregon, I can't keep on making the payments. And they'll take my car back again to pay the debt."

That's where his little sister comes into the story. She knew her brother wanted to help an Oregon church whose pastor was in a wheelchair. So she got a vacation job, working at a fast-food place that featured breakfast biscuits.

All summer long, when other high school students were enjoying their holiday by lolling in bed, she had to get up at 4:00 AM. Burning her hands on hot biscuit pans and serving impatient hungry people seemed a long way from being a missionary. But she did manage to make the payments and keep her brother from losing his car.

One day she got a letter that made it all seem worthwhile. Her brother wrote from faraway Oregon: "You are truly in this mission project because without you I would not be here."

Where does a money jug come into the story?

It comes in on the other side of the world from Florida and South Carolina, California and Oregon. In Indonesia people don't use piggy banks. They save money in small narrow-necked clay jugs. And a money jug, like a piggy bank, must be broken to get out what's inside.

There aren't enough schoolteachers to go around for Indonesia's millions of boys and girls. So sometimes an older boy or girl will start teaching right after graduation from a special high school for teacher training.

That's how it happened with one young woman in Bandung, West Java, Indonesia. She really needed the pay from her teaching job. Her young husband was going on to university and somebody had to pay the bills.

Then that young wife heard about a special mission offering. "Let's bring our gifts to Christ at Christmas time," urged the pastor's wife. "Let's give, to help send the good news of great joy to all people everywhere."

When the pastor's wife passed out money jugs, the young schoolteacher took one and brought it home. She didn't have much money to spare. But every time she remembered how much Jesus meant to her, she dropped a coin or a folded bill down that narrow neck.

Then came Christmas. All the money jugs came home to

roost again at church. Each of them was cracked open like an egg. And the young schoolteacher was as surprised as everybody else at the size of her offering: Twenty-five thousand *rupiah!*

"How can you give so much, my dear?" the pastor's wife gently asked. "Your husband is still in university. And I know you don't get a big salary teaching school."

The young Indonesian woman smiled and shrugged her shoulders. "I just put it in a little at a time," she said. "And I'm glad to give it all to Christ on His birthday."

Bandung: BAHN-doong   rupiah: roo-PEE-ah

25
When Lightning Strikes a Church

What happens when lightning strikes a church?

That depends on what kind of lightning you mean. Whether it's real lightning, or lightning used as a figure of speech for something else that strikes suddenly, the church is likely never to be the same again.

Lightning struck a church in Texas one day in April. Neighbors saw it hit the steeple, but they didn't realize till too late that the little country church had caught on fire. Before the fire department could get there from town, the church had burned to the ground.

It was a small church in more ways than one: not just the size of its building but the size of its membership, too. Those few members gathered with their seventy-four-year-old pastor who had tried to get them to let him retire years before.

The church members faced big problems. Rebuilding would cost about seven times as much as they had, even counting what they got from their fire insurance.

"Then let's *not* rebuild," suggested one of the members. "Let's join other nearby churches instead. And let's give to missions all the money that's left."

Everybody liked the idea. After all, the little church had always given a lot to missions. For years they had sent one dollar out of every four in the collection plate, to help other people hear the story of Jesus. When their pastor was younger, they had even paid his way to Brazil for three weeks, so he could preach the good news there.

Now they divided up the money still left in the church's treasury: First, enough for the old pastor to retire with a comfortable place to live. Then, all the rest went to missions —in Brazil, Texas, and places in between.

When lightning struck in Texas, a church died. But because of the love and generosity of its members, other churches will live and grow strong.

A different kind of lightning struck a church in Guatemala. This "lightning" was a couple of new ideas that struck a Guatemalan pastor. He had been pastoring for several years without much success. For awhile he even dropped out of seminary. Then he went back to school while working as a salesman to pay expenses for his family.

The two ideas that hit him like lightning were these: "A church doesn't have to have a building. And a pastor doesn't have to be full time."

Really, both ideas are as old as the New Testament: Paul worked as a tentmaker while he was a missionary. And none of the churches Paul started had buildings of their own.

But sometimes old ideas can be forgotten. When they spring up again, they seem like new ones. Churches without buildings, part-time pastors—those are still new ideas in Guatemala as they are in many other parts of the world.

The Guatemalan pastor and his wife started visiting their neighbors on Sunday afternoons. Just four months later, several neighbors had believed in Jesus and were baptized. The next year, twenty-eight people gathered in the pastor's home to start *Iglesia Bautista El Camino* (The Way Baptist Church).

Question: When will The Way Baptist Church buy more chairs, since they have only thirty-six of them?

Answer: They don't plan to. The members bring other chairs with them from home when they come to church.

Question: When will the church move out of the pastor's home?

Answer: They don't plan to. They're too busy starting other churches instead.

Soon there were three other congregations meeting in church members' homes. One of these missions grew so fast that it spilled out into the street. The members did put up a small chapel in the yard for the 150 people who attended there, but it still didn't look much like a fancy church building. The pulpit was just pieces of a packing crate nailed together.

Question: Why are these Guatemalan congregations growing so fast?

Answer: Because the church members care more about people than about things. Because when a neighbor gets sick, women of the church go and clean house for her. Because neighborhood boys are invited to learn first aid and self-defense, along with lessons from the Bible. Because men witness to other men at places where they work.

When a family accepts Jesus Christ as Lord and Savior, right then a new Bible study group starts in their home. Men teach men, women teach women, young people teach young people.

Here's what one missionary said about *Iglesia Bautista El Camino,* with all its neighborhood congregations: "If they keep on growing this way, in a few years there'll be ninety new churches here in Guatemala City!"

Not ninety new church buildings, mind you: ninety new *churches.*

That's what can happen when lightning strikes a church.

Iglesia: ee-GLAY-see-ah   El Camino: ell-kah-MEE-no
Bautista: bah-oo-TEES-tah

III.
Might-Have-Been
Mission Stories

All of the stories in section III of this book are true. Yet they are called "Might-Have-Been Mission Stories." Why?

Because the conversations in the stories might or might not have been the exact words that were really spoken. Because two or three real people might have been telescoped into one character, to make the story run smoother.

Yet these stories are fact, not fiction. I have seen (and heard!) the diesel-powered corn mill described in "A Church in Lunga-og" (chapter 26). I have spent several days and nights in a Filipino village home like Caridad's. I have watched boys like Tono pumping bellows at a blacksmith's shop near Baptist Hospital in Kediri, East Java, Indonesia (chapter 30).

I have talked with one of the men who sailed on the "Voyage of the *Messenger*" (chapter 31). I have ridden (but never crashed!) in a missionary airplane like the ones told about in "Flying Doctor" (chapter 29) and "Elijah and the Jungle Pilot" (chapter 34).

You can read for yourself about the personal involvement of my friends and family and me in "Missionary Kid at the Book Factory" (chapter 27). By the way, Scott Corwin is a grown-up now. Both he and his wife Laurie came back as bivocational missionaries to teach at the big international high school in Jakarta, Indonesia's capital, from which Scott himself had graduated a few years before.

So every event in these stories really happened. But they

might or might not have all happened to the same people in the same order as I have told them.

That's why these are called "Might-Have-Been Mission Stories." But mind you, they're not make-believe!

26
A Church in Lunga-og

Felicisimo saw Caridad outside the door. She motioned to him. He slid down from his perch atop the corn mill and sauntered toward her.

"Sim! Where are you going?" yelled Uncle Moreno above the throb of the mill's diesel motor.

Felicisimo (Sim for short) shook his head. "Nowhere, Uncle. Just going to see what Cari wants. Don't worry, I'll be back up there in plenty of time."

A tropical sunset was throwing long shadows across the great plains of Mindanao Island in the Philippines. Sim found Caridad leaning against a huge fallen tree trunk that reached to the belt of her faded dress.

"Is your uncle going to keep on running that mill all night?" she asked.

Sim shrugged. "This is the busy season, Cari, you know that. People keep on coming up the Lunga-og trail with carabao sledges. And every sledge is loaded with corn to grind. What can we do?"

Caridad turned away, squinting into the twilight. "What can *we* do, Sim?" she softly echoed his question. "What if the preacher comes tonight? As long as that motor is running, we can hardly even hear ourselves sing. How can we possibly hear what the preacher says?"

"Who cares?" Fourteen-year-old Sim knotted his dark eyebrows. "We don't want to listen to him anyway—or listen to you, either!"

Uncle Moreno started frowning. Sim scampered back up to the top of the mill. He leaned over to shake the hopper, so that each grain of corn would be sure to strike the grinders and make its share of golden-white meal.

Sim tried to forget the slim figure that still leaned against the fallen log for several minutes after that. Then Cari slipped away into the night.

"Silly girl!" he thought. "Why did she think I would care if the diesel drowns out the sound of their singing?"

Yet he started thinking of Caridad again next morning as he helped tug the Philippine flag up the pole in front of the Lunga-og village school. After classes were over that afternoon, he somehow found himself wandering down the muddy lane toward her house.

The white watchdog barked at him from force of habit. Sim fondled the dog's tattered ears; they were old friends.

The dog leaped before him up the steps into Caridad's home. Like most houses in Lunga-og, its split-bamboo floor was built high off the ground to catch occasional breezes that stirred the heat.

Sim thought he heard a man's deep voice. But when he reached the top step, he saw only Caridad and her mother. The two of them had their hands full of hemp strands from plants that grew in burned-off fields nearby. Deftly they were twisting the long white fibers into string.

"What's that for?" asked Sim.

"We're still hoping the preacher will get here sometime this week," Caridad explained. "Maybe even today. He always brings his own mosquito net with him. But our old strings to hold up the corners of it have all rotted."

Sim realized now that the deep voice he had heard was coming from a transistor radio. High on a shelf it sat, sharing the place of honor with a tinted photograph of Caridad's grandfather and an out-of-date calendar with a picture of Christ.

The man on the radio was speaking about Christ, too. Sim noticed he was speaking very clearly, in good Cebuano.

"Who's that talking, Cari?"

Caridad smiled. "That's the preacher we're waiting for."

"Silly!" hooted the boy. "How in the world do you think he can be broadcasting from Davao City and be on his way here at the same time?"

Caridad finished her string and suddenly whipped it around Sim's neck. "If you're so smart, why haven't you ever heard of tape recordings?"

Sim blushed as he wriggled out of her lasso. He bolted down the steps. "Silly girl!"

He heard the diesel motor coughing as Uncle Moreno tried to start it up. That meant he ought to hurry to his place. But somehow Sim didn't want to climb back up on top of the corn mill just yet. In the gathering shadows he ambled along between rows of Manila hemp toward a gully that cut across the trail.

What was that sound? The diesel at the mill again?

No, this sound was coming from another direction, from the Davao City road.

Was it an automobile? Automobiles were events in Lunga-og. Sim decided to wait at least long enough to see what kind of car it was.

By this time he had reached the edge of the gully. He stepped onto one of the two planed-down logs that made a little bridge—and nearly tumbled headfirst into the creek!

Sim looked at the log more closely. Somehow one side of it had sagged into the mud so that it no longer gave a flat surface to walk on . . . or to drive on.

The automobile was nearer now. Its headlights flared up into his eyes.

"Stop, stop!" Sim jumped up and down, waving his arms.

The jeep's muddy tires slithered to a halt a few feet from the gully.

"What's the matter, lad? Bridge out?"

The voice spoke in Cebuano, Sim's own language. The accent sounded foreign, yet strangely familiar.

"No sir, not exactly," Sim replied. "But the log on this side has gotten turned. I'm afraid you'll slide off if you try to cross."

The driver's white hands glistened in the car lights as he reached down to feel the sidewise angle of the log.

"You're right," he said. "Can we push it back into place?"

Sim dropped onto his stomach and curled his tan arms all the way around the log. "Can't do it, sir," he grunted. "Too heavy for just the two of us."

The *Americano* drew a long breath. "Well! What do we do now? I need to get to Lunga-og. Lots of people there would like to see the colored slides I have here."

Sim's eyes opened wider. "Colored slides? How can you show them in Lunga-og, with no electric lights?"

"No problem." The man smiled. "My projector is battery powered. But how do I get it there? Maybe it's near enough to walk . . . but I can't just leave the jeep sitting out here."

"Just a minute, sir," Sim said quickly. "I'll run get the other boys to help us roll the log over again."

Sim's heartbeats seemed to double the speed of his flying feet. Soon he could hear again the diesel motor of the corn mill. "Let it roar!" thought Sim. "I've got something better to do."

Before long, a laughing, jostling crew of teenagers stood knee-deep in mud and water to wrestle the log back into place. The *Americano* inched his four-wheel drive jeep across the rough bridge. Then the boys tumbled on top of one another into the jeep—mud and all.

After the overloaded car had groaned and bumped its way to the edge of Lunga-og, Sim heard the driver ask, "Let's see, Caridad's mother still lives down there near the corn mill, doesn't she?"

"Caridad! You know Cari?"

"Of course," answered the *Americano*. "That's where I

usually stay when I come. And that's where we usually hold our services."

Then it dawned on Sim: This must be the preacher from Davao City!

Soon Sim was chattering with his friends as they sat on the dirt basketball court outside the school building. Gasoline pressure lanterns gave the preacher enough light to adjust the strong battery-powered beam from his projector. Other people had also heard the chug-chug of the jeep, and the school yard was already full.

Then chatter died away as the hissing lamps were shut down. Colored slides loomed up one by one against the whitewashed wall of the school. Even the roar of the corn mill stopped. Sim wondered whether there was no more grain to grind or whether Uncle Moreno had decided he wanted to watch the show, too.

In smooth Cebuano touched by his *Americano* accent, the visitor told about people shown in the slides: Filipino Christians who had built churches, started schools, operated hospitals. At the same time he talked about the reason why—about the Lord Jesus Christ who wants all people everywhere to know of God's love.

Sim felt something soft against his arm. He turned and faced Caridad.

"Do you see now why we wanted him to come, Sim?" she whispered. "Do you see why we wanted to able to hear him when he finally got here?"

Sim glanced at the makeshift screen, then back at the girl's eager face. "Caridad, why couldn't we build a church here in Lunga-og, like these other Filipinos have done? Maybe we could put it at the other end of the lane yonder. Then even the noise from the corn mill wouldn't bother."

Sim thought Caridad's eyes were growing larger and larger. Then he heard her say, "I'm sure we can have a church in Lunga-og, Sim—if you and all your friends will help."

Lunga-og: LOONG-ah-awg   carabao: KAH-rah-bah-aw

Felicisimo:
   feh-lee-SEE-seem-aw   Mindanao: mean-dah-NAH-aw

Caridad: KAH-ree-dahd   Cebuano: see-boo-AH-naw

Sim: SEEM   Davao: DAH-vah-aw

Moreno: mo-RAY-naw   Americano:
                                ah-meh-ree-KAH-naw

Cari: KAH-ree

27
Missionary Kid at the Book Factory

Scott Corwin flipped the calendar. "Still three weeks till Christmas," he sighed silently.

He had never known a school vacation could drag by so slowly. Of course, back home in Texas he never got two months off in December and January, either.

Scott remembered his teacher's explanation for the long holiday. He wondered whether some of his Missionary Kid classmates had gotten home yet, on other islands of Indonesia far away.

It was nice that Scott's own parents lived right here in Bandung. "Me, I even get to go home for lunch," Scott mused. "It takes some MKs a week to get home for Christmas."

Scott began humming a Christmas song he had learned at school. Fifth grade wasn't exactly his favorite indoor sport, but anything was better than getting bored. And somehow his little sisters seemed more bothersome than ever these days.

He sighed again as the telephone rang. "Probably for Mother, as usual." Then suddenly he began listening to Mother's replies.

"Yes . . . uh-huh . . . I don't see why not. He's not doing a thing but sitting around the house twiddling his thumbs." Then she covered the mouthpiece. "Scott! Come here and talk to Aunt Mary Alice a minute."

Scott's heart seemed to shift into second gear.

"Hello there, Scott," began Miss Ditsworth. (Scott called her "Aunt" as he did all women missionaries—except Mother, of course.)

"We're getting into our busiest part of the quarter here at the publishing house," she continued. "And one of the young Indonesians who usually works part-time has school exams right now. Would you be interested in helping out awhile?"

It didn't take Scott long to make up his mind. "Yes *ma'am!*"

"OK," said Aunt Mary Alice. "I'll pick you up about 1:30 this afternoon, and we'll give it a try."

Of course Scott had been to the Baptist publishing house before; Mother had bought a book for him there. But he had never seen much that went on back behind the book store.

When Scott and Aunt Mary Alice walked in that afternoon, they were met by tan-skinned Mr. Suyoto. Miss Ditsworth explained in a few words of Indonesian. Then Mr. Suyoto smiled at Scott as he spoke, in slow but correct English: "Come with me, please. Your first job will be putting staples in Sunday School quarterlies."

Two or three times that afternoon Scott wondered whether he would make it through his first half day working at a missionary publication center. Who would ever have thought that stapling could be such hard work? He had to bash the big stapler hard enough to grip twenty-six sheets at a time. It hurt. And the stack of quarterlies to be finished was taller than he was.

Even break time at mid-afternoon wasn't much help. Scott grabbed a glass of tea. Then he began jumping around like a circus juggler. In his thirst he had forgotten that Indonesians usually serve *hot* tea in glasses.

By late afternoon his right hand was sore and swollen from pushing down on the stapler. By bedtime it had turned blue.

But Scott Corwin was no quitter. At 7:30 the next morning he was pumping his bike up the steep hill to the publishing house, like a fullback for the Dallas Cowboys charging into the secondary.

That was the beginning of six full weeks for the husky Missionary Kid—full of work, but full of learning and full of fun, too.

Most of the time he worked alongside two teenage girls, Olga and Dede. Scott didn't tell them he was only eleven. Even at that age, a tall Texan is average height for grown-up Indonesians.

Together the three youngsters—one chocolate colored, one caramel, one divinity fudge—made books by the thousands. No one's hands could stand stapling more than two hours at a stretch, but there were plenty of other jobs to do.

Some days they assembled printed pages into copies of *Suara Baptis*—"The Baptist Voice," a bimonthly magazine. Some days they counted out picture leaflets for little children, ten sheets to a stack. Some days Scott came home sticky fingered after spreading glue on lessons for boys and girls his own age.

As the beginning of a new quarter drew near, the bookmaking was finished. Now Scott and Olga and Dede packed and wrapped and tied till they almost felt like brown-paper packages themselves. Then Scott helped the full-time workers lug boxes to a truck for delivery to the post office.

Sometimes the men let him help in other ways. He and Anton stacked dozens of tracts near the heavy cutter blade. Before Anton swung it to trim off the edges of all the pages at once, he let Scott turn the big wheel that tightened them into place. It felt just like driving a truck.

But the worker he liked best was Mr. Imarto, the darkroom man.

"Come on, ma'am, put your apron on and get busy in the kitchen," he would tease Scott as he held out one of the heavy full-length aprons they had to wear for protection.

The young Chinese-Indonesian man and the American boy would keep on pretending to do kitchen chores as they burned aluminum plates with acid for the offset printing press. They made-believe it was strawberry jam that Scott smeared on the plates, instead of a pasty red lacquer that helped to complete the process.

"Now let's do the dishes," Mr. Imarto would chuckle as they rinsed off the metal with a hose in the sink. Soon all was ready for printing a new Bible-study book and an Indonesian Baptist church calendar for next year.

One hot day in December, Scott wolfed down his lunch, didn't drain his glass of iced tea, and forgot to brush his teeth before leaving home again. That hill seemed steeper than ever as he pedaled back to work in tropical sunlight at 1:00 PM.

Scott was walking his bike up the last little grassy plot in front of the door when it happened. Somehow his knees buckled, and he landed in a heap of spokes and handlebars. Three workmen and a book-store lady rushed to his aid. "I'm all right, I'm all right," he insisted as he scrambled to his feet, cheeks hotter than ever.

After he and Olga and Dede had waded into those piles of quarterlies again, Scott felt as dry mouthed as if he were back in Texas playing football. He knew "Uncle Mac" McElrath, another missionary in publication work, always kept a thermos of cool, pure water nearby. Mumbling an excuse, Scott sidled toward the editorial offices.

The doors were closed; there were no nameplates. "I think this is the right one," Scott breathed. So he knocked.

"*Silakan masuk!*" someone answered.

"Oh, no," the boy groaned to himself. "I've gone and bothered some Indonesian editor instead."

"*Silakan masuk!*" the voice repeated.

Even though he'd only been in Indonesia a few months, Scott knew what those words meant: "Please come in!" Timidly he stuck his head inside the door.

"Hey, Scott!" Uncle Mac greeted him. "What can I do for you?"

So it was the right office, after all. And that cool drinking water felt like snow at Christmastime as it trickled down Scott's gullet.

"Are you working hard?" asked Uncle Mac.

"Yes sir . . . sort of," said Scott. "I'm not making much, but it'll sure help buy Christmas presents!"

The missionary nodded. "Maybe you're getting something better than money, too. Been practicing your Indonesian a lot?"

Scott grinned. "I sure have—that is, when Dede hasn't been practicing her English on me!"

Uncle Mac mirrored Scott's smile. "My little Tim is really impressed with your working here. After he watched you assembling quarterlies the other day, he said, 'Daddy, this is a book factory!' And I guess he's right. We editors and writers and translators are like designers and draftsmen at the drawing boards. Then the typists, artists, and printers put our ideas into production . . ."

Scott finished the sentence. "And then the rest of us pitch in to get the products out to people who need 'em." He set the thermos cup down on the edge of Mr. McElrath's desk. "You know, Uncle Mac, when Tim was watching me that day, I was watching a word: *keselamatan,* the first word on the top line of the middle page. I had to watch that word to make sure each quarterly had all its pages before we stapled it."

"You know what *keselamatan* means, don't you, Scott?" asked the missionary editor.

The boy shook his head.

"It means 'salvation.' " Uncle Mac paused. "A pretty good word to be watching, wouldn't you say? That's the real reason why you and I and all the rest of us are working here."

The eleven-year-old's face grew solemn. "Yes sir. I see what you mean." Then Scott's smile came back. "Thanks for the water, Uncle Mac!" And off he trotted to the workroom.

Bandung: BAHN-doong   Anton: AHN-tawn
Suyoto: soo-YAW-taw   Imarto: ee-MAR-taw
Dede: DEH-deh   Silakan: see-LAH-kahn
Suara: soo-AH-rah   masuk: MAH-sook
Baptis: BAHP-teece   keselamatan:
                               kuh-suh-lah-MAH-tahn

28

A Spirit Who Cannot Be Fooled

Taiwo stopped to wait for his twin brother. "Hurry up, will you?" he fussed. "No wonder they call you Kehinde, 'The One Who Lags Behind'!"

Kehinde sniffed. "If you had to lead this balky old goat, you couldn't walk so fast either. Here, you take him for awhile."

"All right." Taiwo grasped the neck rope. "But you have to carry these yams and bananas."

The two Nigerian thirteen-year-olds plodded on. Their dark faces grew solemn as they passed a fresh mound of earth near their mud-wall home.

Kehinde whispered, "Do you suppose Father is happy down there in the ground?"

Taiwo shook his head and blinked several times. It was hard to believe that only three days ago Father had been strong and well, able to bend over his short-handled hoe for hours in the African sun, working his fields of corn and yams and okra.

The twins reached their front yard. The crowd was getting bigger. Already the singing and dancing had started.

Suddenly Taiwo nudged his twin. "Kehinde! Who's that?"

"Where?" asked Kehinde.

"There, sitting in that chair." Taiwo pointed toward a woman whose skin looked pale and faded near the deep rich flesh tones of their friends and neighbors.

The old men who had come to conduct the funeral told

the boys who she was: a foreign teacher of a strange religion. She lived in the great city of Ibadan, but for one week she had come to visit their village.

"A strange religion!" Taiwo sucked in his breath. "Will the spirits like that? What will they do to my father?"

One of the old men smiled. "It will not matter, young one," said he, "as long as the foreigner does not interfere with what we do."

Now the ceremony began. The balky goat was soon dead. His bloody head lay on the ground, near piles of yams and green bananas.

Then one of the old men brought out a tiny casket, made of strips of bamboo.

"Not even big enough for burying a baby," muttered Kehinde. "How can it fool the spirits into thinking Father is really inside it?"

"Hush, hush!" Taiwo warned him. "How do you know the spirits aren't listening right now?"

On went the fake funeral, with more fooling of the spirits. Into a small round hole in the ground, the old men dumped food for Father's journey to the spirit world: soup, yam cakes, and goat meat. But they used only the head, not the good fleshy parts of the goat. Inside the little bamboo coffin they folded Father's clothes for the trip: only a little white rag, but first they held it next to beautiful woven material, so maybe the spirits wouldn't notice which cloth was being buried.

"Are you ready, Kehinde?" whispered Taiwo.

"Yes, it's our turn now!" answered his twin.

Taiwo picked up one of the yams and smashed it against the hard-packed earth. "My father was strong," he chanted, "strong like nut trees that stand tall against the sky."

Kehinde slung the bunch of green bananas so they went squash! against the ground. "My father was strong," he chanted, "strong like leopards that prowl the jungle."

As the twins wrecked yams and bananas while praising

their father's strength, they kept on glancing toward the white-skinned woman.

"She looks sad, Kehinde," whispered Taiwo a minute later.

"I wonder why?" asked Kehinde. "She didn't even know our father, did she?"

Soon it was all over. The bamboo-strip casket was buried. Then twelve smooth cowrie shells were strung on a stick. A village elder held it out, its shiny shells reflecting the sun.

"Come, Taiwo," he called. "Come, 'The One Who Has First Taste of the World.' To the oldest male of the family we give this sacred *juju*. Though you are still a boy, Taiwo, you have no grandfather, no uncle, no older brother. To you, then, Taiwo, we give this holy symbol of your father who now departs for the spirit world. Guard it well!"

Reverently Taiwo placed the *juju* stick on the altar in the front room of the house. There he and Kehinde and their mother and younger brothers and sisters would worship it, along with other *jujus* that already lay on the altar.

After the ceremony of fooling the spirits, everyone went home. But three days later the twins saw the foreign teacher again. She stopped by their house, along with four Nigerians —two young men, two smiling girls.

In the boys' own Yoruba language, she said: "Come with us to the meeting house tonight. Come hear wonderful stories about God. God loves you, you know. God cares because you are sad."

Taiwo looked at Kehinde. Kehinde looked at Taiwo. Loves? Cares? This didn't sound like the gods they knew about.

The foreigner laid one of her hands on each boy's brown shoulder. "You two make a fine pair," she said. "Which is Taiwo and which is Kehinde?"

The brothers were not surprised that she knew their names. All twins of their tribe—boys or girls—were named Taiwo and Kehinde.

"Do come," the woman urged once more. "We'll be looking for you tonight." The Nigerian young people explained when and where the service would be held. Then they handed each twin a tiny four-page book.

"She's very nice," remarked Kehinde when they had gone. "Even if she does teach about a strange god."

Taiwo was reading the printed Yoruba words in the little book. "She says her God loves us and cares about us. This book says the same thing. I wonder . . ."

Kehinde scratched his head. "Wouldn't it be wonderful, Taiwo, if it were really true?"

Neither said anything to the other about going that night. Neither mentioned the visitors to their mother. But when the time came, both twins slipped out of the house where their father's *juju* lay on the front-room altar.

At the meeting one of the young Nigerian men led in singing. Taiwo and Kehinde shared a song sheet. The other young Nigerian man read from a black-covered book. Then he seemed to be praying to some kind of *juju*—maybe the book itself because the twins couldn't see any other.

The white-skinned woman began to speak: "God loves you. God is Spirit. But He is not like the spirits you fear. He is a loving Spirit, a Holy Spirit. God loves you more than the best father in all the world."

Taiwo pricked up his ears when he heard that.

She went on speaking: "God loves you so much that He sent His only Son to die so your sins could be forgiven. Trust Jesus Christ, God's Son, and you never need to fear the evil spirits any more. Believe in Jesus Christ, and worship Him only. Give up your sticks and stones that cannot save you from sin and sorrow."

As she talked, Taiwo's heart beat faster. He felt he wanted to know this Jesus, this God. He would like to believe in a Spirit who truly loved him, who truly cared about him.

While the people were singing again, Taiwo found himself walking toward the front. "I don't understand it all yet," he murmured to the foreign woman and the young Nigerians. "But I want to know more. I think I want to worship this God who is Spirit . . . all my life long."

"Good for you, Taiwo!" said the foreign teacher. "It's good that one who bears your name should be the first to come forward tonight. But—where is Kehinde?"

"Here I am!" Kehinde had followed Taiwo down the aisle.

The twins sat side by side on a rough bench as their new friends explained what it meant to worship the one true God. "He must be your only God," insisted one of the young Nigerians. "No more *jujus*, no more spirit worship, nothing and no one else except the God whose Son is Jesus Christ. He is the only true one. And He is enough."

Taiwo looked at Kehinde. Kehinde looked at Taiwo.

The older twin took a deep breath. "Very well. I am ready to worship the God who loves us and sent Jesus Christ. But . . . will someone please come home with me to help me get rid of all my old gods?"

"And to explain to our mother?" Kehinde quickly added. "I think we're too big now for her to beat us, but . . ."

Next morning the teacher with two of her friends met the twins' mother. The Nigerian woman shook her head every time they tried to tell her about Jesus Christ. But she did agree to let the boys do as they pleased. "They are the men of the house now," she said. "Let them do as they like. If they do wrong, they will suffer for it."

Taiwo scuffed his foot on the dirt floor. Kehinde glanced at the shadowy corner behind him.

The white-skinned teacher took their hands. "Don't worry, boys," she said with a smile. "God will take care of you. You'll never be sorry you decided to worship Him only. Now, . . . where are those *jujus* you mentioned?"

Taiwo reached out to pick up the stick strung with shells which he had received only four days before. He drew his hand back, then stretched it out again. "Here, take it!" he cried. "Take them all. Let's get rid of them!"

Besides the stick with the cowrie shells, there were some feathers, a piece of iron, and a clay figure with bulging eyes. When all of these objects of worship had been taken away, three coins still lay on the household altar.

"I see you've been giving offerings to your old gods, boys," said the teacher. "It's good you've already learned to do that. Now you'll want to give offerings to the true God. Would you like to give this money at the meeting next Sunday?"

Kehinde began to chuckle. Taiwo giggled. Soon both twins were laughing till tears made trails through the dust on their cheeks.

The teacher looked blank. Then suddenly she smiled. "I know," she said. "You've been trying to fool your old gods with *ijebu* money, haven't you?"

Taiwo and Kehinde nodded, still grinning. Everyone else tried to fool the spirits: Why not give them offerings of counterfeit coins?

The teacher's face reflected their smiles. Then she took the three coins and walked to a deep pit near their house. There she flung the false money—down, down, down toward the *jujus* that had already been shattered to bits at the bottom.

"You can trick a *juju*," she explained as they turned away. "But you can't do that with the true God. He knows. He knows what is counterfeit and what is real—whether money or words or deeds. You can't fool Him."

Taiwo's face was solemn now. "I'm glad," he said. "I'm glad our God is too wise to be fooled by tricks."

"I'm glad too," said Kehinde like an echo. "I'm glad we know the one true God, the loving Spirit who really cares about us."

Taiwo: TIE-woe	juju: JOO-joo
Kehinde: KINE-dee	Yoruba: YAW-roo-bah
Ibadan: ee-BAH-dahn	ijebu: ee-JAY-boo

29
Flying Doctor

"There it is! I hear it!" cried Susanna Coleman, jumping up from the breakfast table.

Her little brother and sister trailed her outside as she ran to the edge of the airstrip. The red and white Cessna 172 was already circling into position. Down it roared, whizzing across flat East African soil till it rolled to a stop.

"Hi, Uncle Don!" yelled Susanna as she trotted toward the plane.

"Hello there, Sus," called the blond pilot as he curled his tall frame through the narrow door. "And Happy New Year!"

"Happy New Year!" chorused Susanna, Stephen, and Priscilla.

Susanna's mother had walked up behind them by then. "I hope you brought us a delayed Christmas present, Don," she chuckled.

"Yes ma'am," answered Don Voris, the missionary pilot. "How about fresh bread and fresh vegetables from the Zambezi River Valley?"

"I'm more interested in the rest of your cargo," said Dr. Coleman, Susanna's father.

Uncle Don smiled as he unloaded several small boxes. "Such as this medicine, maybe?"

Soon the little four-seater was ready to take off again. Susanna gave her father a good-bye hug as the missionary doctor stepped into the plane. Mr. Mlanga, the darkskinned

Zimbabwean orderly, helped stow away more medical supplies, then got in himself.

The Coleman children waved till the Cessna was just a speck disappearing behind white clouds that flecked the sky.

"How long will it take 'em to get there, Mom?" asked Susanna.

"Let's see, they go to Mtanke first," she answered. "That's only about fifty miles, so they should be there in half an hour."

"How long would it take by jeep?" Susanna wondered.

"Oh my, those rough roads." Mom shook her head. "Thanks to Uncle Don, your daddy can help as many sick people in three days as he used to in a week."

"He's my favorite uncle, Mama," said Stephen.

Susanna grinned silently. She was already old enough now to understand that Mr. Voris wasn't really her uncle. But Stevie and Prissy still thought all missionaries were kinfolks.

"Come on, Sus, time for school."

Susanna sighed. No playing hooky when your own mother is the teacher. But then, too, no problem getting lots of extra help with homework.

Monday, Tuesday, and Wednesday passed. Mom had memorized Dad's schedule and kept the three young Colemans up to date. "They've finished at Mtanke by now," she said. "They ought to be on their way to Simchembu." Later, she said: "Maybe they're landing at Nenyunka right now." And on Wednesday afternoon: "They're heading back home, kids!"

After lessons were done, Susanna played near the airstrip. Sure enough, she managed once again to be the first to spot the Cessna 172.

The rest of the family had joined Susanna by the time Uncle Don had braked the plane. Priscilla jumped into her father's arms. Stephen hung onto his other hand. Susanna lugged his black bag.

"How did it go, Jim?" asked Mom.

"Pretty good, Sandra," Dad answered. "I'll tell you more after I wet my whistle. Come on in for a drink of tea, Don, before you go home."

"Aren't you back a little early?" asked Mom as she handed Susanna the glasses to serve.

"Yeah, sure," said Dr. Coleman. "We couldn't land at Nenyunka, so that stop was canceled this time."

"What happened, Dad?" Susanna's eyes opened wide.

"Well, you know how these bush airstrips are. The Zimbabweans cut down trees and dig up stumps. Then one of us missionaries drives a jeep over there, and chains heavy logs to the back, and drags the airstrip till it's smooth."

"Too bad they're not all like the one here," put in Uncle Don. "That was real luck, having the district commissioner come by with a road grader just as you were trying to level it off."

Dr. Coleman nodded. "But at Nenyunka, the people have to take care of the airstrip by themselves. And they don't quite realize what kind of surface it takes for an airplane to land at sixty miles an hour. Today, when Don flew over at about ten feet, we could see several muddy spots that cows and goats had churned up. There was nothing we could do but drop a note, saying we'd try again in two weeks if they'd fix things up by then."

"What would you have done there, Daddy, if you landed?" asked Stephen.

Susanna felt she herself could have answered her little brother's question. But she always liked to hear Dad tell about his work.

"Well, take Mtanke, for instance," began Dr. Coleman as he balanced Priscilla on his knee. "That's always the first stop, on Monday morning. Mr. Hwema is head teacher at the Mtanke school. He helps the church there, too, though he's not really a pastor. Mrs. Hwema is a nurse. Before Uncle Don and I landed, she had already started registering people for the clinic."

"What's re-gis-ter-ing?" asked Stevie.

"That means she writes down their names, and tries to find out what's hurting them, and takes their money."

That part of the story still puzzled Susanna. "Why do you make 'em pay, Dad?" she wondered. "I thought Baptists back in America gave mission offerings so we could help people here in Zimbabwe."

Dr. Coleman took a sip of tea before answering. "That's right, Sus. But we ask the patients to pay just a little bit, too. That keeps people from coming to our clinic with imaginary diseases, or just out of curiosity. It makes 'em feel the medicine we give is worth taking, even if it tastes bad. And it keeps 'em from thinking they *must* become Christians just because a Christian doctor treats 'em free of charge."

"I never thought of that," murmured Susanna.

Dad went on. "After Mrs. Hwema had registered everybody, she told me nobody was too sick to wait a few minutes. So then I opened my Shona-language Bible and preached to 'em."

"Are your sermons like Uncle Bill's, Daddy?" asked Stevie.

The missionary doctor chuckled. "Not exactly, I guess. After all, he's a preacher, and I'm not. I just tell 'em I know they've come because their bodies are sick. I tell 'em we'll give medicine, but only God can heal. And even though they'll still die someday, God can also give 'em eternal life— if they trust the Lord Jesus as their Savior."

"Did any of 'em trust Him this time, Dad?" Susanna wanted to know.

"Well, several said they were interested," Dad answered. "Mr. Hwema talked with 'em a long time. Maybe they'll be ready for Uncle Bill to baptize the next time he comes by Mtanke. Me, I had to get busy just the same as you see me do when we have clinic here: listening to hearts and lungs, looking down throats and up noses, and prescribing shots and doses for the nurse and orderly to give."

"Let's see," said Susanna, trying to show how much she knew, "Mtanke is that place across the river from the hospital, isn't it, Dad?"

Dr. Coleman nodded yes. "When we were stationed at the mission hospital, I had to cross the river on a raft and keep a jeep on the other bank, so I could get to sick people at Mtanke. If it weren't for Don, here, that's what I'd be doing yet. And this time of year, in rainy season, I wouldn't be able to make it to Mtanke at all."

The tall bush pilot smiled. "That's my job, Jim—to be a missionary myself and to fly other missionaries to places they need to go. And speaking of that . . ." He looked at his watch. "There's another wife and three Missionary Kids over at Karanda expecting me home by suppertime."

"Can you really get there that soon, Uncle Don?" questioned Susanna.

"Two hundred miles—that's two hours easy, Sus, if those clouds don't close in too tight. But I'd better be on my way right now."

Susanna Coleman stood with her family, watching the red and white aircraft mount up into the sky. Then they all strolled back together to the square prefab house gleaming in African afternoon sunlight—the home of a flying doctor and his family.

Zambezi: zahm-BEE-zee	Nenyunka: nen-YOON-kah
Mlanga: muh-LAHNG-ah	Hwema: HWAY-mah
Mtanke: muh-TAHN-keh	Shona: SHOW-nah
Simchembu: seem-CHEHM-boo	Karanda: kah-RAHN-dah

30
Begitu Saja! (Just Like That!)

Thump-thump! Thump-thump! Thump-thump!

Like the rod on a locomotive wheel, Tono's arm jerked up and down, up and down, as he and Darminto took turns pumping air into Father's bellows.

From his perch high above the rough clay oven, Tono watched the charcoal winking redder and redder with each blast of air from the bellows. Soon the hoe blade lying on the coals would be hot enough to pound into shape.

"Enough!" Father grunted. With a long pair of pincers he fished out the glowing piece of metal.

Tono sighed as he and Darminto jumped down to the dirt floor of the little Indonesian blacksmith shop. His muscles ached as he hoisted the smallest of the three heavy mallets.

Clang-clang-clang! Clang-clang-clang!

The two young brothers and their father never missed a beat as they hammered out a crude rhythm on the hoe blade.

"It almost sounds like a gamelan," thought Tono. He wished it really were . . . because then it would be cool nighttime, and he would be listening to melodies from his favorite Javanese musical instruments.

Tono's breath came faster and faster. Only thin shorts covered his cinnamon-colored body; yet he felt as if he were wrapped in a prickly grass-fiber mat.

"Enough!" gasped Father.

Tono shook sweat from his eyes as his big brother gave

him a hand up. At least he could catch his breath a bit now as they sat side by side and pumped the bellows.

"We march tomorrow," announced Darminto.

"March? Where? Why?" asked Tono.

"We march past the foreigners' hospital," continued the tall teenager. "And who are you to ask why? The leader of our youth group says we must march. *Begitu saja!*"

Tono frowned. "Pak Suparso is a good leader. But I don't like to do anything just because somebody says so—*begitu saja.* I want to know the reason why. What have the foreigners at the hospital ever done to hurt us?"

Darminto shrugged between pumps. "Pak Suparso says those foreigners are our enemies. They stand in the way of our youth group, and the true political party, and our plans for a better life."

"Enough!" Father grunted again.

Tono picked up the smallest mallet and started pounding away.

Be-gi-tu sa-aa-ja! Be-gi-tu sa-aa-ja!

That was what the three hammers seemed to be saying now. Tono frowned as he worked. He still wanted to know why.

But early the next morning he took his place in the line of march.

"Here, little brother," cried Darminto, "take hold!" Together they helped hoist a huge banner that read:

GANYANG RUMAH SAKIT
ANTEK MUSUH-MUSUH INDONESIA!

Tramp-tramp! Tramp-tramp! To the rhythm of the youth group's drum band Tono marched along. When Pak Suparso gave the signal, Tono and all the rest shouted the slogan on the banner: "Destroy the hospital! Crush the enemy agents!"

Begitu saja, just like that, Tono did what he was told, did what all the others did. But still he wondered why the hospi-

tal ought to be destroyed. He wondered whether the foreigners inside it really were agents of Indonesia's enemies.

It was six weeks later before Tono got a chance to have his
questions answered. With his friends Eko and Untung, he
had gone swimming in the river. The wide Brantas rolled
past their town of Kediri—and sometimes, rolled right
through it, tearing down houses and plastering everything
with mud.

"Look!" shouted Eko as the three boys slipped on their
shorts over legs that still glistened wet in the late afternoon
sun. "There comes the sugar cane train. Who wants to walk
all the way back home? Not Eko!"

Tono's bare feet tickled as the three boys trotted through
the cane fields. The little old wood-burning locomotive
puffed toward them, hauling dozens of narrow-gauge cars
piled high with long stalks of sugar cane.

Eko grabbed the side of a car and swung aboard. Untung
followed. Tono was last.

How it happened, Tono never knew. Perhaps his foot was
still soft and damp from that dip in the river. Perhaps it
slipped on the sun-warmed metal.

Tall cane, banana trees, setting sun, darkening sky seemed
to spin before his eyes as he tumbled down. Then he felt
pain, and blood, and dizziness . . . and then everything
turned black.

When Tono woke up, he was lying on his back. First he
noticed the ceiling—not the thatch of his village home.
Then he turned his head. Nearby lay a young man and
another boy, on white beds—beds like the ones foreigners
used!

Tono tried to sit up. Beds and windows began to whirl
before his eyes.

"Quiet, quiet, little brother," said a soft voice. It was a
woman, her dark face smiling beneath her white cap. "You
must lie very still for awhile to give your leg time to get
well."

"Where—where am I?" whispered Tono. But in his heart he already knew the answer.

He was inside the foreigners' hospital.

In the days that followed, Tono's other questions were answered. At first he hurt too much to notice things around him. His leg had been slashed and broken by the sugar cane train. But little by little Tono groaned less and watched and listened more.

His first discovery was this: It was not correct to call the place "the foreigners' hospital" *begitu saja,* just like that.

Yes, of course, there were foreigners in it. A tall yellow-haired doctor, with a name Tono couldn't pronounce, came by each morning. He joked with Tono in the Indonesian language and looked at his leg. A grey-haired chief nurse gave directions on how Tono should be fed and washed and cared for. There was another foreign woman whom he glimpsed passing the door of the children's ward. The boy in the next bed said—of all things!—that this woman also was a doctor.

But there were so many more of Tono's own people in the hospital than there were foreigners! Aides brought him hot rice, salt fish, and fresh papaya. Orderlies scrubbed the tile floor every single day. Nurses put a strange glass rod into his mouth and gave him medicine for pain. All of these were Indonesians.

So was Tulus. Tulus came every day to chat with Tono and other boys in the ward. He showed them brightly colored pictures. He told them stories about someone named Jesus, who often healed sick and broken bodies. He taught them songs about Jesus, too.

"I'm from a village only a few kilometers away from Kediri, little brother," explained Tulus. He spoke in Javanese, just as Tono did. "I used to swim in the Brantas, too, and hitch rides on the sugar cane train. Since I became a man, I have become a follower of Jesus. Let me tell you more about Him!"

Tulus, like other Indonesians in the hospital, called Tono
by the familiar term "little brother." But still Tono missed
his own family. He wondered whether they wouldn't come
see him because workers in the cane fields had carried him
to "the foreigners' hospital."

Then one day Darminto's tall figure appeared in the door-
way of the ward. "What news, little brother?" he asked
softly.

"Darminto!" cried Tono. "How glad I am to see you! My
news is good; I'm getting well. How are Father and Mother?
Who's taking my place in the blacksmith shop?"

Darminto shook his head. "We miss you, little brother. All
are well. But how my arms throb from pumping the bellows
all alone!"

Tono grinned. "Soon I can help again. My leg is getting
strong because my friends here know how to make it heal.
Why did Pak Suparso tell us to march and shout against this
place? Not all the people here are foreigners. And all of
them are kind to me."

Darminto glanced over his shoulder, then leaned toward
Tono's bed and lowered his voice. "You must be careful
what you say, little brother. Haven't you heard the news?"

Tono blinked. "What news?"

The older boy whispered, "The true political party tried
to take over the government of Indonesia—and failed. Everything is changed now. *Begitu saja.* Pak Suparso is in hiding. And I . . . I'm not even sure which *is* the true political
party anymore."

Tono cleared his throat. "I'm not sure either. But one
thing I am sure of: Our leaders were wrong in calling this
hospital a place of Indonesia's enemies."

That week, as Tono began to hop around with a home-
made crutch, he thought about what he had learned at the
hospital. He looked forward to times when Tulus would
come and teach him more songs and stories.

The yellow-haired foreign doctor also talked with him now and then about that same person called Jesus.

One day Tono got up his courage to ask the doctor a question in Indonesian: "Why did you come to Java, doctor? Why do you help me and my people?"

The tall man answered, speaking in his curious accent: "Tono, we came here because Jesus told us to."

"Begitu saja, ya?"

The doctor chuckled. "I suppose you could say it's as simple as that, Tono. Jesus loves me; Jesus loves you; so Jesus sent me here to tell you about Him—and to help your leg get well."

Tono glanced at the crutch by his bed, then at the pictures of Jesus that Tulus had tacked to the wall. "I'm glad, doctor," he said softly. "I'm glad you're here in Indonesia."

Begitu saja: buh-GHEE-too SAH-jah
Tono: TAW-naw
Darminto: dahr-MEAN-taw
gamelan: GAH-meh-lahn
Pak Suparso: pock soo-PAHR-saw
ganyang: GAHN-yahng
rumah sakit: roo-mah SAH-keet

antek musuh-musuh: AHN-teck moo-soo-MOO-soo
Eko: EH-kaw
Untung: OON-toong
Brantas: BRAHN-tahs

Kediri: keh-DEE-ree
Tulus: TOO-loose
ya: YAH
(Guess what it means!)

31
Voyage of the *Messenger*

"All aboard!" called Pastor Davidson.

"I'm here!" answered Mr. Hardin, the radio engineer.

"Got your Portable Missionaries with you?" asked Pastor Davidson.

"Yessirree, all fifty of 'em!"

Pastor Davidson looked over the group from his church as they stepped aboard the *Messenger*. "One, two, three, four, five, six," he counted. "But where's Clark Bayless?"

"Oh, haven't you heard, Pastor?" replied one of the group. "He's got the mumps."

"Mumps!" exploded Pastor Davidson. "A grown man like him?"

"Yep," came the answer. "The doc says he mustn't get out of bed. And after all those hours he slaved learning hymns in Japanese!"

Pastor Davidson shook his head. He turned to Mr. Martin, the other full-time missionary in their group. "Dale, do you suppose the devil is trying to sabotage our voyage?"

Big Dale Martin grinned as she shook his head. "Let's hope not!" he answered. Then he hurried over to board a smaller craft, the *Anne*.

Soon both boats were churning their way out of the tidal basin on the large island of Okinawa, bound due west. Their destination? The tiny protected harbor of Kume Island, fifty-three miles away.

The *Messenger* belonged to the Fishers of Men, a church

group at Naha, Okinawa. Most of the church members were American servicemen from military bases nearby. They had already been giving tithes and offerings faithfully to help spread the good news. "But we want to do more, Pastor," some of them had said. "We want to do something special."

Pastor Davidson had agreed, especially when they promised that their "something special" wouldn't keep them from giving their usual offerings through the church. So the Fishers of Men had pooled their extra gifts to buy the *Messenger*. On this bright April morning, the forty-three-foot cabin cruiser was making her maiden voyage as a messenger of the gospel.

But they didn't make it to Kume Island that day. The engine on the other cruiser which they had rented for the trip soon began to sputter and growl.

The Fishers of Men checked over the *Anne*'s engine. "Looks bad, Pastor," they reported. "We'd better put in for repairs."

So they stopped to spend the night at Zamami Island. "Now I'm sure the devil is trying to sabotage this voyage!" fumed Pastor Davidson.

"Never mind," said Mr. Hardin, the radio engineer. "Tuesday is just as good a day as Monday to get started installing Portable Missionaries."

But the poor old *Anne* still was not seaworthy when Tuesday morning dawned.

"Let's leave 'er!" cried the Fishers of Men. "The *Messenger* is big enough for all of us."

So they all crowded aboard, and the *Messenger* continued her voyage with a heavier load. Shortly before noon, they docked in Kume harbor.

After lunch the missionaries and servicemen divided into two teams. One team went with Mr. Hardin to start installing what he called his "Portable Missionaries." These were small pretuned radios. Anytime they were turned on, they would be sure to pick up a Japanese Christian radio station.

Its broadcasts featured hymns, other good music, Bible messages, and world news with a gospel slant.

"What's the deal, Al?" one of the military men asked the radio engineer. "Do we give 'em away? Or do we sell 'em?"

"Neither one," Al Hardin explained. "We lend 'em on a one-year contract. Anybody who gets one must promise that as many people as possible will be listening every time he turns it on."

The other team got off the *Messenger* with another part of her cargo: seven thousand Gospels of John in Japanese and ten thousand evangelistic tracts. The team spread out through the village. They handed the little brown-backed booklets to all who would take them.

"Be sure and save some for tonight," the two missionaries warned the eager military men. "Let's make up sets of one of each kind to give to people who come to the services."

It was a busy afternoon. The men barely had time to hurry back to the *Messenger* to change clothes and grab a snack. Then they were off again for their evening's work.

Three meetings they conducted that night, all at the same time: one at a church, one at a kindergarten, and one at a small public hall in the village.

"We might have trouble here," one of the men warned Mr. Martin as he trudged up to the village hall, his big hands grasping a movie projector and its speaker. "For one thing, there doesn't seem to be any electricity. And they say some people around here are opposed to Christianity."

"Problem number one is no problem," the missionary answered with a chuckle. "The current at Kume only comes on from 6:30 till 11:30 each evening, and it's not quite time yet. As for problem number two . . . just pray, fellows, and we'll see."

God answered prayers that night. People crowded in everywhere, to watch the film and listen to Mr. Martin preach in Japanese. No one tried to cause trouble.

"How many folks did we have?" asked Dale Martin afterward, as he mopped sweat from his forehead.

"I counted up to three hundred of those I could see," answered one of the servicemen. "No telling how many more were out there in the dark. With only five hours of electricity a night, I can see why they don't want to waste any of it on outdoor lights!"

Wednesday was even busier than Tuesday. Mr. Martin and Pastor Davidson made a heavy load on a motor scooter. They rode off to the other side of the island to prepare for another village service that evening. The scooter belonged to one of the Fishers of Men. He had bought it on purpose to be used in spreading the gospel.

When the two tired missionaries came buzzing back to the dock at dusk, the Portable Missionary team aboard the *Messenger* shouted good news: "Hey, we set a new record today!"

Mr. Hardin, the radio engineer, nodded his head. "We installed no less than twenty-eight PM's. That's the most I've ever heard of in a single day."

Pastor Davidson grinned back at him. "Lots of folks on Kume Island are going to be hearing the gospel, Al."

They held four services that night and two more on Thursday night. Hundreds of islanders squeezed in to watch and listen. Even with no seats, not even straw mats to soften wooden floors, they sat through movies and messages. Every person received a set of tracts and Gospels. Many asked for extras to give to relatives and friends.

On Friday morning the *Messenger* chugged out of the harbor, heading due east for Okinawa and home.

Pastor Davidson watched Kume Island disappear down the skyline into the dark blue China Sea. He turned to Mr. Martin and asked, "How many people in all came to the meetings, Dale?"

"Well, we totaled about sixteen hundred," replied the big

missionary preacher. "Not counting those who stood outside."

"Why . . . that's more than one out of every ten people on the whole island!" cried Pastor Davidson.

"I'd say the voyage of the *Messenger* was a success, wouldn't you guys agree?" added Mr. Hardin, the radio engineer.

The crew of the *Messenger* knew for sure they had done a good job from something they heard a few days later. They met a serviceman on leave from the small military base on Kume Island.

"Everywhere I went," he told the Fishers of Men, "I saw people reading those little brown books. I don't know any Japanese, so I couldn't tell what they were. When I found out they were Gospels of John, I thought you guys must have dropped 'em from an airplane. You sure covered the island with 'em!"

And so the message goes out—by radio, by film, by tracts, by Bible portions, by preaching, by teaching, by personal witnessing . . . on foot, on a motor scooter, sometimes even on a cabin cruiser named the *Messenger.*

Okinawa:
   oh-key-NAH-wah   Naha: NAH-hah
   Kume: KOO-may   Zamami: zah-MAH-mee

32
Rosalina Finds Friends

Rosalina sidestepped a pile of filth on her way to the water faucet. Only seven other girls and women already stood in line ahead of her—good! That meant she had managed to get up earlier than usual this morning.

"*Bom dia*," Leila greeted her.

"*Bom dia*," said Francisca's mother.

"*Bom dia*," said the woman who had just moved to São Paulo from northern Brazil.

"*Bom dia*," replied Rosalina, setting down her battered cans to wait her turn.

"The water runs too slowly this morning," complained Leila.

"Those rich people who own the water company and everything else in the city!" Francisca's mother burst out. "It's bad enough that our whole *favela* has only one faucet. Some mornings they're even slow sending the man to turn the water on. And some mornings the pressure is so weak it takes forever to get what you need."

"Ah, well," signed Leila, "let's talk of more pleasant things. Did you hear about the fight my brother had with his girl friend last night?"

"Tell me more!" cried the woman from northern Brazil, grinning. "What did he hit her with? What names did he call her?"

Rosalina was glad when the dribble of water had filled her

cans. She hurried away through the mud, away from the ugly talk around the faucet.

For seven of her twelve years, Rosalina had lived in the *favela*, a slum district on the swampy banks of the river. Before that, she could barely remember fresh air and green grass on a farm in northern Brazil. But lack of rain had brought dust and hunger, so Rosalina's father had joined the other millions who looked for work, far to the south in São Paulo.

"But he didn't find work," Rosalina remembered. "He only found more hunger." Her bare foot slid a little on the muddy path, and some of her precious water sloshed out.

She pushed open the rough plank door of the shack. A tattered strip of burlap hung over one small window. In the half-light she saw her mother lying on a dingy hammock.

"You're back quickly, Rosalina," murmured her mother.

"Yes, Mama, there weren't many in line," she answered. "Now I can get an earlier start to work. Is there any coffee?"

Mama groaned. "I'm afraid you'll have to go out without even a cup of coffee to give you strength. And there's not a single *cruzeiro* in the house."

Rosalina's head seemed to swim with hunger as she stooped to collect her burlap sacks.

She wondered: "Would we be better off if my father were still alive? Or worse off?" Rosalina knew that some *favela* men, when they couldn't find work, stopped trying to do anything. They stayed at home, pretended to be sick, and drank strong liquor when they could get it. Their wives and children could beg . . . or starve.

"*Adeus*, Mama." Rosalina started out the door. "I'll try to get home before too late and put something over that hole in the roof before it starts raining again."

Away went Rosalina, collecting waste paper and scrap metal in the streets of Brazil's largest city. She was lucky that day: Before noon her sacks were filled, and she got forty *cruzeiros* at the scrap dealer's. That was enough to buy rice, beans, and salt—but no meat.

Yet her luck still held: As she passed a meat market, a man was throwing out spoiled sausages. Curling her nose at the smell, Rosalina poked through the garbage. Finally, she fished out two that still seemed safe to eat.

Bean and rice soup seasoned with cast-off sausage made a feast in Rosalina's shack that night. Even Mama seemed a little stronger after filling her tin-can bowl twice.

"The next time you have a good day, child, we simply must buy some soap," said Mama. "Then maybe, if I take it slowly, I can get down to the river and scrub the clothes."

Darkness came early. Rosalina's mother couldn't pay the fee charged for an extension line from one of the few *favela* households that had electricity. "And even if we could pay it, I'm not sure I would," Mama explained to Rosalina. "It's against the law for them to make us pay like that."

As they lay on their hammocks, they could hear a neighbor's radio blaring. Christmas carols sounded through the warm night air, for it was December 24.

The next day Rosalina awoke to the patter of rain. She smiled when she saw the new patch in the roof. Mama's hammock wouldn't get soggy as usual. But she frowned when she remembered that rain-swept streets made it hard to search for scrap.

By midmorning the shower had stopped. Rosalina shouldered her sacks again and trudged out through the mud.

Near a small, neat brick house, she found treasure in a trash can: a pair of girl's shoes. Rosalina tried them on. They were almost a perfect fit. Then she noticed a girl standing nearby—a girl about her own age.

"*Bom dia,*" said the girl.

"*Bom dia,*" returned Rosalina, as she fumbled in her hurry to put the shoes inside one of her bags.

"My name is Maria. What's yours?"

"Rosalina." The *favela* girl glanced sidewise at Maria's clean dress, polished shoes, and combed hair.

"I haven't seen you in our neighborhood before," said Maria. "Do you come around often?"

"No," replied Rosalina. "Usually it's my mother who comes here and works. But she's sick."

"Works? Is she a housemaid?"

Rosalina looked down. "Most of the time she just collects trash and sells it—like I'm doing today."

"Is that why you picked up my old shoes?" asked Maria. "To sell them?"

Rosalina grinned. "Oh, no. I won't sell those!"

Both girls giggled.

Rosalina shifted her sacks to the ground again as her new friend went on talking. In answer to Maria's questions, she told about Mama's illness, about hunger in *favela* shacks, about schools that had no room for *favela* kids.

Suddenly Maria straightened up, away from the fence post she had been leaning against. "Will you promise not to go away, Rosalina, if I run inside a minute?"

"Yes, I'll wait." Rosalina watched Maria trot across the narrow yard. She wondered what the girl would bring back —maybe leftover food or a pile of old newspapers, or maybe even a few *cruzeiros*.

The slum girl blinked to see Maria returning with a plump, well-dressed woman.

"Here she is, Mama. This is Rosalina," cried Maria. "She's just three months younger than I am, and we wear the same size shoe."

The plump woman smiled. *"Bom dia*, Rosalina. I am *Senhora* Gruber. Will you eat Christmas dinner with us today?"

Rosalina gasped. *"Senhora!* Me?"

"Yes, my dear," she said, nodding. "Maria suggested it, and her father and I like the idea."

"But . . . but . . ." Rosalina stuttered.

Senhora Gruber smiled again. "You see, Rosalina, we are

all *crentes* in our family; that means we truly believe in Jesus Christ. We're not people who just go to church now and then, and that's the end of it. One way we celebrate Jesus' birthday is by having a new friend as our guest. Now come inside, girls, it's almost ready. Maria, show Rosalina where to wash, please."

Rosalina followed them, dazed.

Maria not only got soap and towels and water. From somewhere she also found the prettiest dress Rosalina had ever worn in her life.

"It's beautiful!" squealed Rosalina, stroking the smooth fabric.

More marvels awaited her in the small combination living room and dining room. A Christmas tree was decorated with cookies; a ribbon ran through a little hole in each one. Below the tree stood a manger scene. It was tiny, but much nicer, so Rosalina thought, than the one the streetcar company always set up in a garage near the *favela*.

"We always hang cookies on our tree," explained *Senhor* Gruber, Maria's father. "That's a custom we learned from my grandfather. When he still lived in Germany, his mother made Christmas cookies like these."

Rosalina was not the only guest. A young woman from North America also sat at the table. And the table itself was crowded with more good things to eat than Rosalina had seen in a year.

"This is one of our missionary friends," said the Gruber family as they introduced her.

The foreign woman smiled. In heavily accented Portuguese she asked, "Has your mother been sick long, Rosalina? Maybe our clinic could help her."

Soon Rosalina got over her worries about which fork to use. These people were her friends; they actually cared about her. They weren't like the rich folks of São Paulo who sometimes came to the *favela* at Christmas and passed out bread rolls or candy, and then were never seen again till next year.

"Let's see, Rosalina," continued the North American woman, "can you tell me somewhere near the *favela* that we could meet tomorrow morning? Then you could guide me to your house. I'm afraid I'd never find it otherwise."

"Tomorrow?" cried Rosalina. "Will you really, truly come?"

Plans were laid by the time dinner was over. A lunch for Mama wrapped with clean plastic lay inside one of Rosalina's sacks. But Rosalina still had one more question: "Please, *Senhor, Senhora*—are you very, very rich? You and your North American friend?"

"Rich?" Maria's father looked blank.

"Rich?" echoed the missionary.

"I'm just a small storekeeper," Maria's father said. "I'm not one of São Paulo's rich people. Surely you can see this little brick house isn't like the mansions on other streets."

"Then—I don't understand," murmured Rosalina. "How can you give food and clothes for Mama and me? And promise to give us other kinds of help, too?"

Senhora Gruber put her arm around Rosalina. "Remember what I told you, my dear. All of us here are *crentes*. Because we truly believe in Jesus, we share what we have, to help other people in Jesus' name. Many *crentes*—some in Brazil, some far away in other lands—put their money together. That's how we can have clinics and schools and mission centers and churches. It's not because we're rich."

An hour later, Rosalina hopped barefooted along the *favela* path. She had changed back to her old dress. The new one, along with the shoes, were safely tucked inside one of the burlap sacks. She wasn't about to let mud and slime spoil them!

"*Boa tarde*, Mama," called Rosalina as she pushed against the splintery boards of the door.

"*Boa tarde*, Rosalina." Then her mother frowned. "You

still have two bags partly full. Did the scrap dealer not open because today is a holiday?"

"I didn't find any scrap, Mama," teased Rosalina.

Mama groaned. "Ah! And so we go hungry again—on Christmas Day! Is there no end to it all?"

Rosalina hugged the thin woman on the hammock.

"What I found today is better than trash, Mama," she said. "Part of what I found is inside these sacks. And just wait till I tell you about the rest!"

Rosalina: ro-sah-LEE-nah	Adeus: ah-day-OOSE
Bom dia: bawm DEE-ah	Senhora: sayn-YORE-ah
Leila: lay-EE-lah	Gruber: GROO-ber
Francisca: frahn-SEESE-kah	crentes: KREHN-tehs
São Paulo: sawm PAW-loo	Senhor: SAYN-yore
favela: fah-VAY-lah	Boa tarde: boe-ah TAR-deh
cruzeiro: kroo-ZEH-roo	

33

Mr. Garden, the Popcorn Preacher

Robin Neal squinted through rain that lashed the windshield. "Dad, do you really think they'll come out on a night like this?" she asked.

Mr. Neal stared ahead into the blackness. "You never can tell, Robin," he said. "A better garden means a better life for these folks."

The ten-year-old chuckled. "I get tickled hearing them call you *Bwana Shamba*—'Mr. Garden.' But I guess that's a pretty good name for you."

Robin's mother nudged her. "Look! There's somebody on his way to the meeting right now—with a banana leaf for an umbrella."

Robin liked helping her parents. She knew how important these field days were in their work as agricultural missionaries in Tanzania, East Africa. But tonight's field trip was different from the others.

"Don't drop those seeds!" Dad warned, as Robin slithered through mud from their parked car to the biggest building in the area. "You know they'll be disappointed if every one of 'em doesn't get a sample of every kind of seed we have."

Out of the black night they came—some walking, some hobbling on bandaged feet, some swinging along on their crutches. Soon more than two hundred people had crowded inside.

Mr. Neal stood up and opened his Bible near the front cover. "And the Lord God planted a garden," he read from

Genesis. "And out of the ground the Lord God made to grow every tree that is pleasant to the sight and good for food."*

Robin could almost give her father's talk by heart now. She liked the simple way Dad explained things.

"Soil gets tired," said Mr. Neal. "It needs help to become fresh and strong again, so it can grow good gardens. That's why we add fertilizer."

Holding up prize vegetables from his own farm, the missionary told how certain foods help guard against diseases. Others help grow healthy bodies. Some help children have strong, straight bones.

"It's important to eat many different kinds of food," he continued. "Just corn and bananas aren't enough."

Now it was Robin's turn to help. She and her mother moved through the crowd, passing out tiny seed packets: carrots, cabbages, okra, turnips, onions, beans.

Like many ten-year-olds, Robin Neal had just as soon some of those vegetables had never been discovered. But as Dad had predicted they would, the Africans raised their hands and yelled if she missed them with even one kind of seed.

Then Robin sat down to enjoy the fun. Popcorn was always the best part of Dad's demonstrations, so Robin thought. It was hard to keep the corners of her mouth from curling up as the people around her watched Mr. Neal pour just half a cup of yellow kernels into a pot.

As that familiar pop-pop-pop filled the awed silence, the crowd began to giggle. When the missionary lifted the lid to show white puffy stuff spilling over, everyone gasped.

"Here, Earline, Robin, help me!" called Dad. The girl and her mother passed out handfuls of crunchy goodness—the first popcorn any African there had ever tasted.

But tonight's crowd was different from others who had come to Dad's demonstrations. Some of them had no hands to hold out for their share. Robin had to pour popcorn into

---

* Genesis 2:8-9, RSV.

their laps, to be picked up between bandaged arms or de-
formed stubs.

Earlier that evening, Robin had wondered why they were
going to a place where government health workers helped
people with Hansen's disease (leprosy). In the car on the
way, Dad had explained to Robin that each patient was
given a small plot of ground when he or she was admitted
for treatment. "Some of 'em get well, and some never do,"
he had added. "But nearly all of 'em can grow their own
food."

Sometimes Mr. Neal would preach after his illustrated
lecture on better farming. Tonight, though, he showed films
on the life of Christ. Robin had seen them all before, but she
still liked them.

She was yawning by the time Dad asked her to help take
down the screen. "Go on out to the car with your mother,"
Dad said. "Some of these folks want to talk with me."

Robin fell asleep on the way home. But not before she
heard Dad say, "They asked me to come back soon and help
start a church."

That night Robin Neal learned one way agriculture can
help missions. She saw other ways, in her father's work from
day to day.

Take Pastor Fungameza, for instance. Like the apostle
Paul, and like most Tanzanian Baptist ministers, Pastor Fungameza worked with his hands six days a week and preached
on Sundays. But his small coffee farm could not support the
ten children who nearly split the sides of his mud-wall house.

Then Robin's dad had picked out fifteen farms for coffee
demonstration trials. Pastor Fungameza had been given fertilizer. Dad had lent him simple tools and taught him how
to use them. He had learned to prune and mulch his old,
worn-out coffee trees.

That had been a long time ago when Robin was only
seven. Now Pastor Fungameza's children left their much
larger mud-brick home every morning and proudly

marched off to school, for now their father could afford to pay school fees. On the way they passed his coffee trees that now bore five times as much as their neighbors' trees did.

Their father had now bought his own tools. When he lent them to his neighbors, he would always say, "Just see how much *Bwana Shamba* has helped me. You should listen to him, too!"

At Robin's own breakfast table every morning, Mom and Dad drank coffee brewed from prize beans Pastor Fungameza had brought to their house in plastic bags.

Dad's work in agricultural missions helped not only friends but also enemies.

Over in Masasi, people were suspicious of Baptists at first. Robin's "Uncle Bob and Aunt Nell" (as she and other Missionary Kids called them) and their four MKs had even been arrested. They had not been allowed to leave their rented house for ten long days.

That was before Robin's dad had started a coconut nursery at Antioch Baptist Church in Masasi. Young coconut palms were given to needy farmers in the area. Now people there knew for sure that Baptists had come to Masasi to help. And many of them had trusted in the Lord Jesus.

Robin's special friend Larry Green also helped tell the story of Jesus and the story of better farming. Larry was a young Missionary Journeyman, not much older than Robin's big brother and sister who were away in school. He had come to work in Africa for two years.

"How much milk do cows here give?" Larry had asked soon after he arrived. Robin knew dairy cattle had been Larry's specialty in 4-H Club and ag school.

"Oh, about a quart a day," people told Larry.

"You've got to be kidding!" he groaned. He knew the Tanzanian government had purebred stock for sale. But he soon learned that few people would buy a fine cow because they couldn't believe she would ever give twelve quarts of milk a day.

So Larry bought two government cows of his own. From bamboo and other local materials, he built a simple but modern dairy barn. He began teaching people about more nutrition from better cows. It wasn't long before they got the message.

Robin knew that Larry, like Dad and Mom, didn't stop with farming only. The young missionary had been helping the Neals only five months when an old, one-legged man came tottering up to him beside the road one day.

"I've heard about your work with cattle," the old man explained. "Now will you please come and tell me and my friends and neighbors how we can become Christians?"

The next Sunday Larry Green started a new church in the one-legged man's community. "When I preached," he said, "six people gave their lives to Jesus Christ!"

As she listened to Larry, Robin Neal wondered what God might want her to do as a grown-up. "I've already seen how spreading better seed can help spread the gospel," she mused. "And I'm not surprised that Baptist churches are beginning to grow fast here in Tanzania. I'm proud to be known as the daughter of Mr. Garden, the popcorn preacher!"

Bwana Shamba:
    BWAH-nah SHAHM-bah   Masasi: mah-SAH-see
Fungameza: foong-ah-MAY-zah

34
Elijah and the Jungle Pilot

Who do you think of when you hear the name "Elijah"?

Probably you think of God's great prophet in olden times. But there is another Elijah growing up on Kalimantan, the huge Indonesian island that some people call Borneo.

In the Indonesian Bible, "Elijah" comes out sounding like *Elia*. But it's still the same name, and young Elijah in Kalimantan knows as well as you do who he was named after.

Elijah was born in a village far from any city, far from any road. Behind his father's house stands his father's pepper garden. Often he helps his father tie up new sprouts to the main trunk of a pepper bush so that each bush looks like a green pyramid. Elijah learned to count by looking down the long rows of neatly pointed plants.

In his childhood Elijah hardly ever saw or heard a motor vehicle. Once in awhile an evangelist would slither into the village on a mud-caked motorcycle. Once in awhile Elijah would walk several miles with his father through jungle paths to a market village where a truck or jeep might turn up now and then ... if the bridge hadn't broken down again.

Then one day when Elijah was a growing fifth grader, he saw and heard a motor vehicle far larger and louder than any he had ever dreamed of. He and his father had gone to the market miles away from home when a roar in the sky made them stop and stare. A moment later, an airplane landed at the edge of the market village.

"Hey! Who's in that plane, Father?" Elijah asked.

"A missionary, no doubt," his father answered.

Elijah knew who missionaries were and what they did. In his own village stood a thatch and bamboo-pole building with a cross on the top. Ever since he was tiny, Elijah had been taken to church there every Sunday. "You must become one of God's people," his father had often told him. "Didn't we give you the name of one of God's prophets?"

Indeed, young Elijah had almost grown up at church. The year before, he had professed faith in Jesus Christ as his Lord and Savior. With other new Christians, he had walked down to the river for a baptismal service.

The little river came tumbling down from a great mountain to the west. Its clear waters felt tingling cold to the skin. But Elijah had no fear about wading out to the deep place to be baptized. The river was also where he bathed every day. And when the evangelist arrived hot and sticky from his trip through the jungle, Elijah often led him to the riverbank for a cooling dip.

Six days a week Elijah studied hard. He and his younger brother left early every morning, heading for the grade school in the market village miles away. They had only one bicycle between them. When it was Elijah's turn to ride, he got to school in just an hour; when he had to walk, it took him two hours.

After Elijah was promoted to sixth grade, he began to ask himself: "How can I go on learning? If grade school is this far away, how much farther must I go to get to junior high school?"

Elijah's father was a plain-talking farmer. But he was proud of his son's thirst for learning. "A boy with the name of a great prophet ought to get a good education," he said.

One Sunday after the morning service, the visiting evangelist parked his muddy motorcycle outside Elijah's house. As they ate chicken and sticky rice cakes and drank hot tea, he told Elijah about the Baptist hostel in Singkawang, a small seaport on the coast of Kalimantan. He told about boys and girls from backwoods Baptist families who lived in the hostel so they could go on to junior high school—and sometimes even beyond junior high.

"Would they let me live there?" Elijah asked eagerly.

"We'll see," the evangelist promised. "I'll try to send word the next time a mission plane comes by."

By now Elijah was used to seeing planes. About once a week a four-seater would zoom down to a grassy strip near his grade school. While waiting to take off again, the tall American pilot would fill his gas tank from big metal drums stored in a shed beside the landing field.

Elijah liked to help the pilot. He held the funnel and watched gasoline gurgling down into the tank. Sometimes he rolled heavy drums into place or lifted down boxes of cargo.

"Who knows, Elijah?" said the friendly pilot in his funny accent. "One of these days you might get to take a ride with me."

"Thanks in advance!" Elijah answered with a grin.

In the rainy season, the roof of Elijah's church sprung as many leaks as there were runners on a pepper bush. Elijah and his father pitched in with other men and boys to make repairs.

"When can we build a better church, Father?" Elijah wanted to know.

"When there are ten of our members who tithe," his father explained. "Then we can ask for special help with building expenses."

"I already give ten *rupiah* from every hundred *rupiah* I get, Father," said Elijah.

His father smiled down at him from the bamboo ladder. "I'm proud of you, Son," he said. "But we must have at least ten heads of families who give regularly to the Lord's work."

Elijah stopped to think a moment. "Who pays expenses for the evangelist who comes here, Father?" he asked. "Gasoline costs a lot, especially when he comes by plane instead of motorcycle."

"Why, it's tithes and offerings from God's people all over the world," his father explained. "We Christians here in Kalimantan must help pay for the Lord's work, too, even though we can't give much money yet."

One day when it was nearly time for school to let out, Elijah heard that now-familiar roar in the sky. He glanced out the window, toward the landing strip.

Then he yelled: "Hey! The plane! It crashed!"

Elijah forgot all about being in a sixth grade classroom. He dashed out the door. The landing strip was empty; just beyond it, a dense thicket of bamboo blocked his view.

Elijah ran a good mile before he found the fallen plane. Panting for breath, he stumbled nearer. Pieces of the aircraft were scattered everywhere.

His heart beat faster. In his mind the same prayer kept spinning around like a tape cassette: "O God, please don't let my friend be dead!"

Then he heard a groan: "Help! Help!" He hurried toward the voice. "Elijah! Help!" The voice was weak and wavering, but Elijah jumped for joy to hear it.

He found the jungle pilot sprawled among smashed seats and seatbelts and dials from the dashboard. "Don't try to move me, Elijah," he warned. "It feels like my back is what's hurt. Oohhh!"

Elijah stuttered a little. "What—what—what must I do?"

The pilot took a long breath. "Let's pray first."

By this time three other sixth graders had followed Elijah's track, along with a teacher still young enough to run. All of them listened in silence as Elijah folded his hands, closed his eyes, and thanked God for saving the jungle pilot's life.

Then the pilot looked around him. "Maybe the radio still works," he muttered. "Elijah, hand me the end of that cable over there." He poked around with wires and switches, and suddenly the radio began to sputter. Holding back pain, the pilot spoke several hurried sentences in English. Then he laid the earphones down again. "Another plane will be coming for me," he explained, just before his eyes closed.

The schoolteacher showed Elijah and the other boys how to make a stretcher out of planks. Gently they eased the pilot's long body onto it, being careful to leave his injured back straight. Sometimes he came to, and gave them directions; sometimes he passed out again.

By the time the second plane appeared, the stretcher was waiting beside the landing strip. "Where are you taking him?" Elijah asked the other pilot, whom he had never seen before.

"To the Baptist Hospital at Serukam," the man answered. He adjusted cabin fittings so the injured airman could be laid down inside. Soon the plane soared into the sky.

The next week Elijah heard two pieces of good news. One was that Elijah's friend the jungle pilot, though he did have a very bad back, was going to get well. And the other was that Elijah himself had been accepted at the Baptist hostel in Singkawang.

"I'm glad!" Elijah told his father. "Yet . . . I'm sad at the same time. Singkawang is a long way from here."

"Don't worry, Son," his father comforted him. "Now and then we'll send you rice from our mountain fields; no valley-grown rice in Singkawang could possibly taste as good! And . . . ," he continued, "if you keep on learning, who knows? Maybe for the second time God will call on Elijah!"

Kalimantan:
  kah-lee-MAHN-tahn   Singkawang: seeng-KAH-wahng
Borneo: BORE-nay-oh   rupiah: roo-PEE-ah
Elia: ay-LEE-ah   Serukam: suh-ROO-kahm

35
A Round-the-World Story
at Miguel's Church

Miguel Del Rio threw the rubber ball against the front of the church.

Thwack! It bounced off the plain brick wall, rebounded against the sidewalk, and almost spun out of Miguel's reach as he jumped sideways.

"Here, Pepito!" he yelled, flinging the ball to his friend.

Thwack! And the game went on.

Pastor Del Rio stuck his head out the door. "Miguel!" he called.

"Yes, Papa?" answered Miguel.

"Come inside, please. I need to talk with you."

The twelve-year-old Spanish boy scampered up the steps. "Thanks for bringing your ball, Pepito," he called down from the top. "Let's play again tomorrow."

Miguel opened the door of what looked like any other apartment building along the street. But once he stepped inside, he was walking through a small church auditorium. He ambled down a hall behind Sunday School rooms, heading toward the part of the building where his family lived.

"Yes, Papa? You wanted me?" he said.

Pastor Del Rio's desk was cluttered with Bibles, books, and papers. He held a pen in his hand. "Sit down a moment, Son, and help me count. How many children usually come to our Sunday School?"

Miguel perched on a chair. "Well," he began, "besides

Blondina and Luisa and Juan and me, there's Pepito, and the three Garcia children, and . . ."

"Don't count the littlest Garcia," interrupted his father. "I think she's too little for Vacation Bible School."

"For what, sir?"

"Vacation Bible School," Pastor Del Rio repeated. "The missionary from Cadiz is going to help us have our first one here next week. It's like Sunday School, but it meets all morning and goes on all week. Now, let's don't count that littlest Garcia, for she's only two and a half. Just help me list those who are four years old and older."

Together father and son counted ten children—four of them Del Rios—who usually came to the tiny church that didn't look like a church. "Maybe others will come, but not many," mused Pastor Del Rio, "since we can't announce it publicly or put up any signs. Maybe fifteen would be a safe guess—fifteen at most."

But he was wrong. On the next Monday morning, when *Senora* Perkins the missionary drove in from Cadiz, an excited Miguel rushed up to her car. *"Senora! Senora!"* he shouted. "Twenty-three children have already come, and it's still half an hour before time to start!"

The young American woman smiled. "That's wonderful, Miguel! Let's just hope we have enough Bibles and paper and pencils and colors and paste to go around."

Latecomers brought the total attendance to an even forty. *Senora* Perkins and *Senora* Garcia and Miguel's father and mother scurried around all morning, trying to take care of so many children. Miguel and his sister Blondina, two of the oldest pupils, helped teach some of the younger ones.

On Tuesday morning there were already fifty-one boys and girls present when the opening worship time was over.

"We simply can't take care of any more," announced *Senora* Perkins. "Pastor Del Rio, shall we just shut the doors and not let any more in?"

Miguel's father nodded. "I don't like to turn anyone

away," he said slowly, "but what can we do? Who would ever have thought so many would come—the very first time we had Vacation Bible School?"

On Wednesday morning there was new excitement for Miguel. He saw not just one car, not just two cars, but three cars drive up to the little unmarked church. Two of them were big shiny American models.

"Hello there, Miguel!"

Miguel recognized *Senora* Thompson.

"Hello, good morning," he replied, using three of the few English words he knew.

Besides *Senora* Thompson, he saw other friends getting out of the American cars: *Senora* Becker, and *Senora* Smith, and several other women whose strange names he had a hard time remembering. All of them lived at the American naval base in Rota. Most of them had come before, at one time or another, when Pastor Del Rio's church needed special help.

"*Senora* Perkins, did you go over to Rota to get them to come and help us?" Miguel asked the missionary.

"No," she answered with a laugh. "But I did send my husband over! We knew that last night was when our Christian friends on the naval base would be gathering for prayer meeting."

It was a good thing those extra helpers came, for the total attendance on Wednesday morning was fifty-nine. None of the navy wives from Rota could speak much Spanish. But they could smile, and show how to paste and color, and serve cookies, and generally make the morning run smoother for everyone. Miguel had fun trying to use his English as he translated questions some of the children asked.

Still more Spanish youngsters found their way to the little church behind the plain brick wall. On Thursday, there were sixty-four of them; on Friday, seventy.

Friday morning brought an extra treat: One of the American ladies told a special story. *Senora* Perkins the missionary stood beside *Senora* Becker as interpreter.

"Boys and girls," the story began, "when I was your age and heard someone say the word *missionary*, I always thought of an American going out to a foreign country and telling people there about Jesus. This morning I want to tell you about an American who went out to a foreign country, and people *there* told *him* about Jesus.

"This American's name is Tom."

"Tom. Tom." Miguel repeated it softly to himself. "Must be short for Tomas."

Senora Perkins continued, translating the other woman's story into Spanish:

"Like many American boys, Tom decided he wanted to be a sailor when he grew up. And that's exactly what he did. After finishing high school, he joined the US Navy.

"Tom had gone to Sunday School some, but he never paid much attention to what he studied there. Now he was eighteen years old and in the navy. He thought he was too big to go to church anymore.

"I'm sorry to say Tom picked up bad habits from his fellow sailors. He began drinking and gambling. He thought it was smart to talk as rough as he could and to get into fights over little things.

"During the next few years, Tom visited many countries. He went on cruises that took him around the world. Sometimes he had shore duty at a naval base somewhere—like the one at Rota where I live now.

"Once Tom was stationed in the Philippines—'way over on the other side of the world from Spain. One night he got drunk and had a terrible fight with three other sailors. When he woke up, he was in the navy jail.

"Most churches in the Philippines use one of the Filipino languages. But there's a church in Manila that holds all its services in English. Some of its members are Americans and

British and Australians. Some are Filipinos who like to worship and study the Bible in the English language.

"As a mission project, this English-speaking church sent some of its members to the navy jail. They talked with prisoners and passed out tracts. That's how it happened that a Filipino man met Tom, the American sailor. Because of what that Filipino Christian said to him, Tom started back to church again after he got out of jail. Not long after that, Tom turned his whole life over to Jesus Christ.

"My, what a difference that made! No more drinking for Tom now—no more gambling, no more rough talk or foolish fights. Now Tom began telling other sailors what Christ meant to him. Changes came in the lives of several of them, too—some in the Philippines, some at other naval bases in other countries where Tom was stationed later on.

"It also made a difference in Tom's family life. For the first time his wife and little children learned what it means to have a Christian home.

"I know about this part of the story especially, boys and girls. Because you see . . . Tom is Machinist First Class Thomas L. Becker, my husband!"

Miguel sucked in his breath. What an unexpected ending!

"I liked that story," he told *Senora* Perkins later. "That man went from America to the Philippines, and there a Filipino told him about Jesus. Then he and his wife came over to Spain to help us tell the story of Jesus right here!"

"I liked the story, too, Miguel," agreed *Senora* Perkins. "It's a good reminder that God's people are scattered all over the world—and that all of us must work together to tell everyone the greatest story in the world!"

(A Postscript: Times have changed in Spain since Miguel heard that round-the-world story at his church. Now all Spanish churches are free to put up signs, announce their services, and advertise. But in many other countries—Communist countries, for instance—Christians still meet in unmarked buildings . . . if they are allowed to meet at all. Still they keep on telling the greatest story in the world. Don't forget to pray for them!)

Miguel: mee-GALE	Garcia: gahr-SEE-ah
Del Rio: dell-REE-aw	Cadiz: kah-DEETH
Pepito: peh-PEE-taw	Senora: sayn-YAW-rah
Blondina: blawn-DEE-nah	Rota: RAW-tah
Luisa: loo-EE-sah	Tomas: TAW-mahs
Juan: HWAHN	Manila: mah-NEE-lah

IV.
Modern-Day Martyrs

When we think about Christian martyrs, usually we tend to think of the first century, or the sixteenth, or the nineteenth. Yet, some people say more Christians have died for their faith in the twentieth century than in all other ages put together.*

All of the *Bold Bearers of the Name* whose stories are found in section IV of this book lived in this present century. In fact, it was only a few years ago when I sat down with three surviving members of the Lesnussa family and heard firsthand about "Two Arrows and a Wedding Ring" (chapter 40).

We sometimes think of "Modern-Day Martyrs" as being people like Dr. Bill Wallace of China, who left America and gave his life as a missionary in a foreign land. But all of the Christian martyrs whose stories are told in this book were people of Asia and Africa. Most of them suffered for the sake of Christ in their own native countries.

God does not call all of us to die for our faith. But He does call all of us to live for our faith, no matter what the cost.

Our Lord Jesus has given us a great challenge, and an even greater promise: "Be faithful unto death, and I will give you the crown of life."**

---

* As quoted from Dr. Paul Carlson in James and Marti Hefley, *By Their Blood: Christian Martyrs of the Twentieth Century* (Milford, Michigan: Mott Media, 1979).
** Revelation 2:10, RSV.

36
Faithful unto Death
The Sohn Family of Korea

Can you imagine a father loving the murderer of his two oldest sons? Can you imagine a father even adopting that murderer as a son and leading him to become a follower of the Son of God?

Sohn Yang Won did both of those things.

Doing hard things started early in life for Sohn Yang Won. In 1909, when his life was little different from that of any other seven-year-old boy in Korea, his father became a Christian.

"Your father follows the foreigners' religion!" neighbors teased him. But Yang Won's father stood fast. A year later his mother became a Christian, too. So little Yang Won and his younger brother started out early in life learning what it means to love the Lord Jesus above all else.

During those years the great Japanese Empire was flexing its muscles. Every morning every pupil in every school in Korea must bow toward the east where the emperor reigned in far-off Tokyo.

"You must not do that!" Yang Won's father warned him. "The Ten Commandments warn us not to worship anyone except the one true God!"

So every morning, two boys stood up straight when everyone else bowed. As you might expect, they were soon sent to the office.

The school principal was Japanese. "Why are you two breaking the rules?" he demanded.

Sohn Yang Won, as elder brother, spoke for both of them. Politely he tried to explain.

"Bah!" sneered the Japanese. "Christianity is only for the superstitious, for ignorant village folk."

"I beg your pardon, sir," Yang Won replied. "Christianity is found all over the world, and many Christians are highly educated."

That did it. With bloody noses and bruised lips the two little boys left the school office. But still they would not bow to anyone but God.

When Yang Won was a short, slight youth of seventeen, his father helped lead nonviolent demonstrations against Japanese colonial rule. For doing that, Deacon Sohn was sent to prison for a year.

As eldest son, Yang Won felt he must help his family. By moving to Seoul, capital city of Korea, he could work to support himself and still stay in school.

His job was selling bakery goods along the streets. What made it hard was, all the other boys made their biggest profits on Sundays. But Yang Won still remembered the Ten Commandments and refused to work on the day of worship.

At first the bakery owner was patient. He knew this stubborn little fellow was the most honest agent he had. But when Yang Won persisted in taking Sundays off even during lunar new year celebrations, the bakery owner fired him.

Winters are cold in Korea. Yang Won had nowhere to go, nothing to eat, and only seventy cents in his pocket. He wouldn't spend even that because it was the tithe on his hard-won earnings.

For three days and nights he wandered the streets of Seoul. Then a telegram came from his mother, sending money and telling him to come back home to the village.

Yang Won felt God had honored his prayers, even though now he had to drop out of school. He stopped by church on his way home, so he could put his seventy cents in the offering.

Later on, to his great surprise Yang Won had an opportunity to finish high school after all—not in Seoul, but in Tokyo! The colonial government selected him for special training.

He still had to support himself, which he did by delivering newspapers after school. But once a week he paid another youth to substitute for him, so he wouldn't lose his job.

What did Sohn Yang Won himself do on Sundays? He beat the big bass drum in a band that marched through the streets of Tokyo playing hymns. After they had attracted a crowd, the Christian youth group began proclaiming the gospel.

Back in Korea again, Sohn Yang Won became a lay evangelist. "Lord, make me drunk with Jesus!" he prayed.

He met and married a Christian girl. All their children were given Bible names: Matthew, John, Rachel, Andrew, Ruth.

When young Matthew was ten years old, his father went back to school again. Sohn Yang Won felt he needed to know more about the Bible. For three years he studied in seminary. Then he was officially ordained.

But . . . where could he be sent to serve as a pastor? The Japanese were pressing Koreans harder yet about bowing to the emperor. Even many Christians were saying, "It's only a patriotic duty, like saluting the flag." But everybody knew Pastor Sohn wouldn't agree. Where could he serve without getting into trouble?

Finally they sent him off to the Garden of Loving Care where seven hundred victims of Hansen's disease lived. In those days most people called the disease "leprosy" and knew next to nothing about treating it.

Those seven hundred unfortunate Koreans had been forced to leave their families. Lonely, homesick, frightened, ill, they needed someone to shepherd them. Sohn Yang Won gladly took the job.

But Pastor Sohn could not forget his years as an evangelist. Now and then he accepted invitations to preach in other places that were not as out-of-the-way as the Garden of Loving Care. And still the word spread that he never bowed toward the east.

Finally in 1940 the Japanese hauled him off to prison. For months Mrs. Sohn had no proof that he was even still alive, except when the jailer sent his worn-out clothes home with a curt order for replacements.

Warned by a dream, she and all the children stood in the street on a day when Pastor Sohn was brought out of jail and marched to the train station. Mrs. Sohn barely had time to find out where they were sending him and to show him a verse in her Bible: "Be faithful unto death, and I will give you the crown of life."*

In prison Pastor Sohn was beaten for refusing to bow to the emperor. He was starved for refusing to work on Sundays. By the time a new police investigator arrived from Japan, Pastor Sohn had to be carried into his office on a stretcher.

The Japanese investigator felt sorry for the little Korean prisoner. "All Japanese, myself included, believe that there are many gods, and the emperor is one of them," he began. "Why do you find this so hard to accept?"

Pastor Sohn replied, "There is only One who has ever revealed God to man. Was the emperor born of a virgin? Has he ever worked any miracles? Did he ever die and rise again on the third day?"

The investigator sighed. Obviously this was a hardened criminal who must be brought to trial.

In the meantime, the Sohn family had had to move out of their house in the Garden of Loving Care. Then they had to move again because they refused to put up a godshelf for the worship of ancestors.

On the day Pastor Sohn was supposed to be set free, the whole family lined up to meet him outside the prison. They

---

* Revelation 2:10, RSV.

brought new clothes for him to wear. Even his old father, Deacon Sohn, stood and waited there.

But Sohn Yang Won did not walk out of prison that day. Investigators had learned he would not change his mind, not even under torture. So they had increased his sentence by two more years.

Matthew and John were teenagers by this time. They had to leave home and school to help support the family by working in a barrel factory.

One day Matthew was given special permission to visit his father. He took a long train ride to the prison. But once he got there, the guards refused to let him see his father unless he bowed to the emperor. In his confusion and disappointment, the boy gave in. Later he wept in shame and resolved to stand true to Christ like his father, whatever the cost.

World War II was nearly over before Sohn Yang Won was finally set free. His father, the old deacon, was no longer alive to greet him. But the rest of the Sohn family had a joyful reunion.

American soldiers had already come to South Korea in those days. Not far from the Garden of Loving Care, they ran a training camp to help Koreans defend their country against Communist attacks from the north.

Matthew and John stayed in a boardinghouse so they could live in a small city where there was a high school. During the years of hardship they had gotten far behind. Matthew especially was teased as "the old high school student."

One day an American soldier accidentally broke a shop window. He apologized and started back to his barracks to get money to pay for the damage. But the Korean shopkeeper didn't understand. Luckily Matthew Sohn passed by and understood enough English to smooth things out.

After that Matthew and John became friends with many of the foreign troops. "Come to America with us!" the young soldiers invited them.

"Maybe so, someday," Matthew and John replied. "But if there ever comes a time when we need to stand up for Christ in our own native land, then we'd better stay right here."

That time came sooner than anyone could have guessed. Communists from the north had infiltrated the training camps. One day in 1948 they rebelled, killing South Korean officers and sending American advisors running for help.

Immediately the Communists began setting up what they called "people's courts." Many Koreans were accused of being "enemies of the revolution."

Matthew and John Sohn were dragged out of the boardinghouse where they lived. "Yankee spies, aren't you?" the Communists sneered as they beat the two young men. "So you want to go to America, eh?"

Behind a government building they were shown piles of corpses. All had been found guilty and immediately shot.

They gave Matthew one last chance. "Join us and live," they cried.

He shook his head. "Even if you torture me, I can never give up Jesus Christ."

"Go ahead and kill him!" they yelled.

John jumped in front of his brother. "Kill me, not him!" he begged.

"Be quiet, John," said Matthew. "You go home and take care of our family."

Even as they were blindfolding him, Matthew said, "Why are you committing this great sin? Turn to Jesus and be saved!"

Pistol shots drowned out his testimony.

John hugged his brother's body. Then he jumped up and flung his arms wide, like a cross. "Why did you kill him? He was innocent. Shoot me, too, so I can go where my brother has gone!"

And John Sohn, like his Lord, died praying for his persecutors.

The "revolution" lasted only a week. South Korean government forces soon rounded up the Communists and put them on trial. One of them was a young man named Ahn Chae Sun. He was accused of helping to murder Matthew and John Sohn.

The South Korean officer conducting the military trial got the shock of his life when word came that Pastor Sohn was asking for Chae Sun to be pardoned!

Could it be that Sohn Yang Won didn't care about his two murdered sons? No one believed that . . . at least no one among the thousands who had crowded into the church at the Garden of Loving Care for that double funeral. Pastor Sohn himself had led the service.

"Thank you, Lord," he had prayed through his tears that day. "Thank you for raising up martyrs from blood as sinful as mine. Give me many spiritual children to replace my two beloved sons!"

The military judge still didn't believe it till he heard it from Pastor Sohn's own daughter. Thirteen-year-old Rachel Sohn bravely brought that strange message from her father: Not only did Pastor Sohn ask that Chae Sun not be punished; he also asked to adopt the young man as his own son!

Finally South Korean authorities granted their permission. Pastor Sohn must take complete responsibility for Ahn Chae Sun's conduct. He turned out to be not a hardened criminal, just a confused youth led astray by Communist teachings. Soon Chae Sun became a follower of Jesus Christ. He even announced that God was calling him to preach the gospel.

Chae Sun's parents also became interested in a faith that could cause such love for a murderer. They asked Rachel Sohn to come and live with them, so they could learn more about the Christian way.

The story of the Sohn family was published in a book called *The Seed Must Die.* It was acted on the stage in South Korea and in other lands as well.

Unfortunately the fight against Communism was not yet over. In June of 1950, North Korea struck with full force.

Sohn Yang Won kept on as usual—pastoring his flock, preaching in evangelistic meetings. But many of his fellow Christians urged him to go south for safety.

"A good shepherd doesn't leave his flock when he sees a wolf coming," answered Sohn Yang Won.

Then Chae Sun turned up one day. He had left his studies at a theological seminary. "I've come to help my father, mother, and little brother and sisters move to a place of safety," he announced.

Pastor Sohn and his wife thanked the earnest young Christian who had truly become their spiritual son. But they said, "There is no place of safety except in the Lord."

Three days after Chae Sun's visit, Communist troops captured the area around the Garden of Loving Care.

At first they made no move against the Christians there. But then stocks of food began to run low.

"Stop holding church services and run up the Communist flag," some people advised. "Then we can ask for rations, just like everybody else."

"Unthinkable!" snapped Pastor Sohn.

Finally they sent for him as he sat in the church office preparing for Wednesday evening prayer meeting. Calmly he laid his watch, fountain pen, and other personal belongings on the desk. Then he walked into the church. When they arrested him, he was kneeling in prayer.

At the police station they handed him a form to be filled out. "What must I write here?" he asked, pointing toward a blank marked "Confession."

"Write down all your misdeeds," they said.

And so Sohn Yang Won began to write: "I have been called by Jesus Christ. But I have not carried out the task of witnessing for Him as I should have . . ."

Soon United Nations troops pushed the North Koreans back. The Communists began to march their prisoners north. But in the middle of the night and the middle of the journey, they started shooting down everyone in sight.

A friend of Pastor Sohn's managed to escape. He told how the stubborn little preacher had even witnessed to the guards till they beat his mouth with rifle butts. The lone survivor led grieving Christians to the place where a small, bloody body lay beside the road.

Chae Sun came home to lead the funeral service. "I stand here today like another Saul of Tarsus," he said to the crowd at the church in the Garden of Loving Care. "Once I persecuted Christians; now I am a preacher of the gospel. And you . . ." His voice broke as he looked down at the casket. "You saved my life!"

Long ago the Lord Jesus said, "Unless a grain of wheat falls into the earth and dies, it remains by itself alone; but if it dies, it bears much fruit. He who loves his life loses it; and he who hates his life in this world shall keep it to life eternal."*

Sohn Yang Won:
SAWN yahng WAWN   Ahn Chae Sun: AHN chay SOON

---

* John 12:24-25, NASB.

37
Gospel Grass Fires
The Wallamo Christians of Ethiopia

If you've ever tried to stamp out a grass fire, you know how hard that can be. Just when you think you've put it out in one place, it flares up in another.

The Wallamo tribe knows about grass fires because grass covers much of the mountains and high valleys of southwestern Ethiopia where they live. But even grass fires never spread like the gospel did when once it came to the land of the Wallamos.

The Wallamos carry themselves with dark-skinned dignity. According to tribal tradition, many of them come from kingly families.

But to other peoples of this century, the Wallamos' age-old way of life seemed strange and primitive. They drank their coffee salted and ate their meat raw. And when Ethiopia's wartime enemies sent planes to drop bombs, some Wallamos thought the world was coming to an end.

The Wallamos first met missionaries in the year 1928. Some of them thought one missionary was a devil because he had four eyes. None of them had ever seen eyeglasses before.

The Wallamos themselves sacrificed bulls to devils. Spells and curses controlled their daily lives.

Gradually a few Wallamos began to listen to the good news about the Lord Jesus Christ. Some even dared to face down witch doctors and escaped without harm. That made others brave enough to believe.

After seven years there were seventeen baptized believers among the Wallamos. Then . . . war! The missionaries were ordered to leave.

For nearly two years the missionaries managed to put off obeying that command. They saw the little Wallamo congregation grow from seventeen to forty-eight.

Finally in April of 1937 the missionaries' time was running out. On the day before enemy army trucks would cart them away, they gathered with Wallamo Christians for the Lord's Supper. As they ate crumbled corn bread and drank honey-sweetened water, they wondered what would happen when they were gone. They looked at the Wallamo believers, one by one:

There was Wandaro—a faithful witness, but so slow-witted the missionaries had nearly given up trying to teach him how to read the Bible.

There was Toro, the missionaries' cook, who had quit his job a few months before and gone home over the mountain to tell the good news. "I didn't want anyone to think I was being a Christian just so I could get the missionaries' money," he explained.

Even if Wandaro and Toro and others like them stayed true, how could they do much, with only the Gospel of Mark translated into the Wallamo dialect? For the rest of the Bible, they must use Amharic, the main language of Ethiopia. To most Wallamos, Amharic is a foreign tongue.

What would happen to the Christians now? Two young missionaries had already been butchered by savage tribes to the east. Would the Wallamos themselves be spared?

With sad faces the missionaries climbed into the army trucks and rode away. All they could do now was to pray that the forty-eight would stay faithful.

It was five years later, in 1942, before any Christians outside the highlands of Ethiopia heard news from the Wallamos. When they heard the news, they thought at first it must be a mistake.

"When the missionaries left," someone said, "it was hard to find a Wallamo who was a Christian. Now, it's hard to find a Wallamo who isn't!"

When the story could be checked, it proved to be almost literal truth. In five years those forty-eight Christians had increased to . . . ten thousand!

How did it happen?

Like a grass fire!

One Wallamo told another about finding peace and happiness in Jesus Christ. Women gossiped the gospel from hut to hut. Men talked about it at house-raisings and funerals.

Church elders traveled from ridge to valley, sharing the good news. New believers helped do the elders' farm work —repairing their fences, bringing them firewood or grain or butter or even a sheep—so the elders themselves could be free to evangelize. And the good news kept on spreading.

Two groups of people frowned to see so many Wallamos becoming Christians. Unbelievers within the tribe itself, especially chiefs and witch doctors, hated new ways. And enemy soldiers occupying Ethiopia grew suspicious, too.

Someone set fire to one of the largest churches. It burned easily, for it was built Wallamo-style, with wooden walls and a grass roof. The Wallamos scraped together enough tithes and offerings to raise a new church with a corrugated iron roof.

An angry chief arrested Wandaro. "Give him forty lashes!" he commanded. The whip had several cords of inch-thick hippo hide, each tipped with sharp metal.

When Wandaro was well again, the chief ordered him to call all his church members together. "Tell them to bring their grass knives," he ordered. The church in Wandaro's village was not a fireproof building. The chief laughed to see Christians forced to cut down wood and grass which they had just been working hard to shape into a house of worship.

"Can you still sing now?" the chief jeered. "Come on, let's hear you!"

Singing hymns of praise to God, the Wallamo Christians marched as ordered to a distant town. On heads and shoulders they carried their own wood and grass. There they were made to leave it all, for use in building something else—not a church.

The chief still wasn't through with Wandaro. Five men took turns beating him in the marketplace till his friends thought he was dead. In jail that night he could only rest on elbows and knees; every other part of his body was raw with wounds.

But the Lord began to heal Wandaro again. Only fifteen days later, the chief put him at hard labor. Wandaro witnessed to the guards—that day and every day during the full year he stayed in prison.

After Wandaro was at last set free, that same chief begged him to bring his church members and help harvest ripe grain. "I tried to kill you, but God gave you life," he said in wonder. A hundred singing Christians joined Wandaro in the chief's golden fields.

Still the chief made threats. "In fifteen days we will meet to talk about this new religion," he ruled. "If it is proved false, three of you will die." But before fifteen days had passed, the chief himself fell backward from his throne, a dead man.

Wandaro was not the only Wallamo Christian who suffered. Toro and fifty other church leaders were arrested. Each was given a hundred lashes—and one man, four hundred lashes. They were herded into a prison yard with no food, no bedding, no protection against cold winds that whistle down from the mountains every night.

Three of the Christians died. The rest survived through ten long months, mainly because church members were faithful to bring them nourishing food every day.

When Toro got out of jail, he went into hiding. But no one could hide how fast Christianity was growing. Like a grass fire, it flared up everywhere when enemies tried to stamp it out.

Again Toro was caught. Again he was whipped—this time, with the terrible hippo-hide lashes. As if that were not enough, an enemy army officer jumped up and down on his chest with hobnailed boots.

Toro thought he was dying that day. He could hardly breathe. But the Lord Jesus Himself appeared in a vision. "Toro, don't be afraid," He said. "You are My faithful servant. Let not your heart be troubled."

Toro lived through that torture . . . and also lived through another day when he was stripped naked in the marketplace, thrown face down in the mud, and beaten a hundred times.

More churches were burned; Scriptures were seized.

The Wallamos met by night. Secretly they baptized new believers and took the Lord's Supper. They hid their precious Gospels of Mark in buried clay pots. They wrapped their handwritten Bible verses in wild banana leaves and stuffed them inside the grass roofs of their homes. And the good news kept on spreading like a grass fire.

One of the Wallamo chiefs himself became a Christian. He gave up his own large house to be a church. Later he even became a preacher.

Sometimes the Lord sent special help to His suffering people as He had done on that day when Toro nearly died. When Wallamo Christians were locked up once again, a huge gust of wind blew the grass roof off the jail. Heavy rains weakened its pole walls till they sagged to the ground. The Christians were free!

The end of war and persecution did not bring an end to growth. During the first three years after missionaries came back to work with Wallamo church leaders, the number of believers climbed again, from ten thousand to fifteen thousand.

No telling how many Wallamo Christians there are by

now. But none of them will ever forget those faithful forty-eight, who increased to ten thousand during five years of pain and death when gospel grass fires swept through the Wallamo country.

| Wallamo: wah-LAH-mo | Toro: TAW-ro |
| Wandaro: wahn-DAH-ro | Amharic: ahm-HAH-rick |

38
Tortured for the Truth
Kartar Singh of India and Tibet

Followers of the Sikh religion have long known what it means to suffer for their faith. Sikhs worship only one god like Muslims, but they are like Hindus in most other ways. Because of this they have often been persecuted by both Muslims and Hindus.

Many Sikhs have become brave soldiers, fighting for what they believe to be the truth. But none was ever braver than Kartar Singh.

He was born to a rich Sikh landlord in northern India, sometime in the late nineteenth century. He was an only son; his family gave him everything money could buy. Young Kartar Singh wore the finest clothes, ate the richest foods, went to the best schools. Yet somehow he felt an emptiness inside. Nothing his Sikh teachers taught him could satisfy his longings.

Then Kartar heard about the Lord Jesus Christ. Little by little he became more and more sure that Christ could fill the hollow in his heart. He was still only a young man when he boldly told his family that he intended to become a Christian.

They were shocked. His father blustered at him and bragged on him. He tried every way he could think of to make Kartar change his mind.

Kartar Singh replied, "I have looked for a Savior everywhere, but found him nowhere. Now at last through God's

Word I know the truth: The Savior is the Lord Jesus Christ. And now I will not leave Him who gave His life for me."

As a last try, Kartar's father called for the pretty girl he had already picked out as Kartar's wife. "Go bring my son to his senses!" he ordered.

The girl did her best. She told Kartar how much she loved him, how happy they could be together.

Kartar loved her, too. "I do not want to give you up," he sighed. "But if I am forced to make a choice . . . Jesus Christ must come first."

When the weeping girl reported to the man who would have become her father-in-law, he exploded in anger. Before the whole family he shouted at Kartar, "You are no longer my son! You have no right to anything that is mine—not even the clothes on your back! Leave everything, and go—now!"

It was a December night in northern India where winters are chill. But Kartar Singh took off everything he was wearing and placed it at his father's feet. "I am not ashamed to lay aside my clothing, Father," he said. "The righteousness of Jesus Christ has covered all my nakedness and sin."

But bold words can do little to warm bare flesh. Kartar Singh nearly died of cold and hunger. He worked as an ordinary laborer—he who had been waited on by servants all his life. Yet he felt peace in his heart.

Soon after Kartar had earned enough to buy clothing, he exchanged it again for the yellow robe of a *sadhu*. A sadhu is a wandering holy man who lives on whatever people give him. He spends his life teaching others.

Kartar Singh now began to roam from village to town in northern India. With him he took the truth that he had learned through personal experience.

Then he began to feel that Christ wanted him to spread the truth in Tibet, beyond the high mountains. For hundreds of years no one had dared to preach the gospel there.

But Kartar knew he must obey his Lord. He turned his face toward the hills.

Somewhere along the way he was baptized by an Indian pastor. When he reached the border, he stopped for several months to study the Tibetan language. Then Kartar Singh climbed over the mountain peaks into Tibet . . . and no one ever heard of him again.

That is, no one ever heard until another brave Christian of India carried the good news into Tibet. There at last he found out how Kartar Singh's story had come to an end, sometime in the early years of this twentieth century.

Kartar's mission to Tibet had been hard going from the first. Tibetan minds seemed closed against the truth. At one place, people were so disgusted with Kartar's message that they tied him up in a cloth. They took turns carrying him on their shoulders like a sack of rice. Finally they dumped him outside the city limits and warned him never to come back again.

But Kartar would not quit. He would not go back home to India. He knew he had the truth—the only truth that could bring Tibetans peace with God. And he kept on telling them the good news.

Finally one day a *lama* (or chief priest of Tibetan Buddhism) ordered him arrested. "You broke our laws, even by crossing the mountains into Tibet," he charged. "And here you are, spreading a foreign religion. I sentence you to death . . . by torture!"

The lama's secretary and all those in that courtroom took a long breath. They knew what was coming. But Kartar Singh never flinched. Even as they marched him toward Execution Hill, he preached to them about Jesus Christ. "I shall not come down again," he predicted. "But after three days I shall rise up to meet my Lord in heaven."

On Execution Hill they tore off his clothes. Then they brought out the skin of a yak or Tibetan ox, soaked to make it stretch. They crammed Kartar's body and limbs inside the skin, then sewed it up as tight as they could.

The sun shone bright on that hilltop. As the yak skin dried, it also shrank. Little by little it tightened its grip on the helpless victim inside. First skin and flesh felt the pinch; by the second day, even bones and joints began to crack.

Still Kartar Singh stayed true to his Lord. He sang hymns of praise. He prayed that God would save his enemies from their sins.

On the third day the jeering mob fell silent. They realized that the bundle of twisted flesh and broken bones inside the yak skin could stand little more.

Gasping with pain, Kartar Singh begged, "Please . . . let my right hand out . . . only for a moment."

Out of curiosity, someone did what he asked. The crippled fingers reached for a small Book which had lain beside him on the ground during his hours of agony. Somehow he found strength to scribble something inside it.

Then he faced the crowd. "Do you want to see how a Christian dies?" he asked. "No! It is death itself that dies here today." Then, as his crushed body weakened, he whispered: "O Lord . . . into Thy hands I commit my spirit . . . for it is Thine." And he was dead.

The lama's secretary stepped forward. He picked up the little Book and took it home.

First he read what Kartar Singh had written on a blank page in the front: "I pray that my love for Christ may not be less than the love of a Hindu widow who gives herself up to be burned with the body of her husband. She has no hope of ever meeting him again. Should I not do much more for my living Lord, who is also the Lord of life?"

Strange words . . . the lama's secretary could not forget them. He began to read the little Book itself. Soon he found out about Jesus Christ, the Lord of life.

It was not long before the secretary stood boldly before the lama and proclaimed, "I, too, am a Christian!"

They treated him just the same as they had Kartar Singh. They even made the torture worse by driving thorns under the secretary's nails. But for some reason they did not carry through to the horrible end. They let their victim out of the yak skin and left him for dead on the city dump.

Somehow the lama's secretary recovered from all his terrible wounds. Other Tibetans thought he must have supernatural powers. They were afraid to trouble him anymore.

In freedom, then, he spread the truth for which Kartar Singh had died. And when another Christian evangelist came over the mountains from India, the lama's secretary told him about the rest of Kartar's life.

But the story does not end even there. For that missionary from India traveled back across the high mountains and found Kartar Singh's father still alive. He told that old landlord the truth for which Kartar Singh had willingly suffered torture. And the man who had thrown out his only son naked into a December night found forgiveness and new life in Jesus Christ!

Sikh: SEEK   lama: LAH-mah
Kartar Singh:
   KAR-tar SEENG   yak: YACK
sadhu: SAH-doo

39

On Guard for the Gospel
Watchman Nee of China

In 1949 a Bamboo Curtain shut off China from the rest of the world. Communists took over the Chinese government. For a quarter of a century, little news filtered out from that quarter of all the world's people who live in China.

Yet during those years of silence, the name of one Chinese became known among Christians all around the globe. He was not a Communist, not a government leader, not a great soldier or statesman. In fact, during the years he became famous, he was locked up in jail!

His name was Watchman Nee. And true to his name, he stood on guard for the gospel in China.

When he was born in 1903, he was called Nee Shu Tsu. He brought special joy to his parents because he was their first son, after two daughters. He joined his sisters in playing with the Chang children along the banks of the River Min. Shu Tsu was the youngest, but often he became the leader in their games.

The little Changs' father was a pastor. So was the little Nees' grandfather. All of them were brought up in Christian homes and sent to Christian schools.

Every morning Shu Tsu and the other boys lined up outside the school. There they had to help one another braid their long pigtails. In those days every Chinese man or boy had to wear a pigtail as a sign that he was ruled by the emperor in faraway Beijing.

But one day when Shu Tsu was eight years old, he and his

classmates shouted, "Hurray! No more pigtails!" Gleefully they cut off those hated signs of submission. The emperor had been driven from his throne, and China was now a republic.

Those were troubled years for Chinese schoolboys. Often their lessons were disturbed by riots and revolutions. Home life was different now, too, for Shu Tsu's mother no longer went to church. Instead, she spent most of her time gambling over mah-jongg games with her friends. "If that's all it means to be a Christian," the boy said to himself, "then why should I bother?"

New teachings crept into the schools. In those early years no one knew to call them by their rightful name: Communist teachings.

No wonder Shu Tsu got bored with Bible study at school. Usually, he made top grades. Now he had trouble learning lessons that seemed to have no meaning. So he began to cheat, writing answers on the palm of his hand.

When Shu Tsu was sixteen, his mother punished him harshly for something he didn't do. He hated her for it. But during a revival meeting not long afterward, his mother became a true follower of Christ, not just a Christian in name only. And the first thing she did after she trusted in the Savior was to confess the wrong she had done and ask her son's forgiveness.

It is almost unheard of in Chinese families for a parent to confess wrong and ask forgiveness of a child. "There must be more to Christianity than I thought," said Shu Tsu to himself. It was not long before he, too, had given his life to Christ.

Now he had to face up to his sin. If he confessed to the school principal that he had been cheating during tests in his Bible course, he would probably be expelled. But he found the courage to tell. And the principal decided not to punish him.

School life was different now. On his prayer list, Shu Tsu

wrote the names of seventy classmates. "Hey, look at the walking Bible store!" friends teased him as he began to carry his Bible with him everywhere. Yet one by one, sixty-nine of those seventy schoolboys came to Christ.

Like many Asian Christians, Shu Tsu wanted to take a new name as a sign of his new life in Christ. His mother suggested the name *To Sheng*. She explained why:

"When we were expecting you, late one night I prayed that God would give us a boy this time. And I promised to give you back to God, like Hannah, Samuel's mother. The night watchman passed just then with his bamboo clapper: *To sheng, to sheng, to sheng*, it sounded through the darkness. So maybe God wants you to be a watchman over his people, like Samuel in Old Testament times. Maybe he wants you to stand on guard for the gospel in China."

Thus an eager young Christian took the name *Nee To Sheng*, later translated into English as *Watchman Nee*. He began to lead his Christian classmates in parades through the streets of old Fuzhou. Beating a gong, they passed out tracts and witnessed to all who would listen.

During school vacation they took the gospel to villages outside the city walls. Once they visited an island at the mouth of the River Min. Villagers there worshiped an idol which they called "The Great King." None of them had ever heard of Jesus Christ before.

"What's the matter with you village people?" demanded one of Watchman's younger friends. "Why don't you believe?"

The islanders explained that for 286 years "The Great King" had always sent good weather for his annual festival, which was due in two more days.

"Very well!" retorted the young evangelist. "The one true God will send rain two days from now!"

Watchman Nee was upset when he heard what his rash young friend had promised. But as he prayed, he became more and more convinced that God would do exactly as that thoughtless boy had said He would.

The next day Watchman and his helpers sailed to a nearby island where pirates roamed. Three families came to Christ. In public view they burned their idols.

It was late when the team of young evangelists returned. They slept till seven the next morning. The sun shone bright when they awoke.

Watchman calmly sat down to breakfast with the rest. Then he said, "I think we might remind God of His promise."

They prayed. Before they had finished one bowl of rice apiece, big drops of rain were falling outside. Before they had finished a second bowlful, the streets began to flood!

That youthful experience was repeated in different ways all through Watchman Nee's life. Sometimes he may have acted unwisely. But always he tried to follow God's will. And again and again God honored Watchman's faith and courage, as in that fishing town where dozens of islanders turned from "The Great King" to the One True God.

In the years that followed, it became plain that God had given Watchman Nee a great gift: an unusual ability to make the meaning of the Bible clear. He was not a fiery preacher, but people listened to what he said. He smiled a lot as he stood tall in the pulpit. Often he used his long arms to draw pictures in the air. If he told a sermon illustration about someone who had not followed the teachings of the Word, he spoke only of his own faults, not the faults of others.

Sometimes Watchman wrote Bible lessons for magazines and tracts and books. Sometimes other people took notes from his preaching and teaching and later put these into permanent form.

Many Chinese turned to Christ because of Watchman Nee. Without quite knowing how it happened, he found himself the leader of the largest Christian movement in all of China.

There were many hardships and hindrances along the way. Once a doctor looked at Watchman's chest x-rays and predicted he had only six months to live. Indeed, for several years tuberculosis sapped his strength, but God healed him at last.

Other Christians often misunderstood Watchman's work. Foreign missionaries in China especially criticized him.

Charity Chang, Watchman's childhood sweetheart, came back into his life . . . but only as a worldly university student. And Watchman stood on guard against anything that would lessen his wholehearted devotion to Chirst.

Now wider opportunities for service came his way. He was invited to Singapore, to Malaysia, to Britain, to America. Everywhere Christian friends were impressed with Watchman's courage in witnessing, his skill in explaining gospel truths.

Back home again, he joined a friend on a long trip by automobile into the interior of China. Roads were still rough, and there were wide rivers to ferry. But Watchman pushed on to places where God's Word had never been heard before, even to the borders of Tibet.

Unexpected joy awaited him when he returned from his long motor trek. Through her sister's influence, Charity Chang had now become a devout Christian. She and Watchman Nee were married in 1934. God gave them no children of their own, but He gave them spiritual sons and daughters all over China.

The great land of China kept on churning with revolution and counterrevolution. The central government could not crush Communist forces that moved from province to province. Invading Japanese armies added to the confusion.

During the troubled days of World War II, Watchman Nee and his friends took what seemed to be a strange step: They set up a drug manufacturing company. But who were its traveling salesmen? Who else but preachers and evangelists needing a means of support during hard times? And what do you suppose they carried all over China, along with medi-cines made in Watchman's factory? What else but the good news of Jesus Christ?

At last the war ended in 1945. But Watchman Nee's China knew no peace. Communists continued their struggle and now seemed to be on the winning side.

Watchman and his friends worked harder than ever to spread the truth of the gospel. Thousands upon thousands repented and believed.

Finally in 1949, the Communists came into power, and a Bamboo Curtain shut off China from the rest of the world. For the remaining years of Watchman Nee's life, no more than scattered bits of news about him reached fellow Chris-tians in other lands. Only after China began to be reopened to foreign contacts in the 1970s did the full story come out.

At first the Communists had seemed friendly enough. Watchman had been able to keep on preaching and teach-ing as usual. But little by little the new rulers of China began to set limits on his work.

During those months when signs of the times were turn-ing darker, Watchman Nee held a revival meeting in Hong Kong. He could have stayed there in safety as many other Chinese Christians did. But Watchman still felt called to stand on guard for the gospel in China. "Didn't the apostles stay in Jerusalem when persecution came?" he reminded his friends. And back he went to Shanghai.

The Communists closed their trap on him in 1952. They used his wartime dealings with the drug company to "prove" that he was a rich man and an oppressor of the poor. They told many other lies about him. Often they used the testimony of so-called Christians. And they sentenced Watchman Nee to fifteen years in prison.

Strange . . . the Communists thought they had silenced Watchman Nee by locking him up in jail.But it was during those years of his imprisonment that his name became known worldwide. Books by Watchman Nee began to spread around the globe. Some he had written himself; more were compiled by others from his spoken words. In many languages Christians found new light from the Scriptures, new strength for daily living.

Many legends about Watchman Nee's prison years began to spread to other lands along with the spread of his books. Most are just that: legends. But this much seems clear:

Other prisoners often heard Watchman singing hymns during forced hard labor. At least one of those who guarded him became a Christian through his influence. When the Communists offered to set him free if he would confess his guilt and pay a large fine, Watchman himself stopped his friends who were trying to collect the money. When the Communists could not brainwash him into believing lies, they added five more years to his sentence.

In 1966, during the cultural revolution, young Red Guards broke into the prison. In the struggle that followed, Watchman Nee was knocked to the floor. He was getting old now and already in weakened health. Both of his arms were broken when he fell.

As 1972 drew near, the old man hoped to be set free after twenty long years in captivity. But some of the life must have gone out of him in late 1971: He heard that his beloved wife Charity would no longer be there to greet him when the prison doors opened at last.

Yet he did not give way to despair. In April 1972, he wrote a letter to Charity's sister. Because the letter must be read by Communist censors, he knew it was useless to quote Scripture or share his testimony. But he cleverly arranged Chinese characters in telling everyday news, so that his sister in Christ would immediately be reminded of a well-known verse: "Ask, and you will receive, that your joy may be made full."*

Thus it was with hope and joy that Watchman Nee

---

* John 16:24, NASB.

home to heaven on June 1, 1972. From a Chinese Communist prison, he passed into the presence of the Lord, where his wife Charity had gone before him nine months before.

Like Samuel with the children of Israel long ago, Watchman Nee had said to his own great nation: "Fear not; . . . do not turn aside from following the Lord, but serve the Lord with all your heart; and do not turn aside after vain things which cannot profit or save. . . . For the Lord will not cast away His people. . . . As for me, far be it from me that I should sin against the Lord by ceasing to pray for you; and I will instruct you in the good and the right way."*

Nee: NEE   mah-jongg: MAH-JONG
Shu Tsu: SHOO T'SOO   To Sheng: TOE SHEHNG
Chang: JAHNG   Fuzhou: FOO-JOE
Min: MEAN   Shanghai: SHAHNG-HAI

---

* 1 Samuel 12:20-23, RSV.

40

Two Arrows and a Wedding Ring
The Lesnussa Family of Indonesia

Jan Lesnussa couldn't remember any other house than a bamboo hut with a bark roof which his own father had built. His father and mother told him about living on other islands of Indonesia. But Jan himself knew only the jungles of Irian. (Foreigners called it Western New Guinea.)

Jan's parents, Ruland and Sien Lesnussa, were Indonesian home missionaries. They had left a comfortable life in the city to move to the Wissel Lakes district of Irian. The lakes were big and beautiful: deep, wide, olive green in color. Strange to say, they held no fish—only shrimp.

Lots of things were strange about living in Irian. Men of the Ekagi tribe cleared and fenced new farmland. But women of the Ekagi tribe had to do all the work on the sweet potato crop after that.

Men had more important things to do: sharpening arrows or fighting wars or hiking for two weeks down river valleys to the seacoast. There they would pick up fresh supplies of white cowrie shells, their only form of money. Men herded the tribe's precious pigs, too, unless there were naked boys old enough to do the job.

Most boys went naked, except for Jan. He saw them running away when his father and mother tried to start a school. Some got caught and had their first lesson sloshing around in shallow water. Jan's parents had to show them how to scrub mud-covered bodies clean. For many of them, it was the first bath of their lives.

Then Jan's father had to swing his rattan stick again to herd everybody into the little bamboo schoolhouse. Once they got inside, some of the children found to their surprise that they liked school. But others were like kids anywhere: They decided learning wasn't as much fun as playing or hunting or netting for shrimp. And some of them were pulled out of class by their fathers to help herd pigs.

Of course starting a school was only part of what the Lesnussas did. More important than teaching about words and numbers was teaching about Jesus Christ. When enough people had believed in Him to start a new church, Jan's parents began to think about moving on to a new village.

New friends and old friends in the Ekagi tribe had a strange way of shaking hands: One person holds out one crooked finger. The other person squeezes it between two crooked fingers. Then the two hands are jerked apart so fast that the knuckles go crack! Little Jan learned the hard way that if you couldn't hear it, it didn't count, and you had to try again.

When Jan turned seven in 1955, his mother was expecting a baby. Jan bubbled with excitement when an airplane roared down and landed on the lake. All three Lesnussas climbed aboard. Just forty-five minutes later, Jan saw the ocean for the first time when he was old enough to remember it.

Then he gasped with fear. The pilot turned away from landing on the water and veered inland. Jan thought sure they were going to crash. But the little plane touched the ground and rolled to a stop on the landing strip. Only after Jan climbed down did he find out that the plane was amphibious, with wheels as well as pontoons.

The trip to the hospital was Jan's very first ride in a car. "Mama," he asked, "why are all those people along the road walking backward?"

"Oh, Jan, they're not," she chuckled. "It only looks that

way because we're moving so fast in the car."

So many new experiences for a little boy from the jungle! One of them was a sad experience: The baby born to Jan's mother lived only a few hours.

Later that same year, the Lesnussas moved to a new village: Obano, where a river flows into one of the Wissel Lakes. Not long after that, Jan left home. In Enarotali across the lake, there was a good school for small boys. So Jan moved in with another home missionary family at Enarotali.

In early 1956, a mission school for older children opened in Obano. So two other Indonesian Missionary Kids crossed the lake to live with Jan's father and mother: Robby, a thirteen-year-old boy, and Marta, a twelve-year-old girl. Soon the little bamboo house by the river would be running over, for Jan's mother was expecting again.

Jan got to go back home on the first Saturday in November, 1956, to see something special: a shiny new Cessna that had been flown in to its new base at Obano. Dutch, American, and Indonesian missionaries joined the crowd at the dedication service for the new missionary airplane.

Jan also saw two Indonesian policemen living in a tent near the plane. His father explained why: "Our Ekagi neighbors don't understand about airplanes yet. Some of them might start their cooking fires too close to it."

Jan's father didn't tell him the other reason why there were policemen in Obano. There had been talk that the tribal peoples were becoming restless. . . . But Ruland Lesnussa was not the kind of man to be scared away by rumors.

After the dedication service, Jan begged to stay over the weekend. His mother was ready to say yes. But his father reminded him, "Jan, if you stay here till Monday morning, the boat won't get across to Enarotali in time, and you'll be late to school. You'd better go on back with the others now."

His mother comforted him: "It doesn't really matter, my little Jan. After all, I promise we'll see you again on Monday.

We're coming over to buy fresh supplies."

The next morning Jan went to Sunday School and church, the same as usual. But Sunday dinner was interrupted by strange news: Somebody was trying to send signals from Obano by flashing a mirror in the sun!

Jan and the others ran outside to see. Clouds of smoke billowed up from Obano, five miles away across the lake. Jan climbed a hill. From there he could see sunlight glinting on metal—not just at one place but at many places. Had something happened to that shiny new plane?

Late that Sunday afternoon, Ekagi Christians stumbled out of the jungle. Their bodies were smeared with mud; Jan knew this was a sign of mourning. Their eyes were wide and staring as they wailed:

"*Aduh, ahuh!* They're all dead; Pastor Lesnussa and his wife, young Robby and Marta, the policemen—all shot with arrows. The church is burned down. The new school, our houses—all, all burned. And the great metal bird has been chopped to bits with axes. *Aduh, aduh!*"

Jan shivered. It was hard to believe: On that sunny Sunday he had become an orphan. What was more, if his parents had let him spend the weekend as he begged to do . . . he too would now be dead.

On Monday, marines began landing by the planeload. They gunned their way down the lake, fighting rebels. Little by little they sent back more news about what had happened.

It seemed the trouble had started with pigs. Many of them had gotten sick and died. Leaders of the Ekagi tribe decided those strange newcomers in their midst must be to blame. They planned to attack on Saturday, with crowds in Obano for the special dedication service. Only heavy rains had made them wait a day.

On that Sunday morning, Ruland Lesnussa had read as his sermon text: "You do not know about tomorrow. What is your life? For you are a mist that appears for a little time and then vanishes."*

After morning worship he stayed at church awhile to talk. Sien Lesnussa, Jan's mother, was tired; her baby was due in only a few more weeks. She walked back home with Robby and Marta.

Pastor Lesnussa heard strange noises near the policemen's tent. He stepped outside the church to see what it was.

Suddenly armed warriors leaped from the jungle. They lifted their bows and began to shoot.

Ruland Lesnussa ran for home—not to save himself but to warn the others.

It was too late. His life was spurting out through arrow wounds by the time he staggered to the front step.

Axes broke the door down. "Take whatever you want," screamed Sien Lesnussa, "but please don't kill us!" Robby hid behind a cabinet. Marta hid under a bed.

None of them escaped. Four bloody forms were left inside that little bamboo house beside the river. Soon flames were licking up toward the bark roof.

By Tuesday the marines had gotten as far as Obano. They gathered up everything they could find that might have once been human; it only filled a very small box. They knew which pile of ashes had been Jan's mother, only because of the twisted, broken wedding ring they dug out.

One part of Jan's father's body did not get burned: In their battle fury, the warriors had hacked off Ruland Lesnussa's thumb. They stuck it high on a pole and paraded it around the lake.

Ekagi Christians took it away from them. With loving care they brought it across to Enarotali. There a sad-eyed boy not quite nine saw it. Then it was buried with his martyred father's bones.

Jan Lesnussa found it hard not to hate. But he was sur-

---

* James 4:14, RSV.

rounded by so much love that forgiveness came in time. He was an orphan now, yet still a part of the Christian community. He stayed first with one home missionary family for awhile, then with another.

When he was fifteen years old, Jan got a letter from a distant island, from someone he had never seen: Grandmother Jacob, his mother's mother. She wrote, "Jan, come live with me here in the city, so you can go to high school."

The years passed—high school in the city, then Bible college. One of Jan's classmates was a pretty girl named Annie. In October 1969, Jan graduated from Bible college. In December 1969, he and Annie got married.

The very next year, Jan and Annie Lesnussa felt the same call that Ruland and Sien Lesnussa had felt many years before: God wanted them to spread the good news in the jungles of Irian. Back they went to the Wissel Lakes. Jan became both a preacher and a Bible school teacher.

It was good to be back in Irian. But an old problem came back, too. When Jan was a little boy at Obano, he had had lots of nosebleeds. He thought he had outgrown it, as most children do. But now his nose bled more than ever—sometimes every day for a week.

A doctor told him why: "It's the high altitude here, Pastor Jan. The Wissel Lakes are a mile above sea level, you know. You'd better move somewhere else if you expect to be healthy."

At about that same time Jan Lesnussa was invited to teach at a different Bible school. This one was at Jayapura, down on the coast of Irian. Yet, somehow Jan felt God still had a special job for him to do in the highlands.

He wondered how long he could last before he got really sick. So he started working harder than ever, before his time ran out. Jan led his Bible school students on hikes through the jungle, a week at a time. At every village they stopped to share the gospel. They crossed lakes. They crossed boundary lines between tribes.

And so at last one day they came . . . to Obano.

It wasn't hard for Jan to find where his family's house had once stood, even though three village huts now crowded into that same plot of ground. Grass grew lush and green there near the river. Jan wondered whether the soil was fertile because of ashes long buried underneath.

As Jan Lesnussa walked village paths, he felt many eyes turn to watch. People would glance at him, then turn away and whisper among themselves. He knew they had heard of a son who escaped the massacre seventeen years before. He knew they thought he had come back to get revenge.

In the Obano village church that week, Jan retold Bible stories about murderers . . . murderers like Moses, and David, and Paul, who turned away from their sins and got right with God. When he gave the invitation, many people came forward. They testified that now they were trusting in Christ. Then they turned in the charms and amulets they had been trusting in before.

One day a man walked to the front of the church with two arrows in his hands.

Jan was puzzled. He knew the Ekagi people did not think of arrows as magic talismans.

One arrow was made of bamboo—dusty, worn out, split with age. The other arrow was also old but still bristling with barbs. Dark stains showed on both.

The man held up the bamboo arrow as he turned toward Jan. "With this arrow," he began, "I shot your mother . . . in the calf of the leg."

He laid it down and picked up the barbed arrow. "With this arrow," he went on, "I killed your father . . . by shooting him in the side."

A hubbub broke out. Many people began to sob and wail.

The Ekagi man went on. He confessed his sins and asked forgiveness—from God, and from Jan Lesnussa.

He was not the only murderer in church that day. Nor was he the only murderer who confessed. Many people had the blood of martyrs on their hands. Many now repented and believed in Jesus Christ.

Jan Lesnussa did not baptize the new Christians in Obano. That was a job for the regular pastor of the village church. And who do you suppose he was? None other than the old father of Robby, that boy-martyr of 1956.

Six months later, Jan and Annie Lesnussa moved away from Irian, along with their little son Danny. Jan felt he had finished the work God sent him there to do. Now they could serve in other places on other islands, where he could enjoy better health.

If you should meet the Lesnussa family in Indonesia some day, be sure to ask Mrs. Annie to show you her wedding ring.

"You see, it's partly my mother's," Pastor Jan will explain. "We decided it would mean more to us this way than as an old blackened keepsake. So we had the goldsmith melt it down and make a new one."

Annie Lesnussa's wedding ring is a memorial to a modern-day martyr. Another memorial stands in Jayapura, Indonesia, on the coast of Irian: In 1973 the school there was renamed the Ruland Lesnussa Bible School.

But an even better memorial is forgiveness in the heart of an orphaned son, and Christ in the heart of a murderer.

Jan Lesnussa:
  YAHN less-NOO-sah   Ekagi: eh-KAH-ghee
Irian: EE-ree-ahn   Obano: oh-BAH-no
Ruland: ROO-lahnd   Enarotali: en-nah-ro-TAH-lee
Sien: SEEN   aduh: ah-DOO-uh
Wissel: WISS-sel   Jayapura: jah-yah-POO-rah

Topical Indexes

All numbers refer to chapters or sections, not pages.
*Asterisks beside chapter or section numbers show major emphases.

Who (People) and When (Dates)

Armstrong, Annie (1850-1938), 8, 23
Azariah, V. Samuel (1874-1945), 13*
Bagby, W. B. (1855-1939), 4
Brett, William H. (1818-1886), 17*
Bruckner, Gottlob (1783-1857), I, 5*
Buhlmaier, Marie (1859-1938), 8*
Carey, William (1761-1834), 2, 5,* 7, 13, 17, II*
Cary, Lott (*ca.* 1780-1828), 7*
Chalmers, James (*ca.* 1845-1901), 9
Deu I. Mahandi (1926-1972), I, 20*
Harris, William Wadé (1853-1926), 18*
Hayes, Ida B. (1856-1920), 12*
Ji-wang (1872-1946), 6*
Journeycake, Charles (1817-1894), 10*
Judson, Adoniram (1788-1850), I, 3,* 7, 14, 21
Kam, Joseph (1769-1833), 15*
Kanzo Uchimura (1861-1929), 11*
Kartar Singh (*ca.* 1870-*ca.* 1905), 38*
Kiayi Paulus Tosari (1812-1881), 1*
Ko Tha Byu (*ca.* 1778-1840), I, 3*
Lesnussa, Ruland (*ca.* 1924-1956), 40*
Lesnussa, Sien (*ca.* 1925-1956), 40*
Livingstone, David (1813-1873), 14

Mahandi, Deu I. (1926-1972), I, 20*
Martyn, Henry (1781-1812), 17
Nee To Sheng (1903-1972), 39*
Nee, Watchman (1903-1972), 39*
Nelson, Erik (1862-1939), I, 4*
Pandita Ramabai (1858-1922), 2*
Ramabai, Pandita (1858-1922), 2*
Ruatoka (1846-1903), 9*
Singh, Kartar (*ca.* 1870-*ca.* 1905), 38*
Slessor, Mary Mitchell (1848-1915), 14*
Smith, Amanda Berry (1837-1915), 19*
Smith, Samuel Francis (1808-1895), 21*
Sohn Yang Won (1902-1950), 36*
Tha Byu, Ko (*ca.* 1778-1840), I, 3*
Tosari, Kiayi Paulus (1812-1881), 1*
Trowt, Thomas (1784-1816), 5
Truett, George W. (1867-1944), 22*
Tungane (*ca.* 1850-*ca.* 1900), 9*
Uchimura, Kanzo (1861-1929), 11*
Wallace, Bill (1908-1951), IV
Watchman Nee (1903-1972), 39*
Whilden, Lula F. (1846-1916), I, 16*
Yang Won Sohn (1902-1950), 36*

Where (Countries and Major Areas)

Africa, 5, 7,* 14,* 18,* 19, 28,* 29,* 33,* 37*

Amazon Valley, 4*
America, Central, 12,* 25*

America, Latin, 4,* 12,* 17,* 23,* 25,* 32*

America, North, I, 4, 7,* 8,* 10,* 11, 12, 16, 19,* 21,* 22,* 23,* 24,* 25,* IV

America, South, 4,* 17,* 23,* 25, 32*

Argentina, 23

Asia, I, 1,* 2,* 3,* 5,* 6,* 7, 9,* 11,* 13,* 15,* 16,* 17, 19, 20,* II, 21, 24,* III, 26,* 27,* 30,* 31,* 34,* 35, IV, 36,* 38,* 39,* 40*

Bangladesh, 13

Barbados, 17

Borneo (Kalimantan), 5, 34*

Brazil, 4,* 25, 32*

Burma, I, 3,* 13, 19, 21

Calabar, 14*

California, 24

Canada, 2, 19

Chile, 23*

China, I, 16,* IV, 38,* 39*

Communist countries, I, 35, 36,* 39*

Cook Islands (Rarotonga), 9*

England, 2, 4, 5, 15, 17, 19, II

Ethiopia, 37*

Europe, 4, 5, 8,* 14,* 15, 17, 19, II, 22, 35*

Florida, 24

France, 18, 22

Georgia, 22

Germany, 5, 8, 15, 32

Ghana, 18*

Guatemala, 25*

Guyana, 17*

Holland, 5, 15

Hong Kong, 39

Illinois, 20

India, I, 2,* 5, 13,* 17, 19, II, 38*

Indonesia, I, 1,* 5,* 15,* 24,* III, 27,* 30,* 34,* IV, 40*

Irian (Western New Guinea), IV, 40*

Ivory Coast, 18*

Japan, 6, 11,* 31,* 36

Java, I, 1,* 5,* 15, 24,* III, 27,* 30*

Kalimantan (Borneo), 5, 34*

Kansas, 4, 10

Kentucky, I, 4, 23*

Korea, 36*

Liberia, 7,* 18,* 19

Luzon, 20, 35

Macao, I, 16

Madura, 1

Maryland, 8,* 16, 19

Massachusetts, 21

Mexico, 12*

Mindanao, 20,* 26*

Missouri, 12

Moluccas, 15*

Netherlands, 5, 15

New Guinea (Irian and Papua), 9,* IV, 40*

New York, 8,* 19

Nigeria, 14,* 28*

Ohio, 10

Okinawa, 31*

Oklahoma, 10*

Oregon, 24

Pakistan, 13

Papua New Guinea, 9*

Pennsylvania, 19

Philippines, I, 20,* III, 26,* 35

Puerto Rico, 12

Rarotonga (Cook Islands), 9*

Scotland, 9, 13, 14,* 19

Sierra Leone, 7*, 19

South Africa, 5

South Carolina, 16, 24

Spain, 35*

Sri Lanka, 13

Sweden, 4

Taiwan, 6*

Tanzania, 33*

Texas, 4, 12, 22,* 25,* 27

Tibet, 38,* 39

USA, I, 2, 4, 7,* 8,* 10,* 11, 12, 16, 19,* II, 21,* 22,* 23,* 24,* 25,* IV

Virginia, 7,* 12, 23

Zimbabwe, 29*

How (Ways and Means of Mission Work)

and

Why (Factors that Influence Mission Work)

agricultural missions, 2, 33*

airplanes, aviation, III, 29,* 34,* 40

animism, 6, 9, 13, 14,* 15, 18, 28,* 37, 39, 40*

Bible distribution, 1, 4, 5,* 6, 7, 8,* 12, 15, 16, 20, 31,* 37

Bible translation, I, 2, 3, 5,* 17*

bivocational workers, 8, 17, II, 25, III, 33

boats, boat people, 4,* 15,* 16, 17, 31*

Buddhism, 3, 38*

chaplains, 20,* 22

child abuse, 2,* 14, 16

children's homes and hostels, 2,* 14, 16, 19, 34

church development, 1, 7,* 9,* 10, 13,* 14, 15,* 25, 27,* 34,* 35,* 36, 37, 39, 40

church planting, 1, 3,* 4,* 6,* 9,* 10, 12, 13,* 14,* 17, 18,* 25,* 26,* 28,* 29,* 31, 33,* 37,* 39,* 40*

city missions, 8,* 14, 16, 32,* 36

Communism, 20, 30,* 35, 36,* 39*

cowboys, 4, 22*

drug abuse, drunkenness, 1, 3, 7, 13, 14, 15, 18, 22, 32, 35

education, 7, 9, 11, 12,* 14, 15, 16,* 17, 18, 22, 39, 40

English-language ministries, 18, 31,* 35*

ethnic minorities, 3,* 6,* 8,* 10,* 12, 16, 37*

evangelism, 1, 3,* 4,* 6,* 8,* 13,* 14,* 16,* 18,* 22,* 25,* 28,* 29,* 30,* 31,* 33, 35, 36,* 37,* 38,* 39,* 40*

gambling, 1, 3, 35, 39

handicapped persons, 2, 16,* 33

Hansen's disease (leprosy), 33, 36*

Hinduism, 2,* 38

home missions, I, 7,* 8,* 10,* 12, 13,* 14, 15, 16, 22,* 24, 40

hunger, 2, 32,* 33*

immigrants, 4, 8,* 7, 12, 16

Indians (American), 10,* 17*

Islam, 1,* 5, 7, 20,* 38

language study, 5,* 6, 9, 10, 13, 14, 16, 17, 31, 38

lay missionaries, 1, 3, 6, 8, 10, 11, 17, III, 31,* 33, 35,* 36, 37

leprosy (Hansen's disease), 4, 33, 36*

literacy, 3, 9, 15, 17, 19, 37

literature, 1, 2, 3, 5, 11,* 13, 15, 21, 27,* 28, 39*

martyrdom, 6, 9, IV,* 36,* 37,* 38,* 39, 40*

mass media, 26,* 31,* 33

medical ministries, 7, 14, 29,* 30,* 32, 34

mission-minded parents, 14,* 15, 16,* 23, 34, 40*

mission support, 2, 4, 7, 11, 12,* 13,* 19, II,* 21,* 22,* 23,* 24,* 25,* 29, 31, 32,* 34*

Missionary biographies, foreword, 7, 14, 15, 17

Missionary Journeymen, 33

MKs (Missionary Kids), 16, 27,* 29,* 33,* 40*

Muslims, 1,* 5, 7, 20,* 38

Nationalism, 6, 11,* 12, 13, 18, 36

orphans' homes and hostels, 2,* 14, 16, 19, 34

overseas Chinese, 6, 16, 27, 39

peace, 6, 9,* 11, 14, 20*

people movements, 3,* 6,* 9, 13,* 17, 18,* 37,* 39*

persecution, 1, 2, 3, 6,* 9, 11, 12, 14, 18, IV,* 36,* 37,* 38,* 39,* 40*

planes, III, 29,* 34,* 40

prayer, 2, 12, 13, 14, 16,* 18, 19,* 20, II, 22, 31, 34, 36, 37, 38, 39

publishing, 1, 2, 3, 5, 11,* 13, 15, 21, 27,* 39*

racial prejudice, 1, 3, 7,* 10,* 13, 17, 19*

schools, 7, 9, 11, 12,* 14, 15, 16,* 17, 18, 22, 39, 40
seamen, 4
Shintoism, 6, 11,* 36*
Sikhism, 38*
social ministries, 2,* 8,* 14, 16,* 25, 32,* 33, 35, 36
street people, 2, 16, 32*
stewardship, 12,* 13,* 22,* 23,* 24,* 25, 28, 31, 32,* 34*
student work, 11, 12, 13*
summer missionaries, 24

Sunday Schools, 14,* 27, 35
support, 2, 4, 7, 11, 12,* 13,* 19, II,* 21,* 22,* 23,* 24,* 25,* 29, 31, 32,* 34*
translation, 2, 3, 5,* 17*
Vacation Bible Schools, 35*
volunteers in missions, 2, 24, 31,* 35*
war, 5, 6, 12, 18, 20, 36,* 37,* 39,* 40
witnessing, 1, 3,* 4,* 6,* 8,* 11, 12, 13,* 14,* 16,* 17, 19, 25,* 28,* 29,* 30,* 31, 33, 35,* 36,* 37,* 38,* 39,* 40*